T0259848

Lecture Notes in Computer Science   7554

Commenced Publication in 1973
Founding and Former Series Editors:
Gerhard Goos, Juris Hartmanis, and Jan van Leeuwen

Francisco Heron de Carvalho Junior
Luis Soares Barbosa (Eds.)

Programming Languages

16th Brazilian Symposium, SBLP 2012
Natal, Brazil, September 23-28, 2012
Proceedings

 Springer

Volume Editors

Francisco Heron de Carvalho Junior
Universidade Federal do Ceará, Departamento de Computação
Campus Universitário do Pici, Bloco 910, 60440-900 Fortaleza, Brazil
E-mail: heron@lia.ufc.br

Luis Soares Barbosa
Universidade do Minho, Departamento de Informática
Campus de Gualtar, 4710-057 Braga, Portugal
E-mail: lsb@di.uminho.pt

ISSN 0302-9743   e-ISSN 1611-3349
ISBN 978-3-642-33181-7   ISBN 978-3-642-33182-4   (eBook)
DOI 10.1007/978-3-642-33182-4
Springer Heidelberg Dordrecht London New York

Library of Congress Control Number: 2012945547

CR Subject Classification (1998): D.3.1-2, D.3.4, D.2.5-6, D.2.9, D.1.5, D.2.11

LNCS Sublibrary: SL 2 – Programming and Software Engineering

Typesetting: Camera-ready by author, data conversion by Scientific Publishing Services, Chennai, India

Printed on acid-free paper

Springer is part of Springer Science+Business Media (www.springer.com)

Preface

The Brazilian Symposium on Programming Languages (SBLP) is an annual conference that has been promoted by the Brazilian Computer Society (SBC) since 1996. In the last three years, it has been organized in the context of CBSOFT (Brazilian Conference on Software: Theory and Practice), co-located with a number of other events on computer science and software engineering.

SBLP 2012 was its 16th edition held in Natal, Brazil. It was organized by the Department of Informatics and Applied Mathematics (DIMAP) of the Federal University of Rio Grande do Norte (UFRN), collocated with the 2012 editions of SBMF (Brazilian Symposium on Formal Methods), SBES (Brazilian Symposium on Software Engineering), and SBCARS (Brazilian Symposium on Software Components, Architecture and Reuse), under CBSOFT 2012. The previous editions of SBLP were held in São Paulo (2011), Salvador (2010), Gramado (2009), Fortaleza (2008), Natal (2007), Itatiaia (2006), Recife (2005), Niterói (2004), Ouro Preto (2003), Rio de Janeiro (2002), Curitiba (2001), Recife (2000), Porto Alegre (1999), Campinas (1997), and Belo Horizonte (1996).

The Program Committee (PC) of SBLP 2012 was formed by 36 members, from 10 countries. The Committee was responsible for selecting 10 full papers and 2 short papers from a total of 27 submissions, with authors from Brazil, Czech Republic, France, Netherlands, Portugal, USA and Uruguay. Each paper was reviewed by at least five reviewers, including 21 reviewers outside the PC. The refereeing reports were discussed by the reviewers, generally leading to a consensus. The final selection was made by the Program Committee Co-chairs, based on the final evaluations but also taking into account the reviewers reports as well as all comments received during the discussion phase. As in previous editions, the authors of the 10 full papers were invited to submit extended versions of their works to be considered for publication in a special issue of a reputed journal in computer science.

The technical program of SBLP 2012 also included keynote talks from Bernhard K. Aichernig (Graz University of Technology, Austria), entitled "The Science of Killing Bugs in a Black Box", and Luis S. Barbosa (Universidade do Minho, Portugal), entitled "Software Components as Invariant-Typed Arrows."

Finally, we would like to thank all members of the PC for their efforts, the referees for their reviews and contribution to the final discussion, the invited speakers for accepting our invitation and enriching the technical program with interesting talks, and all the authors, the sponsors and the Organizing Committee of CBSOFT 2012 for contributing to the success of SBLP 2012.

September 2012   Francisco Heron de Carvalho Junior
                                                              Luis Soares Barbosa

Organization

SBLP 2012 was organized by the Department of Informatics and Applied Mathematics, Federal University of Rio Grande do Norte, and sponsored by the Brazilian Computer Society (SBC), in the context of CBSOFT 2012 (Third Brazilian Conference on Software: Theory and Practice).

Organizing Committee

Nélio Cacho   UFRN, Brazil
Martin Musicante   UFRN, Brazil

Steering Committee

Christiano Braga   UFF, Brazil
Ricardo Massa Ferreira Lima   UFPE, Brazil
André Luis de Medeiros Santos   UFPE, Brazil
Francisco Carvalho Junior   UFC, Brazil

Program Committee Chairs

Francisco Carvalho Junior   UFC, Brazil
Luis Soares Barbosa   Universidade do Minho, Portugal

Program Committee

Alberto Pardo   Universidad de La Republica, Uruguay
Alex Garcia   IME, Brazil
Alvaro Freitas Moreira   UFRGS, Brazil
André Rauber Du Bois   UFPel, Brazil
Andre Santos   UFPE, Brazil
Carlos Camarão   UFMG, Brazil
Christiano Braga   UFF, Brazil
Fernando Castor Filho   UFPE, Brazil
Fernando Quintão Pereira   UFMG, Brazil
João Saraiva   Universidade do Minho, Portugal
João F. Ferreira   Teesside University, UK
Jonathan Aldrich   Carnegie Mellon University, USA
José Luiz Fiadeiro   University of Leicester, UK
Lucilia Figueiredo   UFOP, Brazil
Manuel António Martins   Universidade de Aveiro, Portugal

Marcelo A. Maia	UFU, Brazil
Marcello Bonsangue	Leiden University/CWI, The Netherlands
Marcelo d'Amorim	UFPE, Brazil
Marco Tulio Valente	UFMG, Brazil
Mariza A. S. Bigonha	UFMG, Brazil
Martin A. Musicante	UFRN, Brazil
Noemi Rodriguez	PUC-Rio, Brazil
Paulo Borba	UFPE, Brazil
Peter Mosses	Swansea University, UK
Qiu Zongyang	Peking University, China
Rafael Dueire Lins	UFPE, Brazil
Renato Cerqueira	PUC-Rio, Brazil
Ricardo Massa	UFPE, Brazil
Roberto S. Bigonha	UFMG, Brazil
Roberto Ierusalimschy	PUC-Rio, Brazil
Sandro Rigo	UNICAMP, Brazil
Sérgio Soares	UFPE, Brazil
Simon Thompson	University of Kent, UK
Varmo Vene	University of Tartu, Estonian

Additional Referees

T. M. Gawlitza	L. Santos	G. Albuquerque-Junior
V. Vojdani	A. Annamaa	C. Vieira
M. Garcia	P. Martins	H. Rebêlo
J. Mendes	N. Oliveira	J. Saraiva
J. Barbosa	M. Viera	L. Sierra
V. Rebello	H. Yang	
S. Gouw	A. Sanchez	

Sponsoring Institutions

CNPq - Conselho Nacional de Desenvolvimento Científico e Tecnológico
http://www.cnpq.br

CAPES - Coordenação de Aperfeiçoamento de Pessoal de Nível Superior
http://www.capes.gov.br

Ministério da Educação, Brazilian Government
http://www.mec.gov.br

Instituto Nacional de Ciência e Tecnologia para Engenharia de Software
http://www.ines.org.br

Microsoft Research
http://research.microsoft.com

NatalCard
http://www.natalcard.com.br

Table of Contents

Software Components as Invariant-Typed Arrows
(Keynote Talk)

Luis Soares Barbosa

HASLab - High Assurance Software Laboratory,
INESC TEC & Universidade do Minho, Portugal
lsb@di.uminho.pt

Abstract. Invariants are constraints on software components which restrict their behavior in some desirable way, but whose maintenance entails some kind of proof obligation discharge. Such constraints may act not only over the input and output domains, as in a purely functional setting, but also over the underlying state space, as in the case of reactive components. This talk introduces an approach for reasoning about invariants which is both compositional and calculational: compositional because it is based on rules which break the complexity of such proof obligations across the structures involved; calculational because such rules are derived thanks to an algebra of invariants encoded in the language of binary relations. A main tool of this approach is the pointfree transform of the predicate calculus, which opens the possibility of changing the underlying mathematical space so as to enable agile algebraic calculation. The development of a theory of invariant preservation requires a broad, but uniform view of computational processes embodied in software components able to take into account data persistence and continued interaction. Such is the plan for this talk: we first introduce such processes as *arrows*, and then invariants as their *types*.

1   Components as Arrows

Probably the most elementary model of a computational process is that of a *function* $f : I \longrightarrow O$, which specifies a transformation rule between two structures I and O. In a (metaphorical) sense, this may be dubbed as the 'engineer's view' of reality: *here is a recipe to build gnus from gnats*. Often, however, reality is not so simple. For example, one may know how to produce 'gnus' from 'gnats' but not in all cases. This is expressed by observing the output of f in a more refined context: O is replaced by $O + 1$ and f is said to be a *partial* function. In other situations one may recognise that there is some *context* information about 'gnats' that, for some reason, should be hidden from input. It may be the case that such information is huge to be give as a parameter to f, or shared by other functions as well. It might also be the case that building gnus would eventually modify the environment, thus influencing latter production of more 'gnus'. For U a denotation of such context information, the signature of f becomes $f : I \longrightarrow (O \times U)^{U}$. In both cases f can be typed as $f : I \longrightarrow TO$,

F.H. de Carvalho Junior and L.S. Barbosa (Eds.): SBLP 2012, LNCS 7554, pp. 1–5, 2012.

for $T = \mathsf{Id} + \mathbf{1}$ and $T = (\mathsf{Id} \times U)^U$, respectively, where, intuitively, T is a type transformer providing a *shape* for the output of f. Technically, T is a *functor* which, to facilitate composition and manipulation of such functions, is often required to be a *monad*. In this way, the 'universe' in which $f : I \longrightarrow TO$ lives and is reasoned about is the *Kleisli category* for T. In fact, monads in functional programming offer a general technique to smoothly incorporate, and delimit, 'computational effects' of this kind without compromising the purely functional semantics of such languages, in particular, referential transparency.

A function computed within a context is often referred to as 'state-based', in the sense the word 'state' has in automata theory — the memory which both constrains and is constrained by the execution of actions. In fact, the 'nature' of $f : I \longrightarrow (O \times U)^U$ as a 'state-based function' is made more explicit by rewriting its signature as $f : U \longrightarrow (O \times U)^I$

This, in turn, may suggest an alternative model for computations, which (again in a metaphorical sense) one may dub as the 'natural scientist's view'. Instead of a recipe to build 'gnus' from 'gnats', the simple awareness that *there exist gnus and gnats and that their evolution can be observed*. That *observation* may entail some form of *interference* is well known, even from Physics, and thus the underlying notion of computation is not necessarily a passive one.

The able 'natural scientist' will equip herself with the right 'lens' — that is, a tool to observe with, which necessarily entails a particular shape for observation. Similarly, the engineer will resort to a 'tool box' emphasizing the possibility of at least some (essentially finite) things being not only observed, but actually *built*. In summary,

an *observation structure*:	universe $\xrightarrow{c}$ ◯⌢◯	universe
an *assembly process*:	⊔ artifact $\xrightarrow{a}$	artifact

Assembly processes are specified in a similar (but dual) way to *observation structures*. Note that in the picture 'artifact' has replaced 'universe', to stress that one is now dealing with 'culture' (as opposed to 'nature') and, what is far more relevant, that the arrow has been *reversed*. Formally, both 'lenses' and 'toolboxes' are functors. And, therefore, an *observation structure* is a ◯⌢◯-coalgebra, and an *assembly process* is a ⊔-algebra.

Algebras and coalgebras for a functor [13] provide abstract models of essentially construction (or *data*-oriented) and observation (or *behaviour*-oriented) computational processes, respectively. Construction *compatibility* and *indistinguishability* under observation emerge as the basic notions of equivalence which, moreover, are characterized in a way which is parametric on the particular 'toolbox' or 'lens' used, respectively. Algebraic compatibility and bisimilarity *acquire a shape*, which is the source of abstraction such models are proud of. Moreover, it is well known that, if 'toolboxs' or 'lens' are 'smooth enough', there exist *canonical* representations of all 'artifacts' or 'behaviours into an initial (respectively, final) algebra (respectively, coalgebra).

Both *assembly* and *observation* processes, as discussed above, can be modeled by functions, or more generally, by arrows in a suitable category, between the *universes-of-interest*. Both aspects can be combined in a single arrow

$$\boxed{}\ U \quad \overset{d}{\longrightarrow} \quad \bigcirc\!\!\frown\!\!\bigcirc\ U$$

formally known as a *dialgebra*. Initially defined in [14], their theory was developed in [15,1] and later by [16] in the style of *universal algebra*. In Computer Science, dialgebras were firstly used in [7] to deal with data types in a purely categorical way and more recently in [11], as a generalization of both algebras and coalgebras. In [12], they are used to specify systems whose states may have an algebraic structure, i.e., as models of evolving algebras [6].

Dialgebras $(d : \mathsf{F}\,U \longrightarrow \mathsf{G}\,U)$ generalize many interesting computational structures, among which algebras $(a : \mathsf{F}\,U \longrightarrow U)$ and coalgebras $(c : U \longrightarrow \mathsf{G}\,U)$ as the simplest instantiations. A basic example is provided by transition systems with specified initial states. If the transition shape is given by G, functor $Id + \mathbf{1}$ introduces initial states as constants. This makes possible, for example, to introduce initial states on models of automata, as in $d : Q + 1 \longrightarrow Q^{In} \times 2$. Another example are components whose services may have a non deterministic output. If functor F captures an algebraic signature, $d : \mathsf{F}\,U \longrightarrow \mathcal{P}(U)$ caters for non deterministic outcomes.

2   Invariants as Types

If dialgebras provide a very general model for computational processes regarded as arrows between the *universes-of-interest*, one has also to be precise on what such 'universes' really are. A key observation is that, along their lifetime, computer systems are expected to maintain a certain number of properties on which depend their consistency and data integrity. On the other hand, they are subject to the permanent stress of ever changing business rules, which materialise into (either static or dynamic) properties of the underlying code.

Both integrity constraints and domain business rules are examples of *invariant* properties. The word 'invariant' captures the idea that such desirable properties are to be maintained *invariant*, that is, unharmed across all transactions which are embodied in the system's functionality.

Invariants are ubiquitous in systems design. Actually, they take several forms and are defined not only over the input and output domains, as in a purely functional setting, but also over the underlying state space, as in imperative programming or reactive systems design. Software evolution and reconfiguration, on the other hand, entails the need for invariant checking whenever running code is upgraded or even dynamically reconfigured. While testing is the most widely used technique for such purpose, it is highly costly and does not ensure correctness. Ideally, one should be able to *formally verify* that the new invariants are enforced without running the (new) code at all.

This calls for a general theory of invariant preservation upon which one could base such an extended static checking mechanism. This talk sums up a number of steps towards such a theory which is both

- *compositional*: based on rules which break the complexity of the relevant proof obligations across the structures involved
- *calculational*: amenable to agile algebraic manipulation

Our starting point is the explicit use of relational techniques, a body of knowledge often referred to as the *algebra of programming* [5]. In particular an invariant $P \subseteq X$ is represented as a binary relation $y \; \Phi_P \; x \; \equiv \; y = x \; \wedge \; x \in P$, which is called *coreflexive* because it is a fragment of the identity relation, *i.e.*, $\Phi_P \subseteq id$. Notice this is one of the standard ways of encoding a set as a binary relation. Since predicates and coreflexives are in one to one correspondence, we will use uppercase Greek letters to denote such coreflexives and will refer to them as 'invariants' with no further explanation.

Then, we resort to such relations to model types for arrows representing computational processes. Actually, if one regards invariants as *types*, the computational processes they type are *arrows*:

$$\mathsf{F}\,\Phi_P \xrightarrow{\;d\;} \mathsf{G}\,\Phi_P \qquad (1)$$

where $\mathsf{F}\,\Phi$ and $\mathsf{G}\,\Phi$ represent invariant Φ placed in a *context* abstracted by functors F and G, in the sense discussed above.

Typing computational processes (modelled as dialgebras) by invariants encodes a *proof obligation*. Actually the meaning of arrow (1) is

$$d \cdot \mathsf{F}\,\Phi_P \subseteq \mathsf{G}\,\Phi_P \cdot d \qquad (2)$$

which is computed as the relational counterpart to the following first-order formula $\langle \forall \, u \; :: \; u \in \mathsf{F}(P) \; \Rightarrow \; d(u) \in \mathsf{G}(P) \rangle$.

The intuition behind this move is that a dialgebra typed by a predicate is a structure for which such a predicate is to be maintained along its evolution. We will show how this can generalised in the context of a category whose objects are predicates and arrows encode proof obligations, cf,

- for general functions: $\Phi \xrightarrow{\;f\;} \Psi$
- for *reactive processes* modelled as dialgebras $\mathsf{F}\Phi \xrightarrow{\;d\;} \mathsf{G}\Phi$
- for *imperative programs*: $\Phi_{pre} \xrightarrow{\;R\;} \Phi_{post}$ corresponding to *Hoare triples* $\{post\}R\{pre\}$. This requires a generalization of the invariant calculus to *relations*, to capture the calculus of weakest pre-conditions.

In each case, a calculus of invariants' proof obligation discharge is developed, generalising our previous work. References [2,8,3,9] provide a roadmap through our research on (coalgebraic) calculi for components-as-arrows. Most results on typing such arrows by predicates first appeared in [4], with further developments in [10].

Acknowlegments. Long time collaboration with J. N. Oliveira (Minho), Alexandra Silva (Nijmegen) and Manuel A. Martins (Aveiro), is deeply acknowledged. This work is funded by ERDF - European Regional Development Fund through the COMPETE Programme (operational programme for competitiveness) and by National Funds through the FCT - the Portuguese Foundation for Science and Technology within project **FCOMP-01-0124-FEDER-010047**.

References

1. Adámek, J.: Limits and colimits in generalized algebraic categories. Czechoslovak Mathematical Journal 26, 55–64 (1976)
2. Barbosa, L.S.: Towards a Calculus of State-based Software Components. Journal of Universal Computer Science 9(8), 891–909 (2003)
3. Barbosa, L.S., Oliveira, J.N.: Transposing partial components: an exercise on coalgebraic refinement. Theor. Comp. Sci. 365(1-2), 2–22 (2006)
4. Barbosa, L.S., Oliveira, J.N., Silva, A.: Calculating Invariants as Coreflexive Bisimulations. In: Meseguer, J., Roşu, G. (eds.) AMAST 2008. LNCS, vol. 5140, pp. 83–99. Springer, Heidelberg (2008)
5. Bird, R., Moor, O.: The Algebra of Programming. Series in Computer Science. Prentice Hall (1997)
6. Börger, E., Stärk, R.: Abstract state machines: A method for high-level system design and analysis. Springer (2003)
7. Hagino, T.: A Typed Lambda Calculus with Categorical Type Constructors. In: Pitt, D.H., Rydeheard, D.E., Poigné, A. (eds.) Category Theory and Computer Science. LNCS, vol. 283, pp. 140–157. Springer, Heidelberg (1987)
8. Meng, S., Barbosa, L.S.: Components as coalgebras: The refinement dimension. Theor. Comp. Sci. 351, 276–294 (2005)
9. Meng, S., Barbosa, L.S.: Towards the introduction of qos information in a component model. In: Shin, S.Y., Ossowski, S., Schumacher, M., Palakal, M.J., Hung, C.-C. (eds.) Proceedings of the 2010 ACM Symposium on Applied Computing, Sierre, Switzerland, pp. 2045–2046. ACM (2010)
10. Oliveira, J.N.: Extended Static Checking by Calculation Using the Pointfree Transform. In: Bove, A., Barbosa, L.S., Pardo, A., Pinto, J.S. (eds.) LerNet 2008. LNCS, vol. 5520, pp. 195–251. Springer, Heidelberg (2009)
11. Poll, E., Zwanenburg, J.: From algebras and coalgebras to dialgebras. In: CMCS 2001. ENTCS, vol. 44, pp. 1–19. Elsevier (2001)
12. Reichel, H.: Unifying adt– and evolving algebra specifications. EATCS Bulletin 59, 112–126 (1996)
13. Rutten, J.: Universal coalgebra: a theory of systems. Theoretical Computer Science 249, 3–80 (2000)
14. Trnková, V., Goralcík, P.: On products in generalized algebraic categories. Commentationes Mathematicae Universitatis Carolinae 1, 49–89 (1972)
15. Trnková, V.: On descriptive classification of set-functors. I. Commentat. Math. Univ. Carol. 12, 143–174 (1971)
16. Voutsadakis, G.: Universal dialgebra: Unifying universal algebra and coalgebra. Far East Journal of Mathematical Sciences 44(1) (2010)

The Science of Killing Bugs in a Black Box
(Keynote Talk)

Bernhard Klaus Aichernig

Institute for Software Technology,
Graz University of Technology, Austria
`aichernig@ist.tugraz.at`

Abstract. In this talk I will discuss the combination of model-based testing and mutation testing. Model-based testing is a black-box testing technique that avoids the labour of manually writing hundreds of test cases, but instead advocates the capturing of the expected behaviour in a model of the system under test. The test cases are automatically generated from this model. The technique is receiving growing interest in the embedded-systems domain, where models are the rule rather than the exception.

Mutation testing is a technique for assessing and improving a test suite. A number of faulty versions of a program under test are produced by injecting bugs into its source code. These faulty programs are called mutants. A tester analyses if his test suite can "kill" all mutants. We say that a test kills a mutant if it is able to distinguish it from the original. The tester improves his test suite until all faulty mutants get killed.

In model-based mutation testing, we combine the central ideas of model-based testing and mutation testing: we inject bugs in a model and generate a test suite that will kill these bugs. In this talk, I will discuss its scientific foundations, tools, and results. The foundations include semantics and conformance relations; the supporting tools involve model checkers, constraint solvers and SMT solvers; our experimental results are taken from two European projects on embedded-systems. I will conclude with a proposal how model-based mutation testing can be integrated into an agile, iterative development process.

1 Combining Model-Based and Mutation Testing

In this keynote talk I discuss the results of our ongoing research on model-based mutation testing. Mutation testing is a fault-based white-box testing technique. Model-based testing is a black-box testing technique. Their combination leads to a fault-based black-box testing technique that we call *model-based mutation testing*. Similar to the *Science of Programming* [12], we build our automated testing approach on formal semantics and refinement techniques.

Model-based testing is a black-box testing technique focusing on the external behaviour of a system under test (SUT). Hence, we assume that we have no access to the internals of the SUT, like e.g., the source code. The test stimuli are

F.H. de Carvalho Junior and L.S. Barbosa (Eds.): SBLP 2012, LNCS 7554, pp. 6–11, 2012.

automatically generated from an abstract model of the SUT. This test model is usually derived from the requirements. The model serves also as a test oracle providing the verdict (pass or fail) of a test case execution. The models are expressed in special modelling languages that support the abstract specification of the central properties to be tested. A detailed introduction to model-based testing can be found in [18,19].

Why should practitioners accept the efforts to learn new modelling languages and create models along their implementations? The answer is cost reduction. Testing consumes up to 50% of the development costs in a mission-critical project. Once the models and adaptors are created, the test cases come for free, i.e. they are automatically generated. Furthermore, when requirements change, it is much easier to change an abstract model compared to updating hundreds of hand-written test cases. Similarly, when the interface changes, only the test adaptor, mapping abstract test cases to the concrete implementation level, needs an update. Hence, test automation for saving costs is the major motivation from a practitioner's point of view.

Mutation testing is a way of assessing and improving a test suite by checking if its test cases can detect a number of injected faults in a program. The faults are introduced by syntactically changing the source code following patterns of typical programming errors. These deviations in the code are called mutations. The resulting faulty versions of the program are called mutants. Usually, each mutant includes only one mutation. Examples of typical mutations include renaming of variables, replacing operators, e.g., an assignment for an equivalence operator, and slightly changing Boolean and arithmetic expressions. The number and kind of mutations depend on the programming language and are defined as so-called *mutation operators*.

A mutation operator is a rewrite rule that defines how certain terms in the programming language are replaced by mutations. For every occurrence of the term the mutation operator rewrites the original program into a new mutant. After a set of mutants has been generated, the test cases are run both on the original and on each mutant. If a test case can distinguish a mutant from the original program, i.e. a different output behaviour can be observed, we say that this test case *kills a mutant*. The goal is to develop a test suite that kills all mutants, if possible (some mutants are behaviourally equivalent). This technique is known since the 1970ies and receives growing interest [14]. However, "most work on Mutation Testing has been concerned with the generation of mutants. Comparatively less work has concentrated on the generation of test cases to kill mutants." [14] In our work we address this, by focusing on test case generation.

Model-based mutation testing uses the model for both, generating test vectors and as a test oracle. Hence, we generate test cases from a model in order to test the conformance of a SUT. In contrast to classical model-based testing, only those test cases are generated that would kill a set of mutated models. The generated tests are then executed on the SUT and will detect if a mutated model has been implemented. Hence, model-based mutation testing rather tests against non-conformance, than for conformance. In terms of epistemology, we are rather aiming for falsification than for verification. It is a complementary fault-centred testing approach.

2 From Semantics to Automated Test-Case Generation

Contracts are pre-postcondition specifications added to the source code of a program. Contracts abstract away from the internals of an algorithm. Semantically, they represent relations between the program's state before and after execution.

Our first work on model-based mutation testing was purely theoretical [1,4]. The idea was to mutate the contracts and to derive test cases that would kill implementations of the mutated contract. We exploited the negated refinement laws of the refinement calculus. The result was a condition for a mutation test case for non-deterministic contracts: the input should cover the case where the mutant allows behaviour that is forbidden by the specification. In addition, the tests should cover valid inputs with undefined behaviour in the mutated specification. The insights gained were the key to our following more applied results.

We implemented a tool that took an *UML-OCL* contract and its mutant, translated it to a constraint solving problem, and generated a test case covering the fault in the mutant [8]. Later we applied this concept also to contracts in the C# language [15].

Communication protocols. More recently, we applied model-based mutation testing to several implementations of communication protocols. In this domain we are interested in sequences of observable communication events. Hence, the generated test cases have the form of event sequences in the deterministic case, or they have a tree-like shape in the non-deterministic case. This is in contrast to the work on contracts, where we only generated test cases as input-output vectors.

Our first work in this domain was the model-based testing of the Apache web-server[3]. In this project we modelled parts of the HTTP-protocol in a process algebra. We used counter-examples from conformance checks in the CADP toolbox as test-purposes for the test-case generator TGV [13]. The hundred generated mutation tests did find some unexpected behaviour in the conditional page requests to Apache.

Later, we optimised the technique for testing SIP registrars used in voice-over-IP applications, see e.g. [20]. Here, we developed our own input-output conformance checker (*ioco*) for generating mutation test cases. In one experiment the mutation tests detected one additional fault in the commercial implementation that was not revealed by other model-based testing techniques.

An interesting alternative to process algebras like LOTOS is the coordination language REO [9]. It is a visual modelling language for expressing a network coordinating the communication between a set of components. The coordination is exogenous, which means that the network is responsible for connecting and synchronising the communication. This new language for protocols opens new opportunities for mutation. For example, exchanging one type of a connector by another, changes the coordination pattern of a network. Hence, new fault models can be expressed by single (first order) mutations. The basis for test case generation was a new relational REO semantics [17]. This formulation made it possible to adopt our earlier theoretical results [4].

Embedded systems are another line of research. We developed a tool chain comprising a translator from UML to a version of Back's Action Systems [16] and a newly developed conformance checker for Action System models [11]. The tool can also handle the mutation testing of hybrid systems. Action systems are a kind of guarded command language for modelling concurrent reactive systems [10].

Our test case generator is an *ioco* checker for Action Systems. It takes two Action Systems, an original and a mutated one, and generates a test case that kills the mutant. It expects the actions being labelled as input, output and internal actions. For non-deterministic models a tree-like adaptive test case is generated. The tool was implemented in Sicstus Prolog exploiting the backtracking facilities during the model explorations.

Different strategies for selecting the test cases are supported: linear test cases to each fault, adaptive test cases to each fault, adaptive test cases to one fault. The test-case generator also checks if a given or previously generated test case is able to kill a mutant. Only if none of the test cases in a directory can kill a new mutant, a new test case is generated. Furthermore, the tool is able to generate test cases randomly. Our experiments showed that for complex models it is beneficial to generate first a number of long random tests for killing the most trivial mutants. Only when the randomly generated tests cannot kill a mutant, the computationally more expensive conformance check is started. The different strategies for generating test cases are reported in [2].

3   Symbolic Mutation Testing

We currently investigate different symbolic analysis techniques to address state space explosion: constraint solving and SMT solving are promising candidates. However, for reactive systems with long input-output traces, we cannot simply translate the non-conformance problem to one big formula and let the solvers do the job. A clever combination of normal form transformation, directed search and solving is necessary. Note that the solving of non-deterministic models is complex, since the formula includes negation [7].

First experiments with our tool based on a constraint solver have shown promising results [6]. By now, our symbolic tool has been applied to a car alarm system. The refinement checks for 207 mutants require 19 seconds, whereas our previous explicit *ioco* checker, spends 68 seconds for the same set of mutants [5]. Another implementation using the SMT solver Z3 shows similar good performance.

Generating test cases from mutants is computationally costly. This might be a reason for the limited amount of research in this direction. However, recent results show that for many systems under test this can be put into practise.

Acknowledgement. The recent research has received funding from the ARTEMIS Joint Undertaking under grant agreement N° 269335 and from the Austrian Research Promotion Agency (FFG) under grant agreement N° 829817 for the implementation of the project MBAT, Combined Model-based Analysis and Testing of Embedded Systems. The work was also funded by the Austrian Research Promotion Agency (FFG), program line "Trust in IT Systems", project number 829583, TRUst via Failed FALsification of Complex Dependable Systems Using Automated Test Case Generation through Model Mutation (TRUFAL).

References

1. Aichernig, B.K.: Mutation Testing in the Refinement Calculus. Formal Aspects of Computing 15(2-3), 280–295 (2003)
2. Aichernig, B.K., Brandl, H., Jöbstl, E., Krenn, W.: Efficient mutation killers in action. In: IEEE Fourth International Conference on Software Testing, Verification and Validation, ICST 2011, Berlin, Germany, March 21-25, pp. 120–129. IEEE Computer Society (2011)
3. Aichernig, B.K., Delgado, C.C.: From Faults Via Test Purposes to Test Cases: On the Fault-Based Testing of Concurrent Systems. In: Baresi, L., Heckel, R. (eds.) FASE 2006. LNCS, vol. 3922, pp. 324–338. Springer, Heidelberg (2006)
4. Aichernig, B.K., He, J.: Mutation testing in UTP. Formal Aspects of Computing 21(1-2), 33–64 (2009)
5. Aichernig, B.K., Jöbstl, E.: Efficient refinement checking for model-based mutation testing. In: Proceedings of the 12th International Conference on Quality Software (QSIC 2012). IEEE Computer Society (in press, 2012)
6. Aichernig, B.K., Jöbstl, E.: Towards symbolic model-based mutation testing: Combining reachability and refinement checking. In: 7th Workshop on Model-Based Testing (MBT 2012). EPTCS, vol. 80, pp. 88–102 (2012)
7. Aichernig, B.K., Jöbstl, E.: Towards symbolic model-based mutation testing: Pitfalls in expressing semantics as constraints. In: Workshops Proc. of the 5th Int. Conf. on Software Testing, Verification and Validation (ICST 2012), pp. 752–757. IEEE Computer Society (2012)
8. Aichernig, B.K., Salas, P.A.P.: Test case generation by OCL mutation and constraint solving. In: Cai, K.-Y., Ohnishi, A. (eds.) Fifth International Conference on Quality Software, QSIC 2005, Melbourne, Australia, September 19-21, pp. 64–71. IEEE Computer Society (2005)
9. Arbab, F.: Reo: A Channel-based Coordination Model for Component Composition. Mathematical Structures in Computer Science 14(3), 329–366 (2004)
10. Back, R.-J., Kurki-Suonio, R.: Decentralization of process nets with centralized control. In: 2nd ACM SIGACT-SIGOPS Symposium on Principles of Distributed Computing, PODC 1983, pp. 131–142. ACM (1983)
11. Brandl, H., Weiglhofer, M., Aichernig, B.K.: Automated conformance verification of hybrid systems. In: Wang, J., Chan, W.K., Kuo, F.-C. (eds.) Proceedings of the 10th International Conference on Quality Software, QSIC 2010, Zhangjiajie, China, July 14-15, pp. 3–12. IEEE Computer Society (2010)

12. Gries, D.: The Science of Programming. Texts and Monographs in Computer Science. Springer (1981)
13. Jard, C., Jéron, T.: TGV: theory, principles and algorithms. International Journal on Software Tools for Technology Transfer (STTT) 7(4), 297–315 (2005)
14. Jia, Y., Harman, M.: An analysis and survey of the development of mutation testing. IEEE Transactions on Software Engineering 37(5), 649–678 (2011)
15. Krenn, W., Aichernig, B.K.: Test case generation by contract mutation in Spec#. In: Finkbeiner, B., Gurevich, Y., Petrenko, A.K. (eds.) Proceedings of Fifth Workshop on Model Based Testing (MBT 2009), York, England, March 22. Electronic Notes in Theoretical Computer Science, vol. 253(2), pp. 71–86. Elsevier (October 2009)
16. Krenn, W., Schlick, R., Aichernig, B.K.: Mapping UML to Labeled Transition Systems for Test-Case Generation – A Translation via Object-Oriented Action Systems. In: de Boer, F.S., Bonsangue, M.M., Hallerstede, S., Leuschel, M. (eds.) FMCO 2009. LNCS, vol. 6286, pp. 186–207. Springer, Heidelberg (2010)
17. Meng, S., Arbab, F., Aichernig, B.K., Astefanoaei, L., de Boer, F.S., Rutten, J.: Connectors as designs: Modeling, refinement and test case generation. Science of Computer Programming 77(7-8), 799–822 (2012)
18. Utting, M., Legeard, B.: Practical Model-Based Testing: A Tools Approach. Morgan Kaufmann Publishers (2007)
19. Utting, M., Pretschner, A., Legeard, B.: A taxonomy of model-based testing approaches. Software Testing, Verification and Reliability (2011)
20. Weiglhofer, M., Aichernig, B.K., Wotawa, F.: Fault-based conformance testing in practice. International Journal of Software and Informatics 3(2-3), 375–411 (2009); Special double issue on Formal Methods of Program Development edited by Dines Bjoerner

Spill Code Placement for SIMD Machines

Diogo Nunes Sampaio, Elie Gedeon, Fernando Magno Quintão Pereira,
and Caroline Collange

Departamento de Ciência da Computação – UFMG – Brazil
{diogo,fernando}@dcc.ufmg.br, elie.gedeon@ens-lyon.fr

Abstract. The Single Instruction, Multiple Data (SIMD) execution model has
been receiving renewed attention recently. This awareness stems from the rise of
graphics processing units (GPUs) as a powerful alternative for parallel computing. Many compiler optimizations have been recently proposed for this hardware,
but register allocation is a field yet to be explored. In this context, this paper describes a register spiller for SIMD machines that capitalizes on the opportunity
to share identical data between threads. It provides two different benefits: first, it
uses less memory, as more spilled values are shared among threads. Second, it
improves the access times to spilled values. We have implemented our proposed
allocator in the Ocelot open source compiler, and have been able to speedup the
code produced by this framework by 21%. Although we have designed our algorithm on top of a linear scan register allocator, we claim that our ideas can be
easily adapted to fit the necessities of other register allocators.

1 Introduction

The increasing programmability, allied to the decreasing costs of graphics processing
units (GPUs), is boosting the interest of the industry and the academia in this hardware. Today it is possible to acquire, for a few hundred dollars GPUs with a thousand
processing units on the same board. This possibility is bringing together academics,
engineers and enthusiasts, who join efforts to develop new programming models that fit
the subtleties of the graphics hardware. The compiler community is taking active part
in such efforts. Each day novel analyses and code generation techniques that specifically target GPUs are designed and implemented. Examples of this new breed include
back-end optimizations such as Branch Fusion [10], thread reallocation [29], iteration
delaying [7] and branch distribution [17]. Nevertheless, register allocation, which is ar-
guably the most important compiler optimization, has still to be revisited under the light
of graphics processing units.

Register allocation is the problem of finding locations for the values manipulated by
a program. These values can be stored either in registers, few but fast, or in memory,
plenty but slow. Values mapped to memory are called *spills*. A good allocator keeps
the most used values in registers. Register allocation was already an important issue
when the first compilers where designed, sixty years ago [2]. Since then, this problem
has been explored in a plethora of ways, and today an industrial-strength compiler is as
good as a seasoned assembly programmer at assigning registers to variables. However,
GPUs, with their Single Instruction, Multiple Data (SIMD) execution model, pose new

F.H. de Carvalho Junior and L.S. Barbosa (Eds.): SBLP 2012, LNCS 7554, pp. 12–26, 2012.
© Springer-Verlag Berlin Heidelberg 2012

challenges to traditional register allocators. By taking advantage of explicit data-level parallelism, GPUs provide about ten times the computational throughput of comparable CPUs [19]. They run tens of thousands of instances (or *threads*) of a program at the same time. Such massive parallelism causes intense register pressure, because the register bank is partitioned between all threads. For instance, the GeForce 8800 has 8,192 registers per multiprocessor. This number might seem large at first, but it must be shared with up to 768 threads, leaving each thread with at most 10 registers. It is our goal, in this paper, to describe a register allocator that explores the opportunity to share identical data between threads to relieve register pressure.

In this paper we propose a *Divergence Aware Spilling Strategy*. This algorithm is specifically tailored for SIMD machines. In such model we have many threads, also called *processing elements* (PEs), executing in lock-step. All these PEs see the same set of virtual variable names; however, these names are mapped into different physical locations. Some of these variables, which we call *uniform*, always hold the same value for all the threads at a given point during the program execution. Our register allocator is able to place this common data into fast-access locations that can be shared among many threads. When compared to a traditional allocator, the gains that we can obtain with our divergence aware design are remarkable. We have implemented the register allocator proposed in this paper in the Ocelot open source CUDA compiler [12], and have used it to compile 46 well-known benchmarks to a high-end GPU. The code that we produce outperforms the code produced by Ocelot's original allocator by almost 21%. Notice that we are not comparing against a straw-man: Ocelot is an industrial quality compiler, able to process the whole PTX instruction set, i.e., the intermediate format that NVIDIA uses to represent CUDA programs. The divergence aware capabilities of our allocator have been implemented as re-writing rules on top of Ocelot's allocator. In other words, both register allocators that we empirically evaluate use the same algorithm. Thus, we claim in this paper that most of the traditional register allocation algorithms used in compilers today can be easily adapted to be divergence aware.

2 Background

C for CUDA is a programming language that allows programmers to develop applications to NVIDIA's graphics processing units. This language has a syntax similar to standard C; however, its semantics is substantially different. This language follows the so called Single Instruction, Multiple Thread (SIMT) execution model [14,15,20,21]. In this model, the same program is executed by many virtual threads. Each virtual thread is instantiated to a physical thread, and the maximum number of physical threads simultaneously in execution depends on the capacity of the parallel hardware. In order to keep the hardware cost low, GPUs resort to SIMD execution. Threads are bundled together into groups called *warps* in NVIDIA's jargon, or *wavefronts* in ATI's. Threads in a warp execute in lockstep, which allows them to share a common instruction control logic. As an example, the GeForce GTX 580 has 16 Streaming Multiprocessors, and each of them can run 48 warps of 32 threads. Thus, each warp might perform 32 instances of the same instruction in lockstep mode.

Regular applications, such as scalar vector multiplication, fare very well in GPUs, as we have the same operation being independently performed on different chunks of data.

However, divergences may happen in less regular applications when threads inside the same warp follow different paths after processing the same branch. The branching condition might be true to some threads, and false to others. Given that each warp has access to only one instruction at each time, in face of a divergence, some threads will have to wait, idly, while others execute. Hence, divergences may be a major source of performance degradation. As an example, Baghsorkhi *et al.* [3] have analytically showed that approximately one third of the execution time of the prefix scan benchmark [18], included in the CUDA software development kit (SDK), is lost due to divergences.

Divergence Analysis. A divergence analysis is a static program analysis that identifies variables that hold the same value for all the threads in the same warp. In this paper we will be working with a divergence analysis with affine constraints, which we have implemented previously [25]. This analysis binds each integer variable in the target program to an expression $a_1T_{id}+a_2$, where the special variable T_{id} is the thread identifier, and a_1, a_2 are elements of a lattice C. C is the lattice formed by the set of integers $\mathbb{Z}$ augmented with a top element $\top$ and a bottom element $\bot$, plus a meet operator $\wedge$. We let $c_1 \wedge c_2 = \bot$ if $c_1 \neq c_2$, $c \wedge \top = \top \wedge c = c$, and $c \wedge c = c$. Similarly, we let $c + \bot = \bot + c = \bot$. Notice that C is the lattice normally used to implement constant propagation; hence, for a proof of monotonicity, see Aho *et al* [1, p.633-635]. We define A as the product lattice $C \times C$. If (a_1, a_2) are elements of A, we represent them using the notation $a_1T_{id} + a_2$. We define the meet operator of A as follows:

$$(a_1T_{id} + a_2) \wedge (a_1'T_{id} + a_2') = (a_1 \wedge a_1')T_{id} + (a_2 \wedge a_2') \tag{1}$$

A divergence analysis with affine constraints classifies the program variables in the following groups:

- **Constant:** every processing element sees the variable as a constant. Its abstract state is given by the expression $0T_{id} + c, c \in \mathbb{Z}$.
- **Uniform:** the variable has the same value for all the processing elements, but this value is not constant along the execution of the program. Its abstract state is given by the expression $0T_{id} + \bot$.
- **Constant affine:** the variable is an affine expression of the identifier of the processing element, and the coefficients of this expression are constants known at compilation time. Its abstract state is given by the expression $cT_{id} + c', \{c, c'\} \subset \mathbb{Z}$.
- **Affine:** the variable is an affine expression of the identifier of the processing element, but the free coefficient is not known. Its abstract state is given by the expression $cT_{id} + \bot, c \in \mathbb{Z}$.
- **Divergent:** the variable might have possibly different values for different threads, and these values cannot be reconstructed as an affine expression of the thread identifier. Its abstract state is given by the expression $\bot T_{id} + \bot$.

Figure 1 illustrates how the divergence analysis is used. The kernel in Figure 1(a) averages the columns of a matrix m, placing the results in a vector v. Figure 1(b) shows this kernel in assembly format. We will be working in this representation henceforth. It is clear that all the threads that do useful work, e.g., that enter the gray area in 1(a) iterate the loop the same number of times. Some variables in this program always have

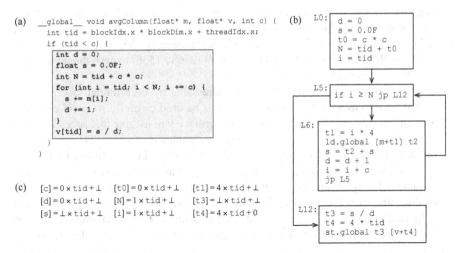

(a)
```
__global__ void avgColumn(float* m, float* v, int c) {
    int tid = blockIdx.x * blockDim.x + threadIdx.x;
    if (tid < c) {
        int d = 0;
        float s = 0.0F;
        int N = tid + c * c;
        for (int i = tid; i < N; i += c) {
            s += m[i];
            d += 1;
        }
        v[tid] = s / d;
    }
}
```

(b)
```
L0:  d = 0
     s = 0.0F
     t0 = c * c
     N = tid + t0
     i = tid

L5:  if i ≥ N jp L12

L6:  t1 = i * 4
     ld.global [m+t1] t2
     s = t2 + s
     d = d + 1
     i = i + c
     jp L5

L12: t3 = s / d
     t4 = 4 * tid
     st.global t3 [v+t4]
```

(c) $[c] = 0 \times tid + \bot$ $[t0] = 0 \times tid + \bot$ $[t1] = 4 \times tid + \bot$
     $[d] = 0 \times tid + \bot$ $[N] = 1 \times tid + \bot$ $[t3] = \bot \times tid + \bot$
     $[s] = \bot \times tid + \bot$ $[i] = 1 \times tid + \bot$ $[t4] = 4 \times tid + 0$

Fig. 1. (a) A kernel, written in C for CUDA, that fills a vector v with the averages of the columns of matrix m. (b) The control flow graph (CFG) of the gray area in the kernel code. (c) The results of a divergence analysis for this kernel.

the same value for all the threads. The constant c, and the base addresses m and v, for instance. Furthermore, variable d, which is incremented once for each iteration is also uniform. Other variables, like i, do not have the same value for all the processing elements, but their values are functions of the thread identifier T_{id}; hence, these variables are classified as affine. The limit of the loop, N, is also an affine expression of T_{id}. Because i and N are both affine expression of T_{id} with the same coefficient 1, their difference is uniform. Therefore, the divergence analysis can conclude that the loop is non-divergent; that is, all the threads that enter the loop iterate it the same number of times. Finally, there are variables that might have a completely different value for each processing element, such as s, the sum of each column, and t3, the final average which depends on s. Figure 1(c) summarizes the results of the divergence analysis.

3 Divergence Aware Register Allocation

In this section we explain why register allocation for GPUs differs from traditional register allocation. We also show how the divergence analysis can improve the results of register allocation. Finally, we close this section discussing some important design decisions that we chose to apply in our implementation.

3.1 Defining the Register Allocation Problem for GPUs

Similar to traditional register allocation we are interested in finding storage area to the values produced during program execution. However, in the context of graphics processing units, we have different types of memory to consider. Thus, in the rest of this paper we assume that a value can be stored in one of the following locations:

- **Registers:** these are the fastest storage regions. A traditional GPU might have a very large number of registers, for instance, one streaming multiprocessor (SM) of a GTX 580 GPU has 32,768 registers. However, running 1536 threads at the same time, this SM can afford at most 21 registers (32768 / 1536) to each thread in order to achieve maximum hardware occupancy.
- **Shared memory:** this fast memory is addressable by each thread in flight, and usually is used as a scratchpad cache. It must be used carefully, to avoid common parallel hazards, such as data races. Henceforth we will assume that accessing data in the shared memory is less than 3 times slower than in registers [24].
- **Local memory:** this off-chip memory is private to each thread. Modern GPUs provide a cache to the local memory, which is as fast as the shared memory. We will assume that a cache miss is 100 times more expensive than a hit.
- **Global memory:** this memory is shared among all the threads in execution, and is located in the same chip area as the local memory. The global memory is also cached. We shall assume that it has the same access times as the local memory.

As we have seen, the local and the global memories might benefit from a cache, which uses the same access machinery as the shared memory. Usually this cache is small: the GTX 580 has 64KB of fast memory, out of which 48KB are given to the shared memory by default, and only 16KB are used as a cache. This cache area must be further divided between global and local memories. Equipped with these different notions of storage space, we define the divergence aware register allocation problem as follows:

Definition 1. *Given a set of variables V, plus a divergence analysis* $D : V \mapsto A$, *find a mapping* $R : V \mapsto M$ *that minimizes the costs paid to access these variables. The possible storage locations M are registers, shared memory, local memory and global memory. Two variables whose live ranges overlap must be given different positions if they are placed on the same location.*

Figure 2 shows the instance of the register allocation problem that we obtain from the program in Figure 1. We use bars to represent the *live ranges* of the variables. The live range of a variable is the collection of program points where that variable is *alive*. A variable v is *alive* at a program point p if v is used at a program point p' that is reachable from p on the control flow graph, and v is not redefined along this path. The colors of the bars represent the abstract state of the variables, as determined by the divergence analysis.

3.2 A Quick Glance at Traditional Register Allocation

Figure 3 shows a possible allocation, as produced by a traditional algorithm, such as the one used in nvcc, NVIDIA's CUDA compiler. In this example we assume that a warp is formed by only two threads, and that each thread can use up to three general purpose registers. For simplicity we consider that the registers are type agnostic and might hold either integer or floating point values. Finally, we assume that the parameters of the kernel, variables c, m and v are already stored in the global memory. A quick inspection of Figure 2 reveals that only three registers are not enough to provide fast storage units to all the variables in this program. For instance, at label L8 we have

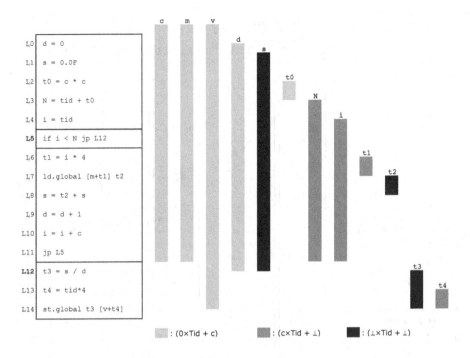

Fig. 2. An instance of the register allocation problem in graphics processing units

eight overlapping live ranges. Therefore, some variables must be mapped to memory, in a process known as *spilling*. The variables that are assigned memory locations are called *spills*. Minimizing the number of spilled values is a well-known NP-complete problem [8,22,26]. Furthermore, minimizing the number of stores and loads in the target program is also NP-complete [13]. Thus, we must use some heuristics to solve register allocation.

There exist many algorithms to perform register allocation. In this paper we adopt an approach called *linear scan* [23], which is used in many industrial strength compilers. The linear scan algorithm sees register allocation as the problem of coloring an interval graph, which has polynomial time solution [16]. However, this correspondence is not perfect: live ranges might have holes, which the intervals in an interval graph do not have. Thus, the linear scan algorithm provides an approximation of the optimal solution to the register allocation problem. This algorithms starts by linearizing the control flow graph of the program, finding an arbitrary ordering of basic blocks, in such a way that each live range is seen as an interval. The left side of Figure 2 shows a possible linearization of the program given in Figure 1(b). After linearizing the program, the allocator scans the live ranges, from the beginning of the program towards the end, assigning variables to registers in the process. If a spill must happen, then a conventional approach is to send to memory the variable with the furthest use from the spilling point onwards. This approach is known as *Belady's Heuristics*, as it has been first described by Belady in the context of virtual page management in operating systems [4].

Program	register file PE0			register file PE1			local PE0			local PE1			global		
	r0	r1	r2	r0	r1	r2	0	1	2	0	1	2	0	1	2
L0 d = 0													c	m	v
L1 st.local d [1]	d			d									c	m	v
L2 s = 0.0F	d			d				d			d		c	m	v
L3 st.local s [0]	d	s		d	s			d			d		c	m	v
L4 ld.global [0] c	d	s		d	s		s	d		s	d		c	m	v
L5 t0 = c * c	d	s	c	d	s	c	s	d		s	d		c	m	v
L6 N = tid + t0	t0	s	c	t0	s	c	s	d		s	d		c	m	v
L7 st.local N [2]	t0	s	N	t0	s	N	s	d		s	d		c	m	v
L8 i = tid	t0	s	N	t0	s	N	s	d	N	s	d	N	c	m	v
L9 ld.local [2] N	i	s	N	i	s	N	s	d	N	s	d	N	c	m	v
L10 if i < N jp L24	i	s	N	i	s	N	s	d	N	s	d	N	c	m	v
L11 t1 = i * 4	i	s	N	i	s	N	s	d	N	s	d	N	c	m	v
L12 ld.global [1] m	i	s	t1	i	s	t1	s	d	N	s	d	N	c	m	v
L13 ld.global [m+t1] t2	i	m	t1	i	m	t1	s	d	N	s	d	N	c	m	v
L14 ld.local [0] s	i	m	t2	i	m	t2	s	d	N	s	d	N	c	m	v
L15 s = t2 + s	i	s	t2	i	s	t2	s	d	N	s	d	N	c	m	v
L16 st.local s [0]	i	s	t2	i	s	t2	s	d	N	s	d	N	c	m	v
L17 ld.local [1] d	i	s	t2	i	s	t2	s	d	N	s	d	N	c	m	v
L18 d = d + 1	i	s	d	i	s	d	s	d	N	s	d	N	c	m	v
L19 st.local d [1]	i	s	d	i	s	d	s	d	N	s	d	N	c	m	v
L20 ld.global [0] c	i	s	d	i	s	d	s	d	N	s	d	N	c	m	v
L21 i = i + c	i	s	c	i	s	c	s	d	N	s	d	N	c	m	v
L22 jp L9	i	s	c	i	s	c	s	d	N	s	d	N	c	m	v
L23 ld.local [1] d	i	s	c	i	s	c	s	d	N	s	d	N	c	m	v
L24 t3 = s / d	i	s	d	i	s	d	s	d	N	s	d	N	c	m	v
L25 t4 = tid*4	t3	s	d	t3	s	d	s	d	N	s	d	N	c	m	v
L26 ld.global [2] v	t3	t4	d	t3	t4	d	s	d	N	s	d	N	c	m	v
L27 st.global t3 [v+t4]	t3	t4	v	t3	t4	v	s	d	N	s	d	N	c	m	v

Fig. 3. Traditional register allocation, with spilled values placed in local memory

Current register allocators for graphics processing units place spilled values in the local memory. Figure 3 illustrates this approach. In this example, variables s, d and N had to be spilled. Thus, each of these variables receive a slot in local memory. The spilled data must be replicated once for each processing element, as each of them has a private local memory area. Accessing data from the local memory is an expensive operation, because this region is off-chip. To mitigate this problem, modern GPUs provide a cache to the local and to the global memories. However, because the number of threads using the cache is large – in the order of thousands – and the cache itself is small, e.g., 16KBs, cache misses are common. In the next section we show that it is possible to improve this situation considerably, by taking the results of the divergence analysis into consideration.

3.3 Divergence Aware Spilling as a Set of Rewriting Rules

Figure 4 shows the code that we generate for the program in Figure 2. The most apparent departure from the allocation given in Figure 3 is the fact that we have moved to shared memory some information that was originally placed in local memory. Our divergence

Program		register file PE0			register file PE1			local PE0 0	local PE1 0	shared 0	shared 1	global 0	global 1	global 2
		r0	r1	r2	r0	r1	r2							
L0	d = 0											c	m	v
L1	st.shared d [0]	d			d							c	m	v
L2	s = 0.0F	d			d					d		c	m	v
L3	st.local s [0]	d	s		d	s				d		c	m	v
L4	ld.global [0] c	d	s		d	s		s	s	d		c	m	v
L5	t0 = c * c	d	s	c	d	s	c	s	s	d		c	m	v
L6	N = tid + t0	t0	s	c	t0	s	c	s	s	d		c	m	v
L7	st.shared t0 [1]	t0	s	N	t0	s	N	s	s	d		c	m	v
L8	i = tid	t0	s	N	t0	s	N	s	s	d	t0	c	m	v
L9	ld.shared [1] t0	i	s	N	i	s	N	s	s	d	t0	c	m	v
L10	N = tid + t0	i	s	t0	i	s	t0	s	s	d	t0	c	m	v
L11	if i < N jp L24	i	s	N	i	s	N	s	s	d	t0	c	m	v
L12	t1 = i * 4	i	s	N	i	s	N	s	s	d	t0	c	m	v
L13	ld.global [1] m	i	s	t1	i	s	t1	s	s	d	t0	c	m	v
L14	ld.global [m+t1] t2	i	m	t1	i	m	t1	s	s	d	t0	c	m	v
L15	ld.local [0] s	i	m	t2	i	m	t2	s	s	d	t0	c	m	v
L16	s = t2 + s	i	s	t2	i	s	t2	s	s	d	t0	c	m	v
L17	st.local s [0]	i	s	t2	i	s	t2	s	s	d	t0	c	m	v
L18	ld.shared [0] d	i	s	t2	i	s	t2	s	s	d	t0	c	m	v
L19	d = d + 1	i	s	d	i	s	d	s	s	d	t0	c	m	v
L20	st.shared d [0]	i	s	d	i	s	d	s	s	d	t0	c	m	v
L21	ld.global [0] c	i	s	d	i	s	d	s	s	d	t0	c	m	v
L22	i = i + c	i	s	c	i	s	c	s	s	d	t0	c	m	v
L23	jp L9	i	s	c	i	s	c	s	s	d	t0	c	m	v
L24	ld.shared [0] d	i	s	c	i	s	c	s	s	d	t0	c	m	v
L25	t3 = s / d	i	s	d	i	s	d	s	s	d	t0	c	m	v
L26	t4 = tid*4	t3	s	d	t3	s	d	s	s	d	t0	c	m	v
L27	ld.global [2] v	t3	t4	d	t3	t4	d	s	s	d	t0	c	m	v
L28	st.global t3 [v+t4]	t3	t4	v	t3	t4	v	s	s	d	t0	c	m	v

Fig. 4. Register allocation with variable sharing

aware register allocator is basically a system of rewriting rules built on top of a host algorithm. We have identified four different ways to rewrite the code produced by the traditional allocator, given the information made available by the divergence analysis. These rules are described in Figure 5. In the rest of this section we will describe each of these rules, and, in the process, explain how we arrived at the allocation given in Figure 4.

Constant Propagation. The divergence analysis discussed in Section 2 marks, as a byproduct, some variables as constants. Thus, it enables us to do constant propagation, a well-known compiler optimization [28]. Indeed, as mentioned before, the lattice that underlies this analysis is the same structure that grounds constant propagation. Variables that are proved to be constant do not need to be mapped into memory. As we see in the Figure 5(a), constant propagation can eliminate all the memory accesses related to the spilled value, cutting the stores off, and replacing the loads by simple variable assignments. In many cases it is possible to fold the constant value directly in the instruction where that value is necessary; thus, even avoiding the copy that replaces loads. In our experiments we did not find many opportunities to do constant propagation, simply because the code that we received from the NVIDIA compiler had already been optimized.

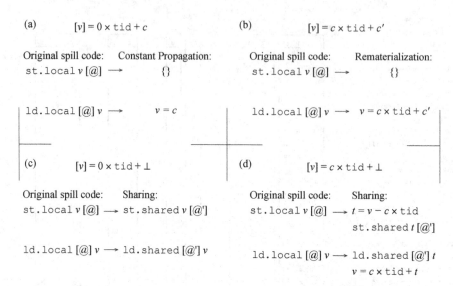

Fig. 5. Rules that rewrite the code produced by a divergent aware register allocator in order to take benefit from divergence information

However, we found many situations that benefit from the next rewriting rules that we describe.

Rematerialization. Variables that the divergence analysis identifies as affine constants can be rematerialized. Rematerialization is a technique proposed by Briggs *et al.* [6] to trade memory accesses by recomputation of values. If all the information necessary to reconstruct a spilled value is available in registers at the point where that value is needed, the register allocator can recompute this value, instead of bringing it back from memory. Like constant propagation, rematerialization is an optimization that completely eliminates all the memory accesses related to the spilled value. Figure 5(b) shows the rewriting rules that we use to rematerialize spilled values. Loads can be completely eliminated. Stores can be replaced by a recomputation of the spilled value, given the thread identifier.

Sharing of Uniform Variables. Threads inside a warp can share uniform variables. Figure 5(c) shows the rewriting rules that we use in this case. Accesses to the local memory are replaced by analogous accesses to the shared memory. In Figure 4 variable d has been shared in this way. Notice how the store in labels L1 and L19 in Figure 3 have been replaced by stores to shared memory in labels L1 and L20 of Figure 4. Similar changes happened to the instructions that load d from local memory in Figure 3.

Sharing of Affine Variables. The last type of rewriting rule, describing the sharing of affine variables, is shown in Figure 5(d). If the spilled variable v is an affine expression of the thread identifier, then its abstract state is $[\![v]\!] = c\mathsf{T}_{id} + t$, where c is a constant known statically, and t is a uniform value. In order to implement variable sharing in this case, we must extract t, the unknown part of v, and store it in shared memory. Whenever necessary to reload v, we must get back from shared memory its dynamic component t, and then rebuild v's value from the thread identifier and t. Notice that only one image of the value t is stored for all the threads in the warp. Thus, the sharing of affine and uniform variables produce the same number of accesses to the shared memory. The difference is that a multiply-add operation is necessary to reconstruct the affine value. Variable N has been spilled in this way in Figure 4. In line L7 we have stored its dynamic component. In lines L9 and L10 we rebuild the value of N, an action that replaces the load from local memory seen at line L9 of Figure 3.

3.4 Implementation Details

Handling Multiple Warps: There is an important implementation detail that deserves attention: a variable is uniform per warp; however, many warps integrate a GPU application. In fact, modern GPUs are implemented as multiple SIMD units [15]. In order to do variable sharing, we partition the shared memory among all the warps that might run simultaneously. This partitioning avoids the need to synchronize accesses to the shared memory between different warps. On the other hand, the register allocator requires more space in the shared memory. That is, if the allocator finds out that a given program demands N bytes to store uniform variables, and the target GPU runs up to M warps simultaneously, then the divergent aware register allocator will need $M \times N$ bytes in shared memory. We had to face an additional difficulty: we do not know, at compilation time, how many warps will run simultaneously. To circumvent this obstacle, our implementation assumes the existence of 32 warps in flight, the maximum number that our hardware supports. If the shared memory does not provide enough space for spilling, then our allocator falls back to the default execution mode, mapping spilled variables to local memory. This kind of situation will happen if the original program is already using too much of the shared memory space.

Spilling Policy. A good spilling policy for a divergent aware register allocator must consider the data type of the spilled variable and this variable's access frequency. For instance, the cost to rematerialize a variable depends on its size. Operations involving 64-bit integer values, on a NVIDIA's Fermi GPU, can be as much as four times slower than similar operations with 32-bits operands. Thus, the re-writing rule that replaces loads in Figure 5(b) and (d) can cost up to eight times more when applied onto doubles. In addition to the variable's data time, its access frequency also plays an important role in the overall cost of spilling it. The access frequency is more important when we consider the spilling of affine variables, as described in Figure 5(d). Each load of an affine variable has a fixed cost that includes reading the shared memory and performing a multiply-add operation to reconstruct the spilled value. If the variable is kept in the local memory, loading it might require an expensive trip to the off-chip memory space. However, if the variable is frequently accessed, then it is likely to be kept in cache from one load to the other. Thus, the cost of reading it from the local memory is amortized over the many times the variable is read or updated. On the other hand, if it is stored in the shared memory, not only the data access fee, but also the multiply-add cost must still be paid whenever the variable is loaded or stored.

SSA Elimination. Many compilers use the Static Single Assignment (SSA) form [11] as the default intermediate representation. Examples include gcc, LLVM, Jikes, and

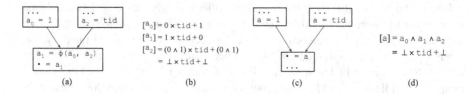

Fig. 6. (a) Program before SSA elimination. (b) Divergent status of the variables before SSA elimination. (c) Program after SSA elimination. (d) Divergent status after SSA elimination.

Ocelot, our target compiler. Programs in this format provide the core property that any variable has only one definition site. To ensure this property, the SSA format relies on a notational abstraction called ϕ-function, which merges the live ranges of different definitions of the same variable, as we show in Figure 6(a). It is possible to perform register allocation on SSA form programs [5]. However, it is more common to precede register allocation with a step called *SSA Elimination*, which replace the ϕ-functions by instructions usually found in assembly languages. There are different ways to perform SSA Elimination. A typical approach is to replace all the variables related by ϕ-functions by the same name [27]. This is the solution that we outline in Figure 6(c). Independent on the strategy used to eliminate ϕ-functions, the compiler must propagate the divergent status of variables when merging variable names. This propagation follows the meet operator that we defined for the lattice A in Equation 1. Continuing with our example, Figure 6(b) shows the divergent status of the variables before SSA Elimination, and Figure 6(d) shows it after. As the divergence analyses are done over SSA intermediate representation no coallesced variable will finish with a undefined value.

4   Experiments

Compiler and Hardware: we have implemented our divergence analysis and divergence aware register allocator in the Ocelot [12] open source compiler, SVN revision 1824 of April 2012. We have tested our implementation on an Intel Xeon X3440 with 8GB RAM equipped with a GPU Geforce GTX 470 with Nvidia's Cuda toolkit 4.1 and Device driver 295.41 (4.2).

Register Allocators: we have implemented two divergence aware register allocators, as re-writing rules on top of Ocelot's original linear scan register allocator. Thus, in this section we compare three different implementations. The first, which we use as a baseline, is the linear scan implementation publicly available in Ocelot. The second, which we call the *divergent* allocator uses Ocelot's default divergence analysis [10]. This analysis only classifies variables as divergent or uniform; hence, it can only use Rule (c) from Figure 5. The other divergence aware register allocator, which we call *affine*, uses the divergence analysis with affine constraints that we describe in [25]. It can use all the four rules in Figure 5. In our experiments we give each allocator only eight registers. For the two divergent aware implementations, this number includes the register necessary to hold the base of the spilling area in the shared memory.

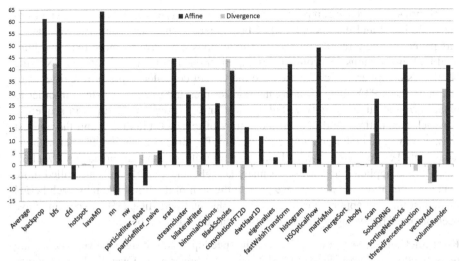

Fig. 7. Runtime results. Each bar gives the percentage of gain of the new allocator over Ocelot's original linear scan. Dark bars: divergence aware allocation with affine constraints – all the four rules in Figure 5. Light gray bars: allocation with simple divergence analysis – only Rule (c) of Figure 5.

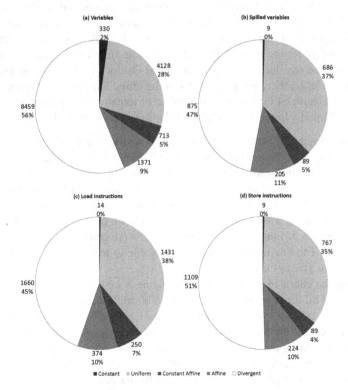

Fig. 8. Overall distribution, into the 5 types of affinity, of divergent states. (a)Variables (b)Spilled variables (c)Load instructions (d)Store instructions

Benchmarks: We have compiled 177 CUDA kernels from 46 applications taken from the Rodinia [9] and the NVIDIA SDK benchmarks, which are publicly available. In this paper we show results for the 23 applications that gave us more than one hundred PTX instructions. We convert these applications from C for CUDA to PTX using NVIDIA's compiler, nvcc. We then use the Ocelot compiler to perform register allocation on these PTX files, lowering the register pressure to eight registers. In order to obtain runtime numbers, each tested application was executed 11 times in sequence. For each application we discarded the results of the first, the fastest and the slowest runs, and averaged the remaining eight results. The time is given in CPU ticks, and is taken right before each kernel call and right after it exits and all threads are synchronized. Some applications consists of many kernels, and some kernels are called more than once per application. Thus, we present the sum of the times taken by each kernel that constitutes an application. The total average numbers, like 21% of speedup, have been obtained by averaging the sum of the total absolute numbers.

Runtime Comparison: Figure 7 shows the speedup that the different divergence aware register allocators provide over Ocelot's original linear scan. Overall, the divergence aware allocator with affine constraints speeds up the applications by 20.81%. The register allocator that only classifies variables as uniform or divergent provides a speed up of 6.21%. We cut the negative scale of the figure in −20%, but for two applications, Rodinia's nw and NVIDIA's SobolQRNG the affine allocator provides substantial slowdown: -380.55% and -146.55%. We believe that this slowdown is caused by the fact that the affine allocator must reserve two registers to handle spills: one for rematerializing values, and another for the base of the spill stack. The simple divergent aware allocator only spares one register for the spill stack, and Ocelot's linear scan can use all the eight registers. Hence, there are more spills in the affine allocator. Furthermore, these applications deal with 64 bit values, and the cost of rematerializing them, as discussed before, is substantially higher than if 32-bit values were used instead.

Static Results. Figure 8 shows how often each re-writing rules of Figure 5 have been used by the divergent aware register allocator with affine constraints. By analyzing Figure 8(a) we see that, on the average, 56% of the variables were classified as divergent. 28% of the variables were classified as uniform, and thus could be handle by the re-writing rules in Figure 5(c). 9% of the variables were classified as affine, and could be handled by Rule(d). 5% of the variables were shown to be constant affine; hence, fit Rule(b) of Figure 5. Finally, 2% of the variables were constants, and could be handled by Rule(a). The low number of constants is due to nvcc already optimizing the programs that we give to Ocelot.

Comparing the charts in part (a) and (b) of Figure 8 we see that with eight registers, about 13.89% of all the program variables had to be spilled, and thus mapped to memory. From Figure 8(b) we infer that most of the spill code, 47% uses the local memory, reflecting the fact that the majority of the program variables are divergent. 37% of the spilling code uses the shared memory according to Rule (c) from Figure 5. We could replace less than one percent of the spill code by constants, what is due to the low concentration of constants in the code that we obtain from nvcc. The other rules, for affine and constant affine variables account for 16% of the spill code. Figure 8(c) and (d) further distriminate between rules used to re-write stores, and rules used to re-write loads. Looking at these last two pies we observe a proportion of 1.69 uses of spilled variables for each definition. Ocelot adopts a spill-everywhere approach to place loads. According to this policy, each use of a spilled variable is replaced by a load instruction. In the case of divergence aware register allocation, some of these load and store instructions are re-written by the rules in Figure 5.

5   Conclusion

This paper has described what we believe is the first register allocator specifically tailored for the Single Instruction, Multiple Data execution model ever discussed in the compiler related literature. We have implemented the proposed allocator as a set of re-writing rules on top of the linear scan allocator used in an open source PTX compiler. Our code is available for download at http://simdopt.wordpress.com. This webpage also contains raw data, like the absolute numbers that we have used to produce the charts in Section 4. We have presented an extensive evaluation of the proposed allocator, but there are still work to be done in this area. In particular, we are interested in trying different spill policies that take into consideration more information related to the divergent state of program variables. We are also interested in identifying uniform variables that do not need to be replicated among every warp in the target program.

References

1. Aho, A.V., Lam, M.S., Sethi, R., Ullman, J.D.: Compilers: Principles, Techniques, and Tools, 2nd edn. Addison Wesley (2006)
2. Backus, J.: The history of fortran i, ii, and iii. SIGPLAN Not. 13(8), 165–180 (1978)
3. Baghsorkhi, S.S., Delahaye, M., Patel, S.J., Gropp, W.D., Hwu, W.M.W.: An adaptive performance modeling tool for GPU architectures. In: PPoPP, pp. 105–114. ACM (2010)
4. Belady, L.A.: A study of replacement algorithms for a virtual storage computer. IBM Systems Journal 5(2), 78–101 (1966)
5. Bouchez, F.: Allocation de Registres et Vidage en Mémoire. Master's thesis, ENS Lyon (October 2005)
6. Briggs, P., Cooper, K.D., Torczon, L.: Rematerialization. In: PLDI, pp. 311–321. ACM (1992)
7. Carrillo, S., Siegel, J., Li, X.: A control-structure splitting optimization for GPGPU. In: Computing Frontiers, pp. 147–150. ACM (2009)
8. Chaitin, G.J., Auslander, M.A., Chandra, A.K., Cocke, J., Hopkins, M.E., Markstein, P.W.: Register allocation via coloring. Computer Languages 6, 47–57 (1981)
9. Che, S., Boyer, M., Meng, J., Tarjan, D., Sheaffer, J.W., Lee, S.H., Skadron, K.: Rodinia: A benchmark suite for heterogeneous computing. In: IISWC, pp. 44–54. IEEE (2009)
10. Coutinho, B., Sampaio, D., Pereira, F.M.Q., Meira, W.: Divergence analysis and optimizations. In: PACT. IEEE (2011)
11. Cytron, R., Ferrante, J., Rosen, B.K., Wegman, M.N., Zadeck, F.K.: Efficiently computing static single assignment form and the control dependence graph. TOPLAS 13(4), 451–490 (1991)
12. Diamos, G., Kerr, A., Yalamanchili, S., Clark, N.: Ocelot, a dynamic optimization framework for bulk-synchronous applications in heterogeneous systems. In: PACT, pp. 354–364 (2010)

13. Farach-colton, M., Liberatore, V.: On local register allocation. Journal of Algorithms 37(1), 37–65 (2000)
14. Garland, M.: Parallel computing experiences with CUDA. IEEE Micro 28, 13–27 (2008)
15. Garland, M., Kirk, D.B.: Understanding throughput-oriented architectures. Commun. ACM 53, 58–66 (2010)
16. Golumbic, M.C.: Algorithmic Graph Theory and Perfect Graphs, 1st edn. Elsevier (2004)
17. Han, T.D., Abdelrahman, T.S.: Reducing branch divergence in GPU programs. In: GPGPU-4, pp. 3:1–3:8. ACM (2011)
18. Harris, M.: The parallel prefix sum (scan) with CUDA. Tech. Rep. Initial release on February 14, 2007, NVIDIA (2008)
19. Lee, V.W., Kim, C., Chhugani, J., Deisher, M., Kim, D., Nguyen, A.D., Satish, N., Smelyanskiy, M., Chennupaty, S., Hammarlund, P., Singhal, R., Dubey, P.: Debunking the 100X GPU vs. CPU myth: an evaluation of throughput computing on CPU and GPU. In: ISCA, pp. 451–460. ACM (2010)
20. Nickolls, J., Dally, W.J.: The GPU computing era. IEEE Micro 30, 56–69 (2010)
21. Nickolls, J., Kirk, D.: Graphics and Computing GPUs. In: Patterson, Hennessy (eds.) Computer Organization and Design, 4th edn., ch. A, pp. A.1–A.77. Elsevier (2009)
22. Pereira, F.M.Q., Palsberg, J.: Register Allocation After Classical SSA Elimination is NP-Complete. In: Aceto, L., Ingólfsdóttir, A. (eds.) FOSSACS 2006. LNCS, vol. 3921, pp. 79–93. Springer, Heidelberg (2006)
23. Poletto, M., Sarkar, V.: Linear scan register allocation. TOPLAS 21(5), 895–913 (1999)
24. Ryoo, S., Rodrigues, C.I., Baghsorkhi, S.S., Stone, S.S., Kirk, D.B., Hwu, W.M.W.: Optimization principles and application performance evaluation of a multithreaded GPU using CUDA. In: PPoPP, pp. 73–82. ACM (2008)
25. Sampaio, D., Martins, R., Collange, C., Pereira, F.M.Q.: Divergence analysis with affine constraints. Tech. rep., École normale supérieure de Lyon (2011)
26. Sethi, R.: Complete register allocation problems. In: 5th annual ACM Symposium on Theory of Computing, pp. 182–195. ACM Press (1973)
27. Sreedhar, V.C., Gao, G.R.: A linear time algorithm for placing ϕ-nodes. In: POPL, pp. 62–73. ACM (1995)
28. Wegman, M.N., Zadeck, F.K.: Constant propagation with conditional branches. TOPLAS 13(2) (1991)
29. Zhang, E.Z., Jiang, Y., Guo, Z., Tian, K., Shen, X.: On-the-fly elimination of dynamic irregularities for GPU computing. In: ASPLOS, pp. 369–380. ACM (2011)

Left Recursion in Parsing Expression Grammars

Sérgio Medeiros[1], Fabio Mascarenhas[2], and Roberto Ierusalimschy[3]

[1] Department of Computer Science – UFS – Aracaju – Brazil
sergio@ufs.br
[2] Department of Computer Science – UFRJ – Rio de Janeiro – Brazil
fabiom@dcc.ufrj.br
[3] Department of Computer Science – PUC-Rio – Rio de Janeiro – Brazil
roberto@inf.puc-rio.br

Abstract. Parsing Expression Grammars (PEGs) are a formalism that can describe all deterministic context-free languages through a set of rules that specify a top-down parser for some language. PEGs are easy to use, and there are efficient implementations of PEG libraries in several programming languages.

A frequently missed feature of PEGs is left recursion, which is commonly used in Context-Free Grammars (CFGs) to encode left-associative operations. We present a simple conservative extension to the semantics of PEGs that gives useful meaning to direct and indirect left-recursive rules, and show that our extensions make it easy to express left-recursive idioms from CFGs in PEGs, with similar results. We prove the conservativeness of these extensions, and also prove that they work with any left-recursive PEG.

Keywords: parsing expression grammars, parsing, left recursion, natural semantics, packrat parsing.

1 Introduction

Parsing Expression Grammars (PEGs) [3] are a formalism for describing a language's syntax, and an alternative to the commonly used Context Free Grammars (CFGs). Unlike CFGs, PEGs are unambiguous by construction, and their standard semantics is based on recognizing instead of deriving strings. Furthermore, a PEG can be considered both the specification of a language and the specification of a top-down parser for that language.

PEGs use the notion of *limited backtracking*: the parser, when faced with several alternatives, tries them in a deterministic order (left to right), discarding remaining alternatives after one of them succeeds. They also have an expressive syntax, based on the syntax of extended regular expressions, and *syntactic predicates*, a form of unrestricted lookahead where the parser checks whether the rest of the input matches a parsing expression without consuming the input.

The top-down parsing approach of PEGs means that they cannot handle left recursion in grammar rules, as they would make the parser loop forever. Left recursion can be detected structurally, so PEGs with left-recursive rules can be

F.H. de Carvalho Junior and L.S. Barbosa (Eds.): SBLP 2012, LNCS 7554, pp. 27–41, 2012.

simply rejected by PEG implementations instead of leading to parsers that do not terminate, but the lack of support for left recursion is a restriction on the expressiveness of PEGs. The use of left recursion is a common idiom for expressing language constructs in a grammar, and is present in published grammars for programming languages; the use of left recursion can make rewriting an existing grammar as a PEG a difficult task [17].

There are proposals for adding support for left recursion to PEGs, but they either assume a particular PEG implementation approach, *packrat parsing* [23], or support just direct left recursion [21]. Packrat parsing [2] is an optimization of PEGs that uses memoization to guarantee linear time behavior in the presence of backtracking and syntactic predicates, but can be slower in practice [18,14]. Packrat parsing is a common implementation approach for PEGs, but there are others [12]. Indirect left recursion is present in real grammars, and is difficult to untangle [17].

In this paper, we present a novel operational semantics for PEGs that gives a well-defined and useful meaning for PEGs with left-recursive rules. The semantics is given as a conservative extension of the existing semantics, so PEGs that do not have left-recursive rules continue having the same meaning as they had. It is also implementation agnostic, and should be easily implementable on packrat implementations, plain recursive descent implementations, and implementations based on a parsing machine.

We also introduce *parse strings* as a possible semantic value resulting from a PEG parsing some input, in parallel to the parse trees of context-free grammars. We show that the parse strings that left-recursive PEGs yield for the common left-recursive grammar idioms are similar to the parse trees we get from bottom-up parsers and left-recursive CFGs, so the use of left-recursive rules in PEGs with out semantics should be intuitive for grammar writers.

The rest of this paper is organized as follows: Section 2 presents a brief introduction to PEGs and discusses the problem of left recursion in PEGs; Section 3 presents our semantic extensions for PEGs with left-recursive rules; Section 4 reviews some related work on PEGs and left recursion in more detail; finally, Section 5 presents our concluding remarks.

2   Parsing Expression Grammars and Left Recursion

Parsing Expression Grammars borrow the use of non-terminals and rules (or productions) to express context-free recursion, although all non-terminals in a PEG must have only one rule. The syntax of the right side of the rules, the *parsing expressions*, is borrowed from regular expressions and its extensions, in order to make it easier to build parsers that parse directly from characters instead of tokens from a previous lexical analysis step. The semantics of PEGs come from backtracking top-down parsers, but in PEGs the backtracking is local to each choice point.

Our presentation of PEGs is slightly different from Ford's [3], and comes from earlier work [12,13]. This style makes the exposition of our extensions, and their

Empty String
$$\frac{}{G[\varepsilon]\ x \overset{PEG}{\leadsto} (x, \varepsilon)} \text{ (empty.1)}$$

Terminal
$$\frac{}{G[a]\ ax \overset{PEG}{\leadsto} (x, a)} \text{ (char.1)}$$

$$\frac{}{G[b]\ ax \overset{PEG}{\leadsto} \text{fail}}, b \neq a \text{ (char.2)} \qquad \frac{}{G[a]\ \varepsilon \overset{PEG}{\leadsto} \text{fail}} \text{ (char.3)}$$

Variable
$$\frac{G[P(A)]\ xy \overset{PEG}{\leadsto} (y, x')}{G[A]\ xy \overset{PEG}{\leadsto} (y, A[x'])} \text{ (var.1)} \qquad \frac{G[P(A)]\ x \overset{PEG}{\leadsto} \text{fail}}{G[A]\ x \overset{PEG}{\leadsto} \text{fail}} \text{ (var.2)}$$

Concatenation
$$\frac{G[p_1]\ xyz \overset{PEG}{\leadsto} (yz, x') \quad G[p_2]\ yz \overset{PEG}{\leadsto} (z, y')}{G[p_1\ p_2]\ xyz \overset{PEG}{\leadsto} (z, x'y')} \text{ (con.1)}$$

$$\frac{G[p_1]\ xy \overset{PEG}{\leadsto} (y, x') \quad G[p_2]\ y \overset{PEG}{\leadsto} \text{fail}}{G[p_1\ p_2]\ xy \overset{PEG}{\leadsto} \text{fail}} \text{ (con.2)} \qquad \frac{G[p_1]\ x \overset{PEG}{\leadsto} \text{fail}}{G[p_1\ p_2]\ x \overset{PEG}{\leadsto} \text{fail}} \text{ (con.3)}$$

Choice
$$\frac{G[p_1]\ xy \overset{PEG}{\leadsto} (y, x')}{G[p_1\ /\ p_2]\ xy \overset{PEG}{\leadsto} (y, x')} \text{ (ord.1)} \qquad \frac{G[p_1]\ x \overset{PEG}{\leadsto} \text{fail} \quad G[p_2]\ x \overset{PEG}{\leadsto} \text{fail}}{G[p_1\ /\ p_2]\ x \overset{PEG}{\leadsto} \text{fail}} \text{ (ord.2)}$$

$$\frac{G[p_1]\ xy \overset{PEG}{\leadsto} \text{fail} \quad G[p_2]\ xy \overset{PEG}{\leadsto} (y, x')}{G[p_1\ /\ p_2]\ xy \overset{PEG}{\leadsto} (y, x')} \text{ (ord.3)}$$

Not Predicate
$$\frac{G[p]\ x \overset{PEG}{\leadsto} \text{fail}}{G[!p]\ x \overset{PEG}{\leadsto} (x, \varepsilon)} \text{ (not.1)} \qquad \frac{G[p]\ xy \overset{PEG}{\leadsto} (y, x')}{G[!p]\ xy \overset{PEG}{\leadsto} \text{fail}} \text{ (not.2)}$$

Repetition
$$\frac{G[p]\ x \overset{PEG}{\leadsto} \text{fail}}{G[p^*]\ x \overset{PEG}{\leadsto} (x, \varepsilon)} \text{ (rep.1)} \qquad \frac{G[p]\ xyz \overset{PEG}{\leadsto} (yz, x') \quad G[p^*]\ yz \overset{PEG}{\leadsto} (z, y')}{G[p^*]\ xyz \overset{PEG}{\leadsto} (z, x'y')} \text{ (rep.2)}$$

Fig. 1. Semantics of the $\overset{PEG}{\leadsto}$ relation

behavior, easier to understand. We define a PEG G as a tuple (V, T, P, p_S) where V is the finite set of non-terminals, T is the alphabet (finite set of terminals), P is a function from V to parsing expressions, and p_S is the *starting expression*, the one that the PEG matches. Function P is commonly described through a set of rules of the form $A \leftarrow p$, where $A \in V$ and p is a parsing expression.

Parsing expressions are the core of our formalism, and they are defined inductively as the empty expression ε, a terminal symbol a, a non-terminal symbol A, a concatenation $p_1 p_2$ of two parsing expressions p_1 and p_2, an ordered choice p_1/p_2 between two parsing expressions p_1 and p_2, a repetition p^* of a parsing expression p, or a not-predicate $!p$ of a parsing expression p. We leave out extensions such as the dot, character classes, strings, and the and-predicate, as their addition is straightforward.

We define the semantics of PEGs via a relation $\overset{PEG}{\leadsto}$ among a PEG, a parsing expression, a subject, and a result. The notation $G[p]\ xy \overset{PEG}{\leadsto} (y, x')$ means that the expression p matches the input xy, consuming the prefix x, while leaving y

and yielding a *parse string* x' as the output, while resolving any non-terminals using the rules of G. We use $G[p]\ xy \overset{\text{PEG}}{\leadsto} \texttt{fail}$ to express an unsuccessful match. The language of a PEG G is defined as all strings that G's starting expression consumes, that is, the set $\{x \in T^* \mid G[p_s]\ xy \overset{\text{PEG}}{\leadsto} (y, x')\}$.

Figure 1 presents the definition of $\overset{\text{PEG}}{\leadsto}$ using natural semantics [11,25], as a set of inference rules. Intuitively, ε just succeeds and leaves the subject unaffected; a matches and consumes itself, or fails; A tries to match the expression $P(A)$; $p_1 p_2$ tries to match p_1, and if it succeeds tries to match p_2 on the part of the subject that p_1 did not consume; p_1/p_2 tries to match p_1, and if it fails tries to match p_2; p^* repeatedly tries to match p until it fails, thus consuming as much of the subject as it can; finally, $!p$ tries to match p and fails if p succeeds and succeeds if p fails, in any case leaving the subject unaffected. It is easy to see that the result of a match is either failure or a suffix of the subject (not a proper suffix, as the expression may succeed without consuming anything).

Context-Free Grammars have the notion of a *parse tree*, a graphical representation of the structure that a valid subject has, according to the grammar. The proof trees of our semantics can have a similar role, but they have extra information that can obscure the desired structure. This problem will be exacerbated in the proof trees that our rules for left-recursion yield, and is the reason we introduce parse strings to our formalism. A parse string is roughly a linearization of a parse tree, and shows which non-terminals have been used in the process of matching a given subject. Having the result of a parse be an actual tree and having arbitrary semantic actions are straightforward extensions.

When using PEGs for parsing it is important to guarantee that a given grammar will either yield a successful result or $\texttt{fail}$ for every subject, so parsing always terminates. Grammars where this is true are *complete* [3]. In order to guarantee completeness, it is sufficient to check for the absence of direct or indirect *left recursion*, a property that can be checked structurally using the *well-formed* predicate from Ford [3] (abbreviated *WF*).

Inductively, empty expressions and symbol expressions are always well-formed; a non-terminal is well-formed if it has a production and it is well-formed; a choice is well-formed if the alternatives are well-formed; a not predicate is well-formed if the expression it uses is well-formed; a repetition is well-formed if the expression it repeats is well-formed and cannot succeed without consuming input; finally, a concatenation is well-formed if either its first expression is well-formed and cannot succeed without consuming input or both of its expressions are well-formed.

A grammar is well-formed if its non-terminals and starting expression are all well-formed. The test of whether an expression cannot succeed while not consuming input is also computable from the structure of the expression and its grammar from an inductive definition [3]. The rule for well-formedness of repetitions just derives from writing a repetition p^* as a recursion $A \leftarrow pA\ /\ \varepsilon$, so a non-well-formed repetition is just a special case of a left-recursive rule.

Left recursion is not a problem in the popular bottom-up parsing approaches, and is a natural way to express several common parsing idioms. Expressing repetition using left recursion in a CFG yields a left-associative parse tree, which is often desirable when parsing programming languages, either because operations have to be left-associative or because left-associativity is more efficient in bottom-up parsers [6]. For example, the following is a simple left-associative CFG for additive expressions, written in EBNF notation:

$$E \to E + T \mid E - T \mid T$$
$$T \to n \mid (E)$$

Rewriting the above grammar as a PEG, by replacing | with the ordered choice operator, yields a non-well-formed PEG that does not have a proof tree for any subject. We can rewrite the grammar to eliminate the left recursion, giving the following CFG, again in EBNF (the curly brackets are metasymbols of EBNF notation, and express zero-or-more repetition, while the parentheses are terminals):

$$E \to T\{E'\}$$
$$T \to n \mid (E)$$
$$E' \to +T \mid -T$$

This is a simple transformation, but it yields a different parse tree, and obscures the intentions of the grammar writer, even though it is possible to transform the parse tree of the non-left-recursive grammar into the left-associative parse tree of the left-recursive grammar. But at least we can straightforwardly express the non-left-recursive grammar with the following PEG:

$$E \leftarrow T \ E'^*$$
$$T \leftarrow n \ / \ (E)$$
$$E' \leftarrow +T \ / \ -T$$

Indirect left recursion is harder to eliminate, and its elimination changes the structure of the grammar and the resulting trees even more. For example, the following indirectly left-recursive CFG denotes a very simplified grammar for l-values in a language with variables, first-class functions, and records (where x stands for identifiers and n for expressions):

$$L \to P.x \mid x$$
$$P \to P(n) \mid L$$

This grammar generates x and x followed by any number of (n) or $.x$, as long as it ends with $.x$. An l-value is a prefix expression followed by a field access, or a single variable, and a prefix expression is a prefix expression followed by an operand, denoting a function call, or a valid l-value. In the parse trees for this grammar each (n) or $.x$ associates to the left.

Writing a PEG that parses the same language is difficult. We can eliminate the indirect left recursion on L by substitution inside P, getting $P \to P(n) \mid P.x \mid x$, and then eliminate the direct left recursion on P to get the following CFG:

$$L \to P.x \mid x$$
$$P \to x\{P'\}$$
$$P' \to (n) \mid .x$$

But a direct translation of this CFG to a PEG will not work because PEG repetition is greedy; the repetition on P' will consume the last $.x$ of the l-value, and the first alternative of L will always fail. One possible solution is to not use the P non-terminal in L, and encode l-values directly with the following PEG (the bolded parentheses are terminals, the non-bolded parentheses are metasymbols of PEGs that mean grouping):

$$L \gets x \ S^*$$
$$S \gets (\ (n) \ )^*.x$$

The above uses of left recursion are common in published grammars, with more complex versions (involving more rules and a deeper level of indirection) appearing in the grammars in the specifications of Java [5] and Lua [10]. Having a straightforward way of expressing these in a PEG would make the process of translating a grammar specification from an EBNF CFG to a PEG easier and less error-prone.

In the next session we will propose a semantic extension to the PEG formalism that will give meaningful proof trees to left-recursive grammars. In particular, we want to have the straightforward translation of common left-recursive idioms such as left-associative expressions to yield parse strings that are similar in structure to parse trees of the original CFGs.

3 Bounded Left Recursion

Intuitively, *bounded left recursion* is a use of a non-terminal where we limit the number of left-recursive uses it may have. This is the basis of our extension for supporting left recursion in PEGs. We use the notation A^n to mean a non-terminal where we can have less than n left-recursive uses, with A^0 being an expression that always fails. Any left-recursive use of A^n will use A^{n-1}, any left-recursive use of A^{n-1} will use A^{n-2}, and so on, with A^1 using A^0 for any left-recursive use, so left recursion will fail for A^1.

For the left-recursive definition $E \gets E + n \ / \ n$ we have the following progression, where we write expressions equivalent to E^n on the right side:

$$E^0 \gets \texttt{fail}$$
$$E^1 \gets E^0 + n \ / \ n \ = \ \bot + n \ / \ n \ = \ n$$
$$E^2 \gets E^1 + n \ / \ n \ = \ n + n \ / \ n$$
$$E^3 \gets E^2 + n \ / \ n \ = \ (n + n \ / \ n) + n \ / \ n$$
$$\vdots$$
$$E^n \gets E^{n-1} + n \ / \ n$$

Table 1. Matching E with different bounds

Subject	E^0	E^1	E^2	E^3	E^4	E^5	E^6
n	fail	ε	ε	ε	ε	ε	ε
n+n	fail	+n	ε	+n	ε	+n	ε
n+n+n	fail	+n+n	+n	ε	+n+n	+n	ε

It would be natural to expect that increasing the bound will eventually reach a fixed point with respect to a given subject, but the behavior of the ordered choice operator breaks this expectation. For example, with a subject n+n and the previous PEG, E^2 will match the whole subject, while E^3 will match just the first n. Table 1 summarizes the results of trying to match some subjects against E with different left-recursive bounds (they show the suffix that remains, not the matched prefix).

The fact that increasing the bound can lead to matching a smaller prefix means we have to pick the bound carefully if we wish to match as much of the subject as possible. Fortunately, it is sufficient to increase the bound until the size of the matched prefix stops increasing. In the above example, we would pick 1 as the bound for n, 2 as the bound for n+n, and 3 as the bound for n+n+n.

When the bound of a non-terminal A is 1 we are effectively prohibiting a match via any left-recursive path, as all left-recursive uses of A will fail. A^{n+1} uses A^n on all its left-recursive paths, so if A^n matches a prefix of length k, A^{n+1} matching a prefix of length k or less means that either there is nothing to do after matching A^n (the grammar is cyclic), in which case it is pointless to increase the bound after A^n, or all paths starting with A^n failed, and the match actually used a non-left-recursive path, so A^{n+1} is equivalent with A^1. Either option means that n is the bound that makes A match the longest prefix of the subject.

We can easily see this dynamic in the $E \leftarrow E + n \ / \ n$ example. To match E^{n+1} we have to match $E^n + n \ /n$. Assume E^n matches a prefix x of the input. We then try to match the rest of the input with $+n$, if this succeeds we will have matched x+n, a prefix bigger than x. If this fails we will have matched just n, which is the same prefix matched by E^1.

Indirect, and even mutual, left recursion is not a problem, as the bounds are on left-recursive *uses* of a non-terminal, which are a property of the proof tree, and not of the structure of the PEG. The bounds on two mutually recursive non-terminals A and B will depend on which non-terminal is being matched first, if it is A then the bound of A is fixed while varying the bound of B, and vice-versa. A particular case of mutual left recursion is when a non-terminal is both left and right-recursive, such as $E \leftarrow E + E/n$. In our semantics, E^n will match $E^{n-1} + E/n$, where the right-recursive use of E will have its own bound. Later in this section we will elaborate on the behavior of both kinds of mutual recursion.

In order to extend the semantics of PEGs with bounded left recursion, we will show a conservative extension of the rules in Figure 1, with new rules for

Left-Recursive Variable

$$\frac{(A, xyz) \notin \mathcal{L} \quad G[P(A)] \ xyz \ \mathcal{L}[(A, xyz) \mapsto \mathtt{fail}] \overset{\text{PEG}}{\rightsquigarrow} (yz, x') \quad G[P(A)] \ xyz \ \mathcal{L}[(A, xyz) \mapsto (yz, x')] \overset{\text{INC}}{\rightsquigarrow} (z, (xy)')}{G[A] \ xyz \ \mathcal{L} \overset{\text{PEG}}{\rightsquigarrow} (z, A[(xy)'])} \quad \text{(lvar.1)}$$

$$\frac{(A, x) \notin \mathcal{L} \quad G[P(A)] \ x \ \mathcal{L}[(A, x) \mapsto \mathtt{fail}] \overset{\text{PEG}}{\rightsquigarrow} \mathtt{fail}}{G[A] \ x \ \mathcal{L} \overset{\text{PEG}}{\rightsquigarrow} \mathtt{fail}} \quad \text{(lvar.2)}$$

$$\frac{\mathcal{L}(A, xy) = \mathtt{fail}}{G[A] \ xy \ \mathcal{L} \overset{\text{PEG}}{\rightsquigarrow} \mathtt{fail}} \quad \text{(lvar.3)} \qquad \frac{\mathcal{L}(A, xy) = (y, x')}{G[A] \ xy \ \mathcal{L} \overset{\text{PEG}}{\rightsquigarrow} (y, A[x'])} \quad \text{(lvar.4)}$$

Increase Bound

$$\frac{G[P(A)] \ xyzw \ \mathcal{L}[(A, xyzw) \mapsto (yzw, x')] \overset{\text{PEG}}{\rightsquigarrow} (zw, (xy)') \quad G[P(A)] \ xyzw \ \mathcal{L}[(A, xyzw) \mapsto (zw, (xy)')] \overset{\text{INC}}{\rightsquigarrow} (w, (xyz)')}{G[P(A)] \ xyzw \ \mathcal{L}[(A, xyzw) \mapsto (yzw, x')] \overset{\text{INC}}{\rightsquigarrow} (w, (xyz)')} \ , \text{where } y \neq \varepsilon \ \text{(inc.1)}$$

$$\frac{G[P(A)] \ x \ \mathcal{L} \overset{\text{PEG}}{\rightsquigarrow} \mathtt{fail}}{G[P(A)] \ x \ \mathcal{L} \overset{\text{INC}}{\rightsquigarrow} \mathcal{L}(A, x)} \quad \text{(inc.2)} \qquad \frac{G[P(A)] \ xyz \ \mathcal{L}[(A, xyz) \mapsto (z, (xy)')] \overset{\text{PEG}}{\rightsquigarrow} (yz, x')}{G[P(A)] \ xyz \ \mathcal{L}[(A, xyz) \mapsto (z, (xy)')] \overset{\text{INC}}{\rightsquigarrow} (z, (xy)')} \quad \text{(inc.3)}$$

Fig. 2. Semantics for PEGs with left-recursive non-terminals

left-recursive non-terminals. For non-left-recursive non-terminals we will still use rules **var.1** and **var.2**, although we will later prove that this is unnecessary, and the new rules for non-terminals can replace the current ones. The basic idea of the extension is to use A^1 when matching a left-recursive non-terminal A for the first time, and then try to increase the bound, while using a memoization table $\mathcal{L}$ to keep the result of the current bound. We use a different relation, with its own inference rules, for this iterative process of increasing the bound.

Figure 2 presents the new rules. We give the behavior of the memoization table $\mathcal{L}$ in the usual substitution style, where $\mathcal{L}[(A, x) \mapsto X](B, y) = \mathcal{L}(B, y)$ if $B \neq A$ or $y \neq x$ and $\mathcal{L}[(A, x) \mapsto X](A, x) = X$ otherwise. All of the rules in Figure 1 just ignore this extra parameter of relation $\overset{\text{PEG}}{\rightsquigarrow}$. We also have rules for the new relation $\overset{\text{INC}}{\rightsquigarrow}$, responsible for the iterative process of finding the correct bound for a given left-recursive use of a non-terminal.

Rules **lvar.1** and **lvar.2** apply the first time a left-recursive non-terminal is used with a given subject, and they try to match A^1 by trying to match the production of A using $\mathtt{fail}$ for any left-recursive use of A (those uses will fail through rule **lvar.3**). If A^1 fails we do not try bigger bounds (rule **lvar.2**), but if A^1 succeeds we store the result in $\mathcal{L}$ and try to find a bigger bound (rule **lvar.1**). Rule **lvar.4** is used for left-recursive invocations of A^n in the process of matching A^{n+1}.

Relation $\overset{\text{INC}}{\rightsquigarrow}$ tries to find the bound where A matches the longest prefix. Which rule applies depends on whether matching the production of A using the memoized value for the current bound leads to a longer match or not; rule **inc.1** covers the first case, where we use relation $\overset{\text{INC}}{\leadsto}$ again to continue increasing the bound after updating $\mathcal{L}$. Rules **inc.2** and **inc.3** cover the second case, where the current bound is the correct one and we just return its result.

Let us walk through an example, again using $E \leftarrow E + n \;/\; n$ as our PEG, with n+n+n as the subject. When first matching E against n+n+n we have $(E, n + n + n) \notin \mathcal{L}$, as $\mathcal{L}$ is initially empty, so we have to match $E + n \;/\; n$ against n+n+n with $\mathcal{L} = \{(E, n + n + n) \mapsto \texttt{fail}\}$. We now have to match $E + n$ against n+n+n, which means matching E again, but now we use rule **lvar.3**. The first alternative, $E + n$, fails, and we have $G[E + n \;/n] \; n + n + n \; \{(E, n + n + n) \mapsto \texttt{fail}\} \overset{\text{PEG}}{\leadsto} (+n + n, n)$ using the second alternative, n, and rule **ord.3**.

In order to finish rule **lvar.1** and the initial match we have to try to increase the bound through relation $\overset{\text{INC}}{\leadsto}$ with $\mathcal{L} = \{(E, n + n + n) \mapsto (+n + n, n)\}$. This means we must try to match $E + n \;/\; n$ against n+n+n again, using the new $\mathcal{L}$. When we try the first alternative and match E with n+n+n the result will be $(+n + n, E[n])$ via **lvar.4**, and we can then use **con.1** to match $E + n$ yielding $(+n, E[n]+n)$. We have successfully increased the bound, and are in rule **inc.1**, with $x = n$, $y = +n$, and $zw = +n$.

In order to finish rule **inc.1** we have to try to increase the bound again using relation $\overset{\text{INC}}{\leadsto}$, now with $\mathcal{L} = \{(E, n + n + n) \mapsto (+n, E[n]+n)\}$. We try to match $P(E)$ again with this new $\mathcal{L}$, and this yields $(\varepsilon, E[E[n]+n]+n)$ via **lvar.4**, **con.1**, and **ord.1**. We have successfully increased the bound and are using rule **inc.1** again, with $x = n + n$, $y = +n$, and $zw = \varepsilon$.

We are in rule **inc.1**, and have to try to increase the bound a third time with $\overset{\text{INC}}{\leadsto}$, with $\mathcal{L} = \{(E, n + n + n) \mapsto (\varepsilon, E[E[n]+n]+n)\}$. We have to match $E + n \;/n$ against n+n+n again, using this $\mathcal{L}$. In the first alternative E matches and yields $(\varepsilon, E[E[E[n]+n]+n])$ via **lvar.4**, but the first alternative itself fails via **con.2**. We then have to match $E + n \;/\; n$ against n+n+n using **ord.2**, yielding $(+n + n, n)$. The attempt to increase the bound for the third time failed (we are back to the same result we had when $\mathcal{L} = \{(A, n + n + n) \mapsto \texttt{fail}\}$), and we use rule **inc.3** once and rule **inc.1** twice to propagate $(\varepsilon, E[E[n]+n]+n)$ back to rule **lvar.1**, and use this rule to get the final result, $G[E] \; n + n + n \; \{\} \overset{\text{PEG}}{\leadsto} (\varepsilon, E[E[E[n]+n]+n])$.

We can see that the parse string $E[E[E[n]+n]+n]$ implies left-associativity in the $+$ operations, as intended by the use of a left-recursive rule.

More complex grammars, that encode different precedences and associativities, behave as expected. For example, the following grammar has a right-associative $+$ with a left-associative $-$:

$$E \leftarrow M + E \;/\; M$$
$$M \leftarrow M - n \;/\; n$$

Matching E with n+n+n yields $E[M[n]+E[M[n]+E[M[n]]]]$, as matching M against n+n+n, n+n, and n all consume just the first n while generating $M[n]$, because $G[M - n \;/\; n] \; n + n + n \; \{(M, n + n + n) \mapsto \texttt{fail}\} \overset{\text{PEG}}{\leadsto} (+n + n, n)$ via **lvar.3**, **con.3**, and **ord.3**, and $G[M - n \;/\; n] \; n + n + n \; \{(M, n + n + n) \mapsto (+n + n, n)\} \overset{\text{INC}}{\leadsto} (+n + n, n)$ via **inc.3**. The same holds for subjects n+n and n with different suffixes. Now, when E matches n+n+n we will have M in $M + E$ matching the first n, while E recursively matching the second n+n, with M again matching the first n and E recursively matching the last n via the second alternative.

Matching E with n-n-n will yield $E[M[M[M[n]-n]-n]]$, as M now matches n-n-n with a proof tree similar to our first example ($E \leftarrow E + n \ / \ n$ against n+n+n). The first alternative of E fails because M consumed the whole subject, and the second alternative yields the final result via **ord.3** and **var.1**.

The semantics of Figure 2 also handles indirect and mutual left recursion well. The following mutually left-recursive PEG is a direct translation of the CFG used as the last example of Section 2:

$$L \leftarrow P.x \ / \ x$$
$$P \leftarrow P(n) \ / \ L$$

It is instructive to work out what happens when matching L with a subject such as x(n)(n).x(n).x. We will use our superscript notation for bounded recursion, but it is easy to check that the explanation corresponds exactly with what is happening with the semantics using $\mathcal{L}$.

The first alternative of L^1 will fail because both alternatives of P^1 fail, as they use P^0, due to the direct left recursion on P, and L^0, due to the indirect left recursion on L. The second alternative of L^1 matches the first x of the subject. Now L^2 will try to match P^1 again, and the first alternative of P^1 fails because it uses P^0, while the second alternative uses L^1 and matches the first x, and so P^1 now matches x, and we have to try P^2, which will match x(n) through the first alternative, now using P^1. P^3 uses P^2 and matches x(n)(n) with the first alternative, but P^4 matches just x again, so P^3 is the answer, and L^2 matches x(n)(n).x via its first alternative.

L^3 will try to match P^1 again, but P^1 now matches x(n)(n).x via its second alternative, as it uses L^2. This means P^2 will match x(n)(n).x(n), while P^3 will match x(n)(n).x again, so P^2 is the correct bound, and L^3 matches x(n)(n).x(n).x, the entire subject. It is easy to see that L^4 will match just x again, as P^1 will now match the whole subject using L^3, and the first alternative of L^4 will fail.

Intuitively, the mutual recursion is playing as nested repetitions, with the inner repetition consuming (n) and the outer repetition consuming the result of the inner repetition plus .x. The result is a PEG equivalent to the PEG for l-values in the end of Section 2 in the subjects it matches, but that yields parse strings that are correctly left-associative on each (n) and .x.

We presented the new rules as extensions intended only for non-terminals with left-recursive rules, but this is not necessary: the **lvar** rules can replace **var** without changing the result of any proof tree. If a non-terminal does not appear in a left-recursive position then rules **lvar.3** and **lvar.4** can never apply by definition. These rules are the only place in the semantics where the contents of $\mathcal{L}$ affects the result, so **lvar.2** is equivalent to **var.2** in the absence of left recursion. Analogously, if $G[(P(A)] \ xy \ \mathcal{L}[(A, xy) \mapsto \texttt{fail}] \overset{\text{PEG}}{\rightsquigarrow} (y, x')$ then

$G[(P(A)] \; xy \; \mathcal{L}[(A, xy) \mapsto (y, x')] \overset{PEG}{\leadsto} (y, x')$ in the absence of left recursion, so we will always have $G[A] \; xy \; \mathcal{L}[(A, xy) \mapsto (y, x')] \overset{INC}{\leadsto} (y, x')$ via **inc.3**, and **lvar.1** is equivalent to **var.1**. We can formalize this argument with the following lemma:

Lemma 1 (Conservativeness). *Given a PEG G, a parsing expression p and a subject xy, we have one of the following: if $G[p] \; xy \overset{PEG}{\leadsto} X$, where X is* fail *or (y, x'), then $G[p] \; xy \; \mathcal{L} \overset{PEG}{\leadsto} X$, as long as $(A, w) \notin \mathcal{L}$ for any non-terminal A and subject w appearing as $G[A] \; w$ in the proof tree of if $G[p] \; xy \overset{PEG}{\leadsto} X$.*

Proof. By induction on the height of the proof tree for $G[p] \; xy \overset{PEG}{\leadsto} X$. Most cases are trivial, as the extension of their rules with $\mathcal{L}$ does not change the table. The interesting cases are **var.1** and **var.2**.

For case **var.2** we need to use rule **lvar.2**. We introduce $(A, xy) \mapsto$ fail in $\mathcal{L}$, but $G[A] \; xy$ cannot appear in any part of the proof tree of $G[P(A)] \; xy \overset{PEG}{\leadsto}$ fail, so we can just use the induction hypothesis.

For case **var.1** we need to use rule **lvar.1**. Again we have $(A, xy) \mapsto$ fail in $\mathcal{L}$, but we can use the induction hypothesis on $G[P(A)] \; xy \; \mathcal{L}[(A, xy) \mapsto$ fail] to get (y, x'). We also use **inc.3** to get $G[P(A)] \; xy \; \mathcal{L}[(A, xy) \mapsto (y, x') \overset{INC}{\leadsto} (y, x')]$ from $G[P(A)] \; xy \; \mathcal{L}[(A, xy) \mapsto (y, x')]$, using the induction hypothesis, finishing **lvar.1**.

A non-obvious consequence of our bounded left recursion semantics is that a rule that mixes left and right recursion is right-associative. For example, matching $E \leftarrow E + E \; / \; n$ against n+n+n yields the parse string $E[E[n] + E[E[n] + E[n]]]$. The reason is that E^2 already matches the whole string:

$$E^1 \leftarrow E^0 + E \; / \; n = n$$
$$E^2 \leftarrow E^1 + E \; / \; n = n + E \; / \; n$$

We have the first alternative of E^2 matching n+ and then trying to match E with n+n. Again we will have E^2 matching the whole string, with the first alternative matching n+ and then matching E with n via E^1. In practice this behavior is not a problem, as similar constructions are also problematic in parsing CFGs, and grammar writers are aware of them.

An implementation of our semantics can use *ad-hoc* extensions to control associativity in this kind of PEG, by having a right-recursive use of non-terminal A with a pending left-recursive use match through A^1 directly instead of going through the regular process. Similar extensions can be used to have different associativities and precedences in operator grammars such as $E \leftarrow E + E \; / \; E - E \; / \; E * E \; / \; (E) \; / \; n$.

In order to prove that our semantics for PEGs with left-recursion gives meaning to any closed PEG (that is, any PEG G where $P(A)$ is defined for all non-terminals in G) we have to fix the case where a repetition may not terminate (p in p^* has not failed but not consumed any input). We can add a $x \neq \varepsilon$ predicate to rule **rep.2** and then add a new rule:

$$\frac{G[p] \ x \ \mathcal{L} \ \overset{PEG}{\rightsquigarrow} \ (x, \varepsilon)}{G[p^*] \ x \ \mathcal{L} \ \overset{PEG}{\rightsquigarrow} \ (x, \varepsilon)} \ \textbf{(rep.3)}$$

We also need a well-founded ordering $<$ among the elements of the left side of relation $\overset{PEG}{\rightsquigarrow}$. For the subject we can use $x < y$ if and only if x is a proper suffix of y as the order, for the parsing expression we can use $p_1 < p_2$ if and only if p_1 is a proper part of the structure of p_2, and for $\mathcal{L}$ we can use $\mathcal{L}[A \mapsto (x, y)] < \mathcal{L}$ if and only if either $\mathcal{L}(A)$ is not defined or $x < z$, where $\mathcal{L}(A) = (z, w)$. Now we can prove the following lemma:

Lemma 2 (Completeness). *Given a closed PEG G, a parsing expression p, a subject xy, and a memoization table $\mathcal{L}$, we have either $G[p] \ xy \ \mathcal{L} \ \overset{PEG}{\rightsquigarrow} \ (y, x')$ or $G[p] \ xy \ \mathcal{L} \ \overset{PEG}{\rightsquigarrow}$ fail.*

Proof. By induction on the triple $(\mathcal{L}, xy, p)$. It is straightforward to check that we can always use the induction hypothesis on the antecedent of the rules of our semantics.

4 Related Work

Warth et al. [23] describes a modification of the packrat parsing algorithm to support both direct and indirect left recursion. The algorithm uses the packrat memoization table to detect left recursion, and then begins an iterative process that is similar to the process of finding the correct bound in our semantics.

Warth et al.'s algorithm is tightly coupled to the packrat parsing approach, and its full version, with support for indirect left recursion, is complex, as noted by the authors [22]. The release versions of the authors' PEG parsing library, OMeta [24], only implement support for direct left recursion to avoid the extra complexity [22].

The algorithm also produces surprising results with some grammars, both directly and indirectly left-recursive, due to the way it tries to reuse the packrat memoization table [1]. Our semantics does not share these issues, although it shows that a left-recursive packrat parser cannot index the packrat memoization table just by a parsing expression and a subject, as the $\mathcal{L}$ table is also involved. One solution to this issue is to have a scoped packrat memoization table, with a new entry to $\mathcal{L}$ introducing a new scope. We believe this solution is simpler to implement in a packrat parser than Warth et al.'s.

Tratt [21] presents an algorithm for supporting direct left recursion in PEGs, based on Warth et al.'s, that does not use a packrat memoization table and does not assume a packrat parser. The algorithm is simple, although Tratt also presents a more complex algorithm that tries to "fix" the right-recursive bias in productions that have both left and right recursion, like the $E \leftarrow E + E \ / \ n$ example we discussed at the end of Section 3. We do not believe this bias is a problem, although it can be fixed in our semantics with ad-hoc methods.

IronMeta [20] is a PEG library for the Microsoft Common Language Runtime, based on OMeta [24], that supports direct and indirect left recursion using an implementation of an unpublished preliminary version of our semantics. This preliminary version is essentially the same, apart from notational details, so IronMeta can be considered a working implementation of our semantics. Initial versions of IronMeta used Warth et al.'s algorithm for left recursion [23], but in version 2.0 the author switched to an implementation of our semantics, which he considered "much simpler and more general" [20].

Parser combinators [8] are a top-down parsing method that is similar to PEGs, being another way to declaratively specify a recursive descent parser for a language, and share with PEGs the same issues of non-termination in the presence of left recursion. Frost et al. [4] describes an approach for supporting left recursion in parser combinators where a count of the number of left-recursive uses of a non-terminal is kept, and the non-terminal fails if the count exceeds the number of tokens of the input. We have shown in Section 3 that such an approach would not work with PEGs, because of the semantics of ordered choice (parser combinators use the same non-deterministic choice operator as CFGs). Ridge [19] presents another way of implementing the same approach for handling left recursion, and has the same issues regarding its application to PEGs.

ANTLR [16] is a popular parser generator that produces top-down parsers for Context-Free Grammars based on LL(*), an extension of LL(k) parsing. Version 4 of ANTLR will have support for direct left recursion that is specialized for expression parsers [15], handling precedence and associativity by rewriting the grammar to encode a *precedence climbing* parser [7]. This support is heavily dependent on ANTLR extensions such as semantic predicates and backtracking.

5   Conclusion

We presented a conservative extension to the semantics of PEGs that gives an useful meaning for PEGs with left-recursive rules. It is the first extension that is not based on packrat parsing as the parsing approach, while supporting both direct and indirect left recursion. The extension is based on bounded left recursion, where we limit the number of left-recursive uses a non-terminal may have, guaranteeing termination, and we use an iterative process to find the smallest bound that gives the longest match for a particular use of the non-terminal.

We also presented some examples that show how grammar writers can use our extension to express in PEGs common left-recursive idioms from Context-Free Grammars, such as using left recursion for left-associative repetition in expression grammars, and the use of mutual left recursion for nested left-associative repetition. We augmented the semantics with *parse strings* to show how we get a similar structure with left-recursive PEGs that we get with the parse trees of left-recursive CFGs.

Finally, we have proved the conservativeness of our extension, and also proved that all PEGs are complete with the extension, so termination is guaranteed for the parsing of any subject with any PEG, removing the need for any static checks of well-formedness beyond the simple check that every non-terminal in the grammar has a rule.

Our semantics has already been implemented in a PEG library that uses packrat parsing [20]. We are now working on adapting the semantics to a PEG parsing machine [12], as the first step towards an alternative implementation based on LPEG [9]. This implementation will incorporate ad-hoc extensions for controlling precedence and associativity in grammars mixing left and right recursion in the same rule, leading to more concise grammars.

References

1. Cooney, D.: Problem with nullable left recursion and trailing rules in Packrat Parsers Can Support Left Recursion. PEG Mailing List (2009),
   https://lists.csail.mit.edu/pipermail/peg/2009-November/000244.html
2. Ford, B.: Packrat parsing: Simple, powerful, lazy, linear time. In: Proceedings of the 7th ACM SIGPLAN International Conference on Functional Programming, ICFP 2002, pp. 36–47. ACM, New York (2002)
3. Ford, B.: Parsing expression grammars: a recognition-based syntactic foundation. In: POPL 2004: Proceedings of the 31st ACM SIGPLAN-SIGACT Symposium on Principles of Programming Languages, pp. 111–122. ACM, New York (2004)
4. Frost, R.A., Hafiz, R., Callaghan, P.: Parser Combinators for Ambiguous Left-Recursive Grammars. In: Hudak, P., Warren, D.S. (eds.) PADL 2008. LNCS, vol. 4902, pp. 167–181. Springer, Heidelberg (2008),
   http://dl.acm.org/citation.cfm?id=1785754.1785766
5. Gosling, J., Joy, B., Steele, G., Bracha, G.: The Java Language Specification. Addison-Wesley Professional (2005)
6. Grune, D., Jacobs, C.J.: Parsing Techniques – A Practical Guide. Ellis Horwood (1991)
7. Hanson, D.R.: Compact recursive-descent parsing of expressions. Software: Practice and Experience 15(12), 1205–1212 (1985),
   http://dx.doi.org/10.1002/spe.4380151206
8. Hutton, G.: Higher-order Functions for Parsing. Journal of Functional Programming 2(3), 323–343 (1992)
9. Ierusalimschy, R.: A text pattern-matching tool based on Parsing Expression Grammars. Software - Practice and Experience 39(3), 221–258 (2009)
10. Ierusalimschy, R., de Figueiredo, L.H., Celes, W.: Lua 5.1 Reference Manual. Lua.Org (2006)
11. Kahn, G.: Natural Semantics. In: Brandenburg, F.J., Wirsing, M., Vidal-Naquet, G. (eds.) STACS 1987. LNCS, vol. 247, pp. 22–39. Springer, Heidelberg (1987)
12. Medeiros, S., Ierusalimschy, R.: A parsing machine for PEGs. In: DLS 2008: Dynamic Languages Symposium, pp. 1–12. ACM, New York (2008)
13. Medeiros, S., Mascarenhas, F., Ierusalimschy, R.: From Regular Expressions to Parsing Expression Grammars. In: SBLP 2011: Brazilian Programming Languages Symposium (2011)
14. Mizushima, K., Maeda, A., Yamaguchi, Y.: Packrat parsers can handle practical grammars in mostly constant space. In: Proceedings of the 9th ACM SIGPLAN-SIGSOFT Workshop on Program Analysis for Software Tools and Engineering, PASTE 2010, pp. 29–36. ACM, New York (2010)
15. Parr, T.: ANTLR's left-recursion prototype. PEG mailing list (2011),
    https://lists.csail.mit.edu/pipermail/peg/2011-April/000414.html

16. Parr, T., Fisher, K.: LL(*): the foundation of the ANTLR parser generator. In: Proceedings of the 32nd ACM SIGPLAN Conference on Programming Language Design and Implementation, PLDI 2011, pp. 425–436. ACM, New York (2011), `http://doi.acm.org/10.1145/1993498.1993548`
17. Redziejowski, R.R.: Parsing expression grammar as a primitive recursive-descent parser with backtracking. Fundamenta Informaticae 79(3-4), 513–524 (2008)
18. Redziejowski, R.R.: Some aspects of parsing expression grammar. Fundamenta Informaticae 85, 441–451 (2008)
19. Ridge, T.: Simple, Functional, Sound and Complete Parsing for All Context-Free Grammars. In: Jouannaud, J.-P., Shao, Z. (eds.) CPP 2011. LNCS, vol. 7086, pp. 103–118. Springer, Heidelberg (2011), `http://dx.doi.org/10.1007/978-3-642-25379-9_10`
20. Tisher, G.: IronMeta parser generator (2012), `http://ironmeta.sourceforge.net`
21. Tratt, L.: Direct left-recursive parsing expression grammars. Tech. Rep. EIS-10-01, School of Engineering and Information Sciences, Middlesex University (October 2010)
22. Warth, A.: OMeta squeak left recursion? OMeta Mailing List (June 2008), `http://vpri.org/pipermail/ometa/2008-June/000006.html`
23. Warth, A., Douglass, J., Millstein, T.: Packrat parsers can support left recursion. In: PEPM 2008: Proceedings of the 2008 ACM SIGPLAN Symposium on Partial Evaluation and Semantics-Based Program Manipulation, pp. 103–110. ACM, New York (2008)
24. Warth, A., Piumarta, I.: OMeta: an object-oriented language for pattern matching. In: DLS 2007: Proceedings of the 2007 Symposium on Dynamic Languages, pp. 11–19. ACM, New York (2007)
25. Winskel, G.: The Formal Semantics of Programming Languages: An Introduction. Foundations of Computing. MIT Press (1993)

Speed and Precision in Range Analysis

Victor Hugo Sperle Campos, Raphael Ernani Rodrigues,
Igor Rafael de Assis Costa, and Fernando Magno Quintão Pereira

Department of Computer Science – UFMG – Brazil
{victorsc,raphael,igor,fernando}@dcc.ufmg.br

Abstract. Range analysis is a compiler technique that determines statically the lower and upper values that each integer variable from a target program may assume during this program's execution. This type of inference is very important, because it enables several compiler optimizations, such as dead and redundant code elimination, bitwidth aware register allocation, and detection of program vulnerabilities. In this paper we describe an inter-procedural, context-sensitive range analysis algorithm that we have implemented in the LLVM compiler. During the effort to produce an industrial-quality implementation of our algorithm, we had to face a constant tension between precision and speed. The foremost goal of this paper is to discuss the many engineering choices that, due to this tension, have shaped our implementation. Given the breath of our evaluation, we believe that this paper contains the most comprehensive empirical study of a range analysis algorithm ever presented in the compiler related literature.

1 Introduction

Range analysis is a compiler technique whose objective is to determine statically, for each program variable, limits for the minimum and maximum values that this variable might assume during the program execution. Range analysis is important because it enables many compiler optimizations. Among these optimizations, the most well-known are dead and redundant code elimination. Examples of redundant code elimination include the removal of array bounds checks [3,13,27] and overflow checks [22]. Additionally, range analysis is also used in bitwidth aware register allocation [1,19,26], branch prediction [18] and synthesis of hardware for specific applications [4,12,14,23]. Because of this importance, the programming language community has put much effort in the design and implementation of efficient and precise range analysis algorithms.

However, the compiler related literature does not contain a comprehensive evaluation of range analysis algorithms that scale up to entire programs. Many works on this subject are limited to very small programs [14,21,23], or, given their theoretic perspective, have never been implemented in production compilers [9,10,24,25]. There are implementations of range analysis that deal with very large programs [2,6,13,16]; nevertheless, because these papers focus on applications of range analysis, and not on its implementation, they do not provide a thorough discussion about their engineering decisions. A noticeable exception is

F.H. de Carvalho Junior and L.S. Barbosa (Eds.): SBLP 2012, LNCS 7554, pp. 42–56, 2012.

the recent work of Oh *et al.* [17], which discusses a range analysis algorithm developed for C programs that can handle very large benchmarks. Oh *et al.* present an evaluation of the speed and memory consumption of their implementation. In this paper we claim to push this discussion considerably further.

We have implemented an industrial-quality range analysis algorithm in the LLVM compiler [11]. While designing and implementing our algorithm we had to face several important engineering choices. Many approaches that we have used in an attempt to increase the precision of our implementation would result in runtime slowdowns. Although we cannot determine the optimum spot in this design space, given the vast number of possibilities, we discuss our most important implementation decisions in Section 3. Section 3.1 shows how we can improve runtime and precision substantially by processing data-flow information in the strongly connected components that underly our constraint system. Section 3.2 discuss the importance of choosing a suitable intermediate representation when implementing a sparse data-flow framework. Section 3.3 compares the intra-procedural and the inter-procedural versions of our algorithm. The role of context sensitiveness is discussed in Section 3.4. Finally, Section 3.5 discusses the different widening strategies that we have experimented with.

This work concludes a two years long effort to produce a solid and scalable implementation of range analysis. Our first endeavor to implement such an algorithm was based on Su and Wagner's constraint system [24,25]. However, although we could use their formulation to handle a subset of C-like constructs, their description of how to deal with loops was not very explicit. Thus, in order to solve loops we adopted Gawlitza *et al.*'s [9] approach. This technique uses the Bellman-Ford algorithm to detect increasing or decreasing cycles in the constraint system, and then saturates these cycles via a simple widening operator. A detailed description of our implementation has been published by Couto and Pereira [8]. Nevertheless, the inability to handle comparisons between variables, and the cubic complexity of the Bellman-Ford method eventually led us to seek alternative solutions to range analysis. This quest reached a pinnacle in the present work, which we summarize in this paper.

2   Brief Description of Our Range Analysis Algorithm

The Interval Lattice. Following Gawlitza *et al.*'s notation, we shall be performing arithmetic operations over the lattice $\mathcal{Z} = \mathbb{Z} \cup \{-\infty, +\infty\}$, where the ordering is naturally given by $-\infty < \ldots -1 < 0 < 1 \ldots < +\infty$. We let meet and join be the min and max operators respectively. For any $x > -\infty$ we define:

$$x + \infty = \infty \qquad x - \infty = -\infty$$
$$x \times \infty = \infty \text{ if } x > 0 \quad x \times \infty = -\infty \text{ if } x < 0$$
$$0 \times \infty = 0 \qquad (-\infty) \times \infty = \text{ not defined}$$

From the lattice $\mathcal{Z}$ we define the product lattice $\mathcal{Z}^2$, partially ordered by the subset relation $\sqsubseteq$, and defined as $\mathcal{Z}^2 = \emptyset \cup \{[z_1, z_2] | z_1, z_2 \in \mathcal{Z}, z_1 \leq z_2, -\infty < z_2\}$. The objective of range analysis is to determine a mapping $I : V \mapsto \mathcal{Z}^2$ from

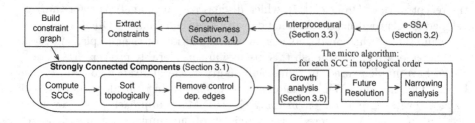

Fig. 1. Our implementation of range analysis. Rounded boxes are optional modules. The grey box is a module implemented in LLVM; the other parts are our contributions.

the set of integer program variables V to intervals, such that, for any variable $v \in V$, if $I(v) = [l, u]$, then, during the execution of the target program, any value i assigned to v is such that $l \leq i \leq u$.

A Holistic View of Our Range Analysis Algorithm. Figure 1 gives a global view of our range analysis algorithm. We perform range analysis in a number of steps, some of which are optional. The optional parts improve the precision of the range analysis, at the expense of a longer running time. In Section 3 we discuss in more detail these tradeoffs.

We will illustrate the mandatory parts of the algorithm via the example program in Figure 2. More details about each phase of the algorithm will be introduced in Section 3, when we discuss our engineering decisions. Figure 2(a) shows an example program taken from the partition function of the quicksort algorithm used by Bodik *et al.* [3]. Figure 2(b) shows one possible way to represent this program internally. As we explain in Section 3.2, a good program representation helps range analysis to find more precise results. In this example we chose a program representation called Extended Static Single Assignment form [3], which lets us solve range analysis via a path sensitive algorithm. This representation uses the ϕ-functions typical in SSA form programs [7], plus *futures* (**ft**), which we shall define later. Figure 2(c) shows the constraints that we extract from the intermediate representation seen in part (b) of this figure. From these constraints we build the *constraint graph* in Figure 2(d). This graph is the main data-structure that we use to solve range analysis. For each variable v in the constraint system, the constraint graph has a node n_v. Similarly, for each constraint $v = f(\ldots, u, \ldots)$ in the constraint system, the graph has an *operation node* n_f. For each constraint $v = f(\ldots, u, \ldots)$ we add two edges to the graph: $\overrightarrow{n_u n_f}$ and $\overrightarrow{n_f n_v}$. Some edges in the constraint graph are dashed. These are called *control dependence edges*. If a constraint $v = f(\ldots, \mathbf{ft}(u), \ldots)$ uses a *future* bound from a variable u, then we add to the constraint graph a control dependence edge $\overrightarrow{n_u n_f}$. The final solution to this instance of the range analysis problem is given in Figure 2(e).

The Micro Algorithm. We find the solution given in Figure 2(e) in a process that we call the micro algorithm. This process is divided into three sub-steps: (i) growth analysis; (ii) future resolution and (iii) narrowing analysis.

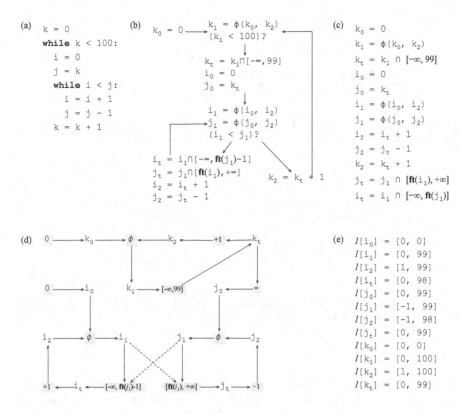

Fig. 2. Range analysis by example. (a) Input program. (b) Internal compiler representation. (c) Constraints of the range analysis problem. (d) The constraint graph. (e) The final solution.

Growth Analysis. The objective of growth analysis is to determine the growth behavior of each program variable. There are four possible behaviors: (a) the variable is bound to a constant interval, such as k_0 in Figure 2(b). (b) The variable is bound to a decreasing interval, i.e., an interval whose lower bound decreases. This is the case of j_1 in our example. (c) The variable is bound to an increasing interval, i.e., its upper bound increases. This is the case of i_1 in the example. (d) The variable is bound to an interval that expands in both directions. The growth analysis uses an infinite lattice, i.e., $\mathcal{Z}^2$. Thus, a careless implementation of an algorithm that infers growth patterns might not terminate. In order to ensure termination, we must rely on a technique called *widening*, first introduced by Cousot and Cousot as a key component of abstract interpretation [5]. There are many different widening strategies. We discuss some of them in Section 3.5.

Future Resolution. In order to learn information from comparisons between variables, such as i < j in Figure 2(a), we bind some intervals to *futures*. Futures are symbolic limits, which will be replaced by actual numbers once we finish the growth analysis. The ranges found by the growth analysis tells us

$$\frac{Y = X \sqcap [l, \mathbf{ft}(V) + c] \qquad I(V)_\uparrow = u}{Y = X \sqcap [l, u + c]} \quad u, c \in \mathbb{Z} \cup \{-\infty, +\infty\}$$

$$\frac{Y = X \sqcap [\mathbf{ft}(V) + c, u] \qquad I(V)_\downarrow = l}{Y = X \sqcap [l + c, u]} \quad l, c \in \mathbb{Z} \cup \{-\infty, +\infty\}$$

Fig. 3. Rules to replace futures by actual bounds. Given an interval $\iota = [l, u]$, we let $\iota_\downarrow = l$, and $\iota_\uparrow = u$

$$\frac{I(V)_\downarrow = -\infty \qquad e(V)_\downarrow > -\infty}{I(V) \leftarrow [e(V)_\downarrow, I(V)_\uparrow]} \qquad \frac{I(V)_\downarrow > e(V)_\downarrow}{I(V) \leftarrow [e(V)_\downarrow, I(V)_\uparrow]}$$

$$\frac{I(V)_\uparrow = +\infty \qquad e(V)_\uparrow < +\infty}{I(V) \leftarrow [I(V)_\downarrow, e(V)_\uparrow]} \qquad \frac{I(V)_\uparrow < e(V)_\uparrow}{I(V) \leftarrow [I(V)_\downarrow, e(V)_\uparrow]}$$

Fig. 4. Cousot and Cousot's narrowing operator. Function $e(V)$ is an abstract evaluation, on the interval lattice, of the instruction that produces V.

which variables have fixed bounds, independent on the intersections in the constraint system. Thus, we can use actual limits to replace intersections bounded by futures. Figure 3 shows the rules to perform these substitutions. In order to correctly replace a future $\mathbf{ft}(v)$ that limits a variable v', we need to have already applied the growth analysis onto v. Had we considered only data dependence edges, then it would be possible that v' be analyzed before v. However, because of control dependence edges, this case cannot happen. The control dependence edges ensure that any topological ordering of the constraint graph either places N_v before $N_{v'}$, or places these nodes in the same strongly connected component. For instance, in Figure 2(d), variables j_1 and i_t are in the same SCC only because of the control dependence edges.

Narrowing Analysis. The growth analysis associates very conservative bounds to each variable. Thus, the last step of our algorithm consists in narrowing these intervals. We accomplish this step via Cousot and Cousot's classic narrowing operator [5, p.248], which we show in Figure 4.

Example. Continuing with our example, Figure 5 shows the application of our algorithm on the last strong component of Figure 2(d). Upon meeting this SCC, we have already determined that the interval $[0, 0]$ is bound to i_0 and that the interval $[100, 100]$ is bound to j_0. We are not guaranteed to find the least fixed point of a constraint system. However, in this example we did it. We emphasize that finding this tight solution was only possible because of the topological ordering of the constraint graph in Figure 2(d). Had we applied the widening

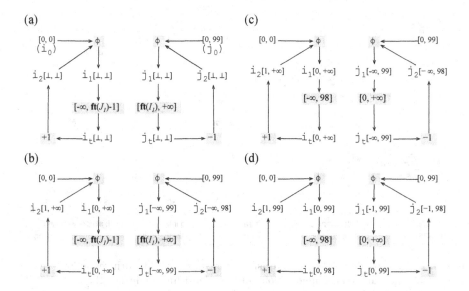

Fig. 5. Four snapshots of the last SCC of Figure 2(d). (a) After removing control dependence edges. (b) After running the growth analysis. (c) After fixing the intersections bound to futures. (d) After running the narrowing analysis.

operator onto the whole graph, then we would have found out that variable j_0 is bound to $[-\infty, +\infty]$, because (i) it receives its interval directly from variable k_t, which is upper bounded by $+\infty$, and (ii) it is part of a negative cycle. On the other hand, by only analyzing j's SCC after we have analyzed k's, k only contributes the constant range $[0, 99]$ to j_0.

3 Design Space

As we see from a cursory glance at Figure 1, our range analysis algorithm has many optional modules. These modules give the user the chance to choose between more precise results, or a faster analysis. Given the number of options, the design space of a range analysis algorithm is vast. In this section we try to cover some of the most important tradeoffs. All the numbers that we show have been obtained as the average of 15 runs in an Intel Core 2 Quad processor with 2.4 GHz, and 3.5 GB of main memory. Figure 6 plots, for the integer programs in the SPEC CPU 2006 benchmark suite, precision versus speed for different configurations of our implementation. Our initial goal when developing this analysis was to support a bitwidth-aware register allocator. Thus, we measure precision by the average number of bits that our analysis allows us to save per program variable. It is very important to notice that we do not consider constants in our statistics of precision. In other words, we only measure bitwidth reduction in variables that a constant propagation step could not remove.

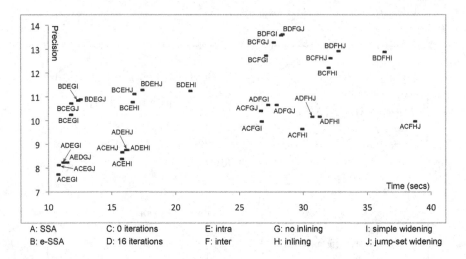

| A: SSA | C: 0 iterations | E: intra | G: no inlining | I: simple widening |
| B: e-SSA | D: 16 iterations | F: inter | H: inlining | J: jump-set widening |

Fig. 6. Design space exploration: precision (percentage of bitwidth reduction) versus speed (secs) for different configurations of our algorithm analyzing the SPEC CPU 2006 integer benchmarks.

3.1 Strongly Connected Components

The greatest source of improvement in our implementation is the use of strongly connected components. To propagate ranges across the constraint graph, we fragment it into strongly connected components, collapse each of these components into single nodes, and sort the resulting directed acyclic graph topologically. We then solve the range analysis problem for each component individually. Once we have solved a component, we propagate its ranges to the next components, and repeat the process until we walk over the entire constraint graph. It is well-known that this technique is essential to speedup constraint solving algorithms [15, Sec 6.3]. In our case, the results are dramatic, mostly in terms of speed, but also in terms of precision. Figure 7 shows the speedup that we gain by using strong components. We show results for the integer programs in the SPEC CPU 2006 benchmark suite. In `xalancbmk`, the analysis on strong components is 450x faster.

According to Figure 7, in some cases, as in `bzip2`, strong components increase our precision by 40%. The gains in precision happen because, by completely resolving a component, we are able to propagate constant intervals to the next components, instead of propagating intervals that can grow in both directions. An an example, in Figure 5 we pass the range $[0, 99]$ from variable k to the component that contains variable j. Had we run the analysis in the entire constraint graph, by the time we applied the growth analysis on j we would still find k bound to $[0, +\infty]$.

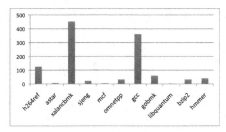 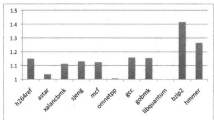

Fig. 7. (Left) Bars give time to run our analysis without building strong components divided by time to run the analysis on strongly connected components. (Right) Bars give precision, in bitwidth reduction, that we obtain with strong components, divided by the precision that we obtain without them.

3.2   The Choice of a Program Representation

If strong components account for the largest gains in speed, the choice of a suitable program representation is responsible for the largest gains in precision. However, here we no longer have a win-win condition: a more expressive program representation decreases our speed, because it increases the size of the target program. We have tried our analysis in two different program representations: the Static Single Assignment (SSA) form [7], and the Extended Static Single Assignment (e-SSA) form [3]. The SSA form gives us a faster, albeit more imprecise, analysis. Any program in e-SSA form has also the SSA core property: any variable name has at most one definition site. The contrary is not true: SSA form programs do not have the core e-SSA property: any use site of a variable that appears in a conditional test post-dominates its definition. The program in Figure 2(b) is in e-SSA form. The live ranges of variables i_1 and j_1 have been split right after the conditional test via the assertions that creates variables i_t and j_t. The e-SSA format serves well analyses that extract information from definition sites and conditional tests, and propagate this information forwardly. Examples include, in addition to range analysis, tainted flow analysis [20] and array bounds checks elimination [3].

Figure 8 compares these two program representations in terms of runtime. As we see in Figure 8(Left), the e-SSA form slows down our analysis. In some cases, as in `xalancbmk`, this slowdown increases execution time by 71%. Runtime increases for two reasons. Firstly, the e-SSA form programs are larger than the SSA form programs, as we show in Figure 8(Right). However, this growth is small: we did not verify any growth larger than 9% in any integer program of SPEC CPU 2006. Second, the e-SSA form program has futures; hence requiring the future resolution phase of our algorithm, which is not necessary in SSA form programs. Nevertheless, whereas the e-SSA form slows down the analysis runtime, its gains in precision are remarkable, as seen in Figure 9. These gains happen because the e-SSA format lets the analysis to use the results of comparisons to narrow the ranges of variables.

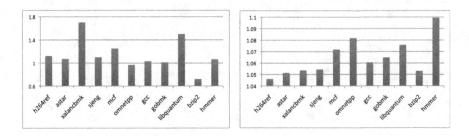

Fig. 8. (Left) Bars give the time to run analysis on e-SSA form programs divided by the time to run analysis on SSA form programs. (Right) Bars give the size of the e-SSA form program, in number of assembly instructions, divided by the size of the SSA form program.

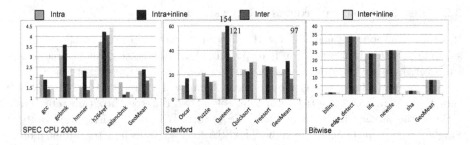

Fig. 9. The impact of the e-SSA transformation on precision for three different benchmark suites. Bars give the ratio of precision (in bitwidth reduction), obtained with e-SSA form conversion divided by precision without e-SSA form conversion.

3.3   Intra versus Inter-procedural Analysis

A naive implementation of range analysis would be intra-procedural; that is, would solve the range analysis problem once per each function. However, we can gain in precision by performing it inter-procedurally. An inter-procedural implementation allows the results found for a function f to flow into other functions that f calls. Figure 10 illustrates the inter-procedural analysis for the program seen in Figure 2(a). The trivial way to produce an inter-procedural implementation is to insert into the constraint system assignments from the actual parameter names to the formal parameter names. In our example of Figure 10, our constraint graph contains a flow of information from 0, the actual parameter, to k_0, the formal parameter of function foo.

Figure 12 compares the precision of the intra and inter-procedural analyses for the five largest programs in three different categories of benchmarks: SPEC CPU 2006, the Stanford Suite[1] and Bitwise [23]. Our results for the SPEC programs were disappointing: on average, for the five largest programs,

---

[1] http://classes.engineering.wustl.edu/cse465/docs/BCCExamples/stanford.c

```
main():
    foo(0, 100)

foo(k, N):
    while k < N:
        i = 0
        j = k
        while i < j:
            i = i + 1
            j = j - 1
        k = k + 1
```

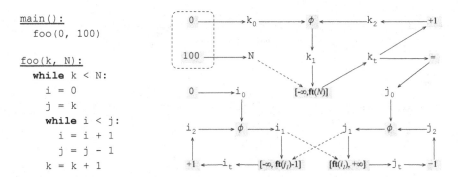

Fig. 10. Example where an inter-procedural analysis is more precise than an intra-procedural analysis

the intra-procedural version of our analysis saves 5.23% of bits per variable. The inter-procedural version increases this number to 8.89%. A manual inspection of the SPEC programs reveals that this result is expected: these programs use many external library functions, which we cannot analyze, and their source codes do not provide enough explicit constants to power our analysis up. However, with numerical benchmarks we fare much better. On average, our inter-procedural algorithm reduces the bitwidth of the Stanford benchmarks by 36.24%. For Bitwise we obtain a bitwidth reduction of 12.27%. However, this average is lowered by two outliers: edge_detect and sha, which cannot be reduced. The Bitwise benchmarks were implemented by Stephenson et al. [23] to validate their bitwidth analysis. Our results are on par with those found by the original authors. The Bitwise programs contain only the main function; thus, different versions of our algorithm find the same results when applied onto these programs.

3.4 Context Sensitive versus Context Insensitive Analysis

Another way to increase the precision of range analysis is via a context-sensitive implementation. Context-sensitiveness allows us to distinguish different calling sites of the same function. Figure 11 shows why the ability to make this distinction is important for precision. In Figure 11(a) we have two different calls of function foo. An usual way to perform a data-flow analysis inter-procedurally is to create assignments between formal and actual parameters, as we show in Figure 11(b). If a function is called more than once, then its formal parameters will receive information from many actual parameters. We use the SSA's ϕ-functions to bind this information together into a single flow. However, in this case the multiple assignment of values to parameters makes the ranges of these parameters very large, whereas in reality they are not. As an example, in Figure 11(b), variable k ends up associated with the range $[0, 10^5]$, but in reality this variable contains an interval that is only 100 units long. A way to circumvent this source of imprecision is via function inlining, as we show in Figure 11(c). The results that we can derive for the transformed program are more precise, as each input parameter is assigned a single value.

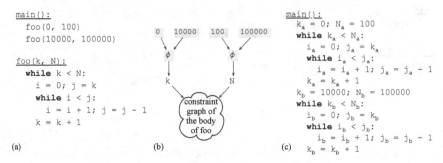

```
main():                                    main():
  foo(0, 100)          0  10000  100  100000   k_a = 0; N_a = 100
  foo(10000, 100000)                           while k_a < N_a:
                                                 i_a = 0; j_a = k_a
foo(k, N):               φ          φ             while i_a < j_a:
  while k < N:                                       i_a = i_a + 1; j_a = j_a - 1
    i = 0; j = k        k          N             k_a = k_a + 1
    while i < j:                               k_b = 10000; N_b = 100000
      i = i + 1; j = j - 1    constraint       while k_b < N_b:
    k = k + 1                 graph of           i_b = 0; j_b = k_b
                             the body            while i_b < j_b:
                              of foo               i_b = i_b + 1; j_b = j_b - 1
 (a)                  (b)                      k_b = k_b + 1
                                            (c)
```

Fig. 11. Example where a context-sensitive implementation improves the results of range analysis

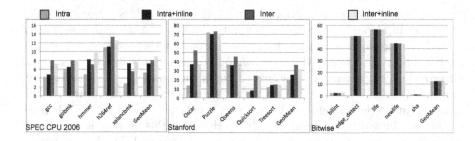

Fig. 12. The impact of whole program analysis on precision. Each bar gives precision in %bitwidth reduction.

Figure 12 shows how function inlining modifies the precision of our results. It is difficult to find an adequate way to compare the precision of our analysis with, and without inlining. This difficulty stems from the fact that this transformation tends to change the target program too much. In absolute numbers, we always reduce the bitwidth of more variables after function inlining. However, proportionally function inlining leads to a smaller percentage of bitwidth reduction for many benchmarks. In the Stanford Collection, for instance, where most of the functions are called in only one location, inlining leads to worse precision results. On the other hand, for the SPEC programs, inlining, even in terms of percentage of reduction, tends to increase our measure of precision.

Intra vs Inter-procedural Runtimes. Figure 13(Right) compares three different execution modes. Bars are normalized to the time to run the intra-procedural analysis without inlining. On average, the intra-procedural mode is 28.92% faster than the inter-procedural mode. If we perform function inlining, then this difference is 45.87%. These numbers are close because our runtime is bound to the size of the strong components. We have observed that function inlining does not increase too much these components.

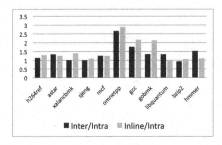

Fig. 13. Runtime comparison between intra, inter and inter+inline versions of our algorithm. The bars are normalized to the time to run the intra-procedural analysis.

$$[-\infty, +\infty]$$

$$[-\infty, c] \qquad [c, +\infty]$$

$$[c_1, c_2]$$

$$[\bot, \bot]$$

$$\frac{I(V) = [\bot, \bot]}{I(V) \leftarrow e(V)} \qquad \frac{e(V)_{\downarrow} < I(V)_{\downarrow} \qquad e(V)_{\uparrow} > I(V)_{\uparrow}}{I(V) \leftarrow [-\infty, +\infty]}$$

$$\frac{e(V)_{\downarrow} < I(V)_{\downarrow}}{I(V) \leftarrow [-\infty, I(V)_{\uparrow}]} \qquad \frac{e(V)_{\uparrow} > I(V)_{\uparrow}}{I(V) \leftarrow [I(V)_{\downarrow}, +\infty]}$$

Fig. 14. (Left) The lattice used in the simple widening strategy. (Right) Cousot and Cousot's widening operator. We evaluate the rules from left-to-right, top-to-bottom, and stop upon finding a pattern matching.

3.5   Choosing a Widening Strategy

We have implemented the widening operator used in the growth analysis in two different ways. The first way, which we call *simple*, is based on Cousot and Cousot's original widening operator [5]. This operator is shown in Figure 14, and it is the one used in Figure 5(b). The second widening strategy, which we call *jump-set widening* consists in using the constants that appear in the program text, in sorted order, as the next limits of each interval after widening is applied. This operator is common in implementations of range analysis [15, p.228]. There are situations in which jump-set widening produces better results than the simple operator. Figure 15 shows an example taken from the code of SPEC CPU bzip2. Part of the constraint graph of the program in Figure 15(a) is given in Figure 15(b). The result of applying the simple operator is shown in Figure 15(c). Jump-set widening would use the lattice in Figure 15(d), instead of the lattice in Figure 14(Right). This lattice yields the result given in Figure 15(e), which is more precise.

Another way to improve the precision of growth analysis is to perform a few rounds of abstract interpretation on the constraint graph, and to apply widening only if this process does not reach a fixed point. Each round of abstract interpretation consists in evaluating all the constraints, and then updating the

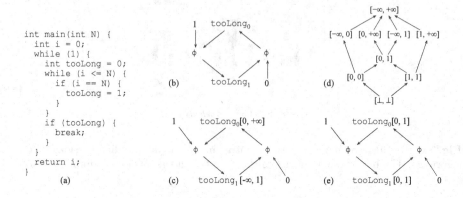

Fig. 15. An example where jump-set widening is more precise

Benchmark	Size	0 + Simple	16 + Simple	0 + Jump	16 + Jump
hmmer	38,409	9.98	11.40 (12.45)	10.98 (9.11)	11.40 (12.45)
gobmk	84,846	8.15	9.93 (17.92)	9.02 (9.64)	10.13 (19.54)
h264ref	97,494	12.58	13.11 (4.04)	13.00 (3.23)	13.11 (4.04)
xalancbmk	352,423	7.71	7.98 (3.38)	7.95 (3.02)	7.98 (3.38)
gcc	449,442	16.09	16.63 (3.25)	16.41 (1.95)	16.64 (3.31)

Fig. 16. Variation in the precision of our analysis given the widening strategy. The size of each benchmark is given in number of variable nodes in the constraint graph. Precision is given in percentage of bitwidth reduction. Numbers in parenthesis are percentage of gain over 0 + Simple.

intervals that change from one evaluation to the other. For instance, in Figure 15 one round of abstract interpretation, coupled with the simple widening operator, would be enough to reach the fixed point of that constraint system. We have experimented with 0 and 16 iterations before doing widening, and the overall result, for the programs in the SPEC CPU 2006 suite is given in Figure 6. Figure 16 shows some of these results in more detail for the five largest benchmarks in this collection. In general jump-set widening improves the precision of our results in non-trivial ways. Nevertheless, the simple widening operator preceded by 16 rounds of abstract interpretation in general is more precise than jump-set widening without any cycle of pre-evaluation, as we see in Figure 16.

4   Final Remarks

This paper presents what we believe is the most comprehensive evaluation of range analysis in the literature. Altogether we have experimented with 32 different configurations of our range analysis algorithm. Our implementation is publicly available at http://code.google.com/p/range-analysis/.

This repository contains instructions about how to deploy and use our implementation. We provide a gallery of examples, including source codes, CFGs and constraint graphs that we produce for meaningful programs at http://code.google.com/p/range-analysis/wiki/gallery.

References

1. Barik, R., Grothoff, C., Gupta, R., Pandit, V., Udupa, R.: Optimal Bitwise Register Allocation Using Integer Linear Programming. In: Almási, G.S., Caşcaval, C., Wu, P. (eds.) KSEM 2006. LNCS, vol. 4382, pp. 267–282. Springer, Heidelberg (2007)
2. Bertrane, J., Cousot, P., Cousot, R., Feret, J., Mauborgne, L., Miné, A., Rival, X.: Static analysis and verification of aerospace software by abstract interpretation. In: I@A, pp. 1–38. AIAA (2010)
3. Bodik, R., Gupta, R., Sarkar, V.: ABCD: eliminating array bounds checks on demand. In: PLDI, pp. 321–333. ACM (2000)
4. Cong, J., Fan, Y., Han, G., Lin, Y., Xu, J., Zhang, Z., Cheng, X.: Bitwidth-aware scheduling and binding in high-level synthesis. In: Proceedings of the Asia and South Pacific Design Automation Conference, ASP-DAC 2005, January 18-21, vol. 2, pp. 856–861 (2005)
5. Cousot, P., Cousot, R.: Abstract interpretation: a unified lattice model for static analysis of programs by construction or approximation of fixpoints. In: POPL, pp. 238–252. ACM (1977)
6. Cousot, P., Cousot, R., Feret, J., Mauborgne, L., Miné, A., Rival, X.: Why does astrée scale up? Form. Methods Syst. Des. 35(3), 229–264 (2009)
7. Cytron, R., Ferrante, J., Rosen, B.K., Wegman, M.N., Kenneth Zadeck, F.: Efficiently computing static single assignment form and the control dependence graph. TOPLAS 13(4), 451–490 (1991)
8. do Couto Teixeira, D., Pereira, F.M.Q.: The design and implementation of a non-iterative range analysis algorithm on a production compiler. In: SBLP, pp. 45–59. SBC (2011)
9. Gawlitza, T., Leroux, J., Reineke, J., Seidl, H., Sutre, G., Wilhelm, R.: Polynomial precise interval analysis revisited. Efficient Algorithms 1, 422–437 (2009)
10. Lakhdar-Chaouch, L., Jeannet, B., Girault, A.: Widening with Thresholds for Programs with Complex Control Graphs. In: Bultan, T., Hsiung, P.-A. (eds.) ATVA 2011. LNCS, vol. 6996, pp. 492–502. Springer, Heidelberg (2011)
11. Lattner, C., Adve, V.S.: LLVM: A compilation framework for lifelong program analysis & transformation. In: CGO, pp. 75–88. IEEE (2004)
12. Lhairech-Lebreton, G., Coussy, P., Heller, D., Martin, E.: Bitwidth-aware high-level synthesis for designing low-power dsp applications. In: ICECS, pp. 531–534. IEEE (2010)
13. Logozzo, F., Fahndrich, M.: Pentagons: a weakly relational abstract domain for the efficient validation of array accesses. In: SAC, pp. 184–188. ACM (2008)
14. Mahlke, S., Ravindran, R., Schlansker, M., Schreiber, R., Sherwood, T.: Bitwidth cognizant architecture synthesis of custom hardware accelerators. Computer-Aided Design of Integrated Circuits and Systems 20(11), 1355–1371 (2001)
15. Nielson, F., Nielson, H.R., Hankin, C.: Principles of Program Analysis. Springer (1999)
16. Oh, H., Brutschy, L., Yi, K.: Access Analysis-Based Tight Localization of Abstract Memories. In: Jhala, R., Schmidt, D. (eds.) VMCAI 2011. LNCS, vol. 6538, pp. 356–370. Springer, Heidelberg (2011)

17. Oh, H., Heo, K., Lee, W., Lee, W., Yi, K.: Design and implementation of sparse global analyses for C-like languages. In: PLDI, pp. 229–238. ACM (2012)
18. Patterson, J.R.C.: Accurate static branch prediction by value range propagation. In: PLDI, pp. 67–78. ACM (1995)
19. Pereira, F.M.Q., Palsberg, J.: Register allocation by puzzle solving. In: PLDI, pp. 216–226. ACM (2008)
20. Rimsa, A., d'Amorim, M., Pereira, F.M. Q.: Tainted Flow Analysis on e-SSA-Form Programs. In: Knoop, J. (ed.) CC 2011. LNCS, vol. 6601, pp. 124–143. Springer, Heidelberg (2011)
21. Simon, A.: Value-Range Analysis of C Programs: Towards Proving the Absence of Buffer Overflow Vulnerabilities, 1st edn. Springer (2008)
22. Sol, R., Guillon, C., Pereira, F.M.Q., Bigonha, M.A.S.: Dynamic Elimination of Overflow Tests in a Trace Compiler. In: Knoop, J. (ed.) CC 2011. LNCS, vol. 6601, pp. 2–21. Springer, Heidelberg (2011)
23. Stephenson, M., Babb, J., Amarasinghe, S.: Bitwidth analysis with application to silicon compilation. In: PLDI, pp. 108–120. ACM (2000)
24. Su, Z., Wagner, D.: A Class of Polynomially Solvable Range Constraints for Interval Analysis without Widenings and Narrowings. In: Jensen, K., Podelski, A. (eds.) TACAS 2004. LNCS, vol. 2988, pp. 280–295. Springer, Heidelberg (2004)
25. Su, Z., Wagner, D.: A class of polynomially solvable range constraints for interval analysis without widenings. Theoretical Computeter Science 345(1), 122–138 (2005)
26. Tallam, S., Gupta, R.: Bitwidth aware global register allocation. In: POPL, pp. 85–96. ACM (2003)
27. Venet, A., Brat, G.: Precise and efficient static array bound checking for large embedded c programs. SIGPLAN Not. 39, 231–242 (2004)

Parameter Based Constant Propagation

Péricles Rafael Oliveira Alves, Igor Rafael de Assis Costa,
Fernando Magno Quintão Pereira, and Eduardo Lage Figueiredo

Departamento de Ciência da Computação – UFMG
Av. Antônio Carlos, 6627 – 31.270-010 – Belo Horizonte – MG – Brazil
{periclesrafael,igor,fernando,figueiredo}@dcc.ufmg.br

Abstract. JavaScript is nowadays the lingua franca of web browsers. This programming language is not only the main tool that developers have to implement the client side of web applications, but it is also the target of frameworks such as Google Web Toolkit. Given this importance, it is fundamental that JavaScript programs can be executed efficiently. Just-in-time (JIT) compilation is one of the keys to achieve this much necessary efficiency. An advantage that a JIT compiler has over a traditional compiler is the possibility to use runtime values to specialize the target code. In this paper we push JIT speculation to a new extreme: we have empirically observed that many JavaScript functions are called only once during a typical browser section. A natural way to capitalize on this observation is to specialize the code produced by a function to the particular values that are passed to this function as parameters. We have implemented this approach on IonMonkey, the newest JIT compiler used in the Mozilla Firefox browser. By coupling this type of parameter specialization with constant propagation, a classical compiler optimization, we have been able to experimentally observe speedups of up to 25% on well-known algorithms. These gains are even more remarkable because they have been obtained over a worldly known, industrial quality JavaScript runtime environment.

1 Introduction

Dynamically typed programming languages are today widespread in the computer science industry. Testimony of this fact is the ubiquity of PHP, Python and Ruby in the server side of web applications, and the dominance of JavaScript on its client side. This last programming language, JavaScript, today not only works as a tool that developers may use to code programs directly, but also fills the role of an assembly language for the Internet [13]. The Google Web Toolkit, for instance, allows programmers to develop applications in Java or Python, but translates these programs to a combination of JavaScript and HTML [5]. Given this importance, it is fundamental that dynamically typed languages, which are generally interpreted, can be executed efficiently, and the just-in-time (JIT) compilers seem to be a key player to achieve this much needed speed [2].

However, in spite of the undeniable importance of a language such as JavaScript, executing its programs efficiently is still a challenge even for a JIT

F.H. de Carvalho Junior and L.S. Barbosa (Eds.): SBLP 2012, LNCS 7554, pp. 57–71, 2012.

compiler. The combination of dynamic typing and late binding hides from the compiler core information that is necessary to generate good code. The type of the values manipulated by a JavaScript program is only known at runtime, and even then it might change during program execution. Moreover, having a very constrained time window to generate machine code, the JIT compiler many times gives up important optimizations that a traditional translator would probably use. Therefore, it comes as no surprise that the industry and the academic community are investing a huge amount of effort in the advance of JIT technology [11,13]. Our intention in this paper is to contribute further in this effort.

In this paper we discuss a key observation, and a suite of ideas to capitalize on it. After instrumenting the Mozilla Firefox browser, we have empirically observed that almost half the JavaScript functions in the 100 most visited websites in the Alexa index[1] are only called once. This observation motivates us to specialize these functions to their arguments. Hence, we give to the JIT compiler an advantage that a traditional compilation system could never have: the knowledge of the values manipulated at runtime.

We propose a form of constant propagation that treats the arguments passed to the function to be compiled as constants. Such approach is feasible, because we can check the values of these parameters at runtime, during JIT compilation. If the target function is only called once, then we have a win-win condition: we can generate simpler and more effective code, without having to pay any penalty. On the other hand, if the function is called more than once, we must recompile it, this time using a traditional approach, which makes no assumptions about the function arguments.

1.1 Why Parameter Specialization Matters

The main motivation to our work comes out of an observation: most of the JavaScript functions in typical webpages are called only once. To corroborate this statement, Figure 1 plots the percentage of JavaScript functions called N times, $1 \leq N \leq 50$. To obtain this plot we have used the same methodology adopted by Richard *et al.* [10]: we have instrumented the browser, and have used it to navigate through the 100 most visited pages according to the Alexa index. This company offers users a toolbar that, once added to their browsers, tracks data about browsing behavior. This data is then collected and used to rank millions of websites by visiting rate.

From Figure 1 we see that the number of times each JavaScript function is called during a typical browser section clearly obeys a power law. About 47% of the functions are called only once, and about 59% of the functions are called at most twice. Therefore, many functions will be given only one set of arguments. Nevertheless, a traditional just-in-time compiler generates code that is general enough to handle any possible combination of parameters that their types allow. In this paper, we propose the exact opposite: lets specialize functions to their arguments; hence, producing efficient code to the common case. Functions that

[1] http://www.alexa.com/

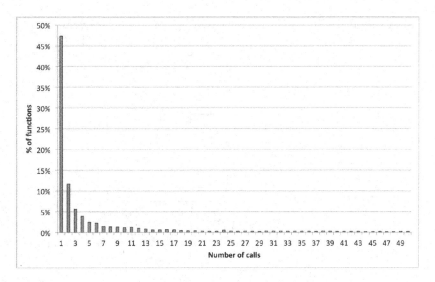

Fig. 1. A plot that shows how many times each different JavaScript function is called in a typical browser section in the 100 most visited pages according to the Alexa website

are called more than once must either be re-compiled or interpreted. In this way we can produce super-specialized binaries, using knowledge that is only available at runtime; thus, achieving an advantage that is beyond the reach of any ordinary static compiler.

2 Parameter Based Method Specialization

In this section we illustrate our approach to runtime code optimization via an example. Then we explain how we can use runtime knowledge to improve constant propagation, a well-known compiler optimization.

2.1 Parameter Based Specialization by Example

We illustrate how a just-in-time compiler can benefit from parameter based specialization via the example program in Figure 2. The function `closest` finds, among the n elements of the array v, the one which has the smallest difference to an integer q. We see the control flow graph (CFG) of this program at the figure's right side. This CFG is given in the Static Single Assignment [9] (SSA) intermediate representation, which is adopted by IonMonkey, our baseline compiler. The SSA format has the core property that each variable name has only one definition site. Special instructions, called ϕ-functions, are used to merge together different definitions of a variable. This program representation simplifies substantially the optimizations that we describe in this paper.

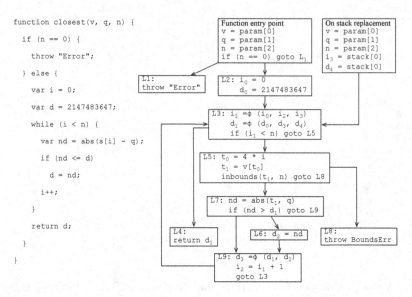

Fig. 2. (Left) The JavaScript program that will be our running example. (Right) A SSA-form, three-address code representation of the example.

The control flow graph in Figure 2(Right) differs from the CFG normally produced by a compiler because it has two entry points. The first, which we call *function entry point*, is the equivalent to the entry point of an ordinary CFG. The second, which we call the *On-Stack Replacement* block (OSR), is created by the just-in-time compiler, in case the function was compiled while being executed. All the functions that we optimize start execution from this block, as they are compiled only once. If a function is executed several times, then subsequent calls will start at the function entry.

The knowledge of the runtime values of the parameters improve some compiler optimizations. In this section we will show how this improvement applies onto four different compiler optimizations: dead-code elimination, array bounds check elimination, loop inversion and constant propagation. Figure 3(a) shows the code that we obtain after a round of dead-code elimination. Because we enter the function from the OSR block, the code that is reachable only from the function entry point is dead, and can be safely removed. This elimination also removes the test that checks if the array has a non zero size. Notice that even if reachable from the OSR block, we would be able to eliminate this test, given that we know that the result would be always positive.

Figure 3(b) shows the result of applying array bounds check elimination onto our example. JavaScript is a strongly typed language; thus, to guarantee the runtime consistency of programs, every array access is checked, so that memory is never indexed out of declared bounds. In our case, a simple combination of range analysis [16], plus dead-code elimination is enough to remove the test performed over the limits of v. This limit, 100, is always greater than any value that the loop counter i can assume throughout program execution.

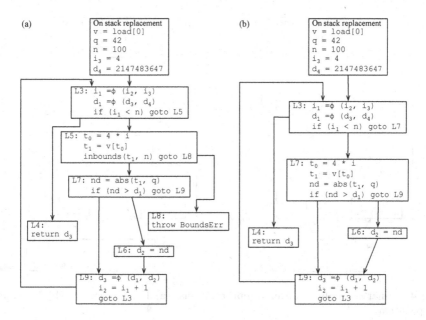

Fig. 3. The code that results from two different optimizations in sequence. (a) Dead-code elimination. (b) Array bounds check elimination.

Figure 4(a) shows the result of applying loop inversion on the example, after dead-code elimination has pruned useless code. Loop inversion [15] converts a while into a do-while loop. The main benefit of this optimization is to replace the combination of conditional and unconditional branches used to implement the while loop by a single conditional jump, used to implement the repeat loop. Under ordinary circumstances an extra conditional test, wrapped around the while, is necessary, to certify that iterations will be performed only on non-null counters. However, given that we know that the loop will be executed at least once, this wrapping is not necessary.

Finally, Figure 4(b) shows the code that we obtain after performing constant propagation. Out of all the optimizations that we have discussed here, constant propagation is the one that most benefits from parameter specialization. Given that the parameters are all treated as constants, this optimization has many opportunities to transform the code. In our example, we have been able to propagate the array limit **n**, and the query distance **q**. Constant propagation is the optimization that we have chosen, in this paper, to demonstrate the effectiveness of parameter based code specialization. In the rest of this paper we will be discussing its implementation in our scenario, and its effectiveness.

2.2   "Constification"

Argument based value specialization works by replacing the references to the parameters of a function about to be JIT compiled by the actual values of these

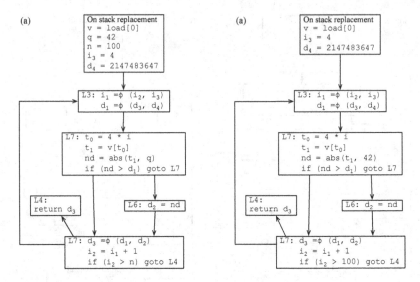

Fig. 4. Final code after two more optimizations. (a) Loop inversion. (b) Constant Propagation.

parameters, in a process that we have dubbed *constification*. Before introducing the basic principles that underlie this technique, we will explain how the interpreter and the native code produced by the just-in-time compiler communicate. In this section we will describe the memory layout used by the SpiderMonkey interpreter; however, this organization is typical in other environments where the interplay between just-in-time compilation and interpretation happens, such as the Java Virtual Machine [2].

Whenever SpiderMonkey needs to interpret a JavaScript program, it allocates a memory space for this script, which, in Mozilla's jargon is called the *stack space*. This memory area will store the global data created by the script, plus the data allocated dynamically, for instance, due to function calls. A functions keep the data that it manipulates in a structure called activation record. This structure contains the function's parameters, its return address, the local variables, a pointer to the previous activation record, and a nesting link, which allows a nested function to find variables in the scope of the enclosing function. Activation records are piled on a stack, as different function calls take place. For instance, Figure 5(a) shows a stack configuration containing the activation records of two functions.

In principle, both the interpreter and the just-in-time compiled program could share the same stack of activation records, and thus we would have a seamless conversation between these two worlds. However, whereas the interpreter is a stack-based architecture, the native code runs on a register based machine. In other words, the two execution modes use different memory layouts. To

---

[2] See **Java SE HotSpot at a Glance**, available on-line

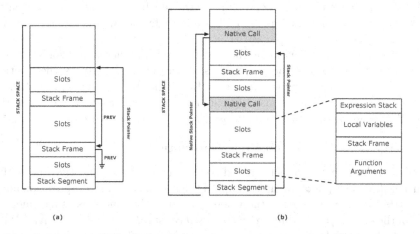

Fig. 5. SpiderMonkey's memory layout. (a) Interpretation. (b) Execution of native code. Data that is not visible to the interpreter is colored in gray. *Stack Segment* contains a pointer to the current top of stack, and to the chain of activation records of the native functions. Each activation record has a fixed-size area called the *stack frame*. *Slots* denote area whose layout depends on the function. Arguments of the function are stored before the stack frame, and the local variables are stored after it.

circumvent this shortcoming, once an initially interpreted function is JIT compiled, its activation record is extended with a new memory area that is only visible to the JITed code. Figure 5(b) illustrates this new layout. In this example, we assume that both functions in execution in Figure 5(a) have been compiled to native code. The native code shares the activation records used by the interpreter – that is how it reads the values of the parameters, or writes back the return value that it produces upon termination. The interpreter, on the other hand, is oblivious to the execution of code produced by the just-in-time compiler.

Reading the Values of Parameters: JavaScript methods, in the Firefox browser, are initially interpreted. Once a method reaches a certain threshold of calls, or a loop reaches a certain threshold of iterations, the interpreter invokes the just-in-time compiler. At this point, a control flow graph is produced, with the two entry blocks that we have described in Section 2.1. Independent on the reason that has triggered just-in-time compilation, number of iterations or number of calls, the function's actual parameters are in the interpreter's stack, and can be easily retrieved. However, we are only interested in compilation due to an excessive number of loop iterations. We do not specialize functions compiled due to an excessive number of calls; these functions are likely to be called many more times in the future. During the generation of the native code, we can find the values bound to the parameters of a function by inspecting its activation record. Reading these parameters has almost zero overhead when compared to the time to compile and execute the program.

After inspecting the parameter values, we redefine them in the two entry blocks of the CFG. For instance, in Figure 2(Right) we would replace the two load instructions, e.g., v = `param[0]` in the function entry and the OSR block, by the value of v at the moment the just-in-time compiler was invoked. Then, we replace all the uses of the parameters in the function body by their actual values. This last phase is trivial in the Static Single Assignment representation, because each variable name has only one definition site; hence, there is not the possibility of we wrongly changing a use that is not a parameter.

2.3   Argument Based Constant Propagation

In order to show that parameter based code specialization is effective and useful to just-in-time compilers, we have adapted the classic constant propagation algorithm [19] to make the most of the values passed to the functions as parameters. We call the ensuing algorithm *argument based constant propagation*, or ABCP for short. We have implemented ABCP in the IonMonkey[3] compiler. This compiler is the newest member of the *Monkey family*, a collection of JavaScript just-in-time engines developed in the Mozilla Foundation to be used in the Firefox browser. We chose to work in this compiler for two reasons. Firstly, because it is an open-source tool, which means that its code can be easily obtained and modified. Secondly, contrary to previous Mozilla compilers, IonMonkey has a clean design and a modern implementation. In particular, because it uses the SSA form, IonMonkey serves as a basis for the implementation of many modern compiler techniques.

Constant propagation, given its simple specification and straightforward implementation, is the canonical example of a compiler optimization [15, p.362]. Constant propagation is a *sparse* optimization. In other words, abstract states are associated directly with variables. The classic approach to constant propagation relies on an iterative algorithm. Initially all the variables are associated with the $\top$ abstract state. Then, those variables that are initialized with constants are added to a work list. If a variable is inserted into the worklist, then we know, as an invariant, that it has a constant value c_1, in which case its abstract state is c_1 itself. In the iterative phase, an arbitrary variable is removed from the worklist, and all its uses in the program code are replaced by the constant that it represents. It is possible that during this updating some instruction i is changed to use only constants in its right side. If such an event occurs, then the variable defined by i, if any, is associated to the value produced by i, and is inserted into the worklist. These iterations happen until the worklist is empty. At the end of the algorithm, each variable is known to have a constant value (C_i) or is not guaranteed to be a constant, and is thus bound to $\bot$.

Constant propagation suits well JIT compilers, because it is fast. The worst-case time complexity of this algorithm is $O(V^2)$, where V is the number of variables in the program. To derive this complexity, we notice that a variable can enter into the worklist at most once, when we find that it holds a constant value. A variable can be used in up to $O(I)$ program instructions, where I is the number of instructions. Normally $O(I) = O(V)$; thus, replacing a variable

---

[3] https://wiki.mozilla.org/IonMonkey

by the constant it represents takes $O(V)$ worst-case time. In practice a variable will be used in a few sites; therefore, constant propagation tends to be $O(V)$.

3 Experiments

In order to validate our approach, we have created a small benchmark that contains 8 well known algorithms, plus three programs from the SunSpider test suite. These benchmarks are publicly available at http://code.google.com/p/im-abcp/source/browse/trunk/tests. Figure 6 describes each of these programs.

Benchmark	LoC	Complexity	Description
SunSpider::math-cordic(R, C, A)	68	$O(R)$	Calls a sequence of transcendental functions R times.
SunSpider::3d-morph(L, X, Z)	56	$O(L \times X \times Z)$	Performs $L \times X \times Z$ calls to the sin transcendental function.
SunSpider::string-base64(T_{64}, B, T_2)	133	$O(|T_{64}|)$	Converts an array of integers to a Base-64 string.
matrix-multiplication(M_1, M_2, K, L, M)	46	$O(K \times L \times M)$	Multiplies a $K \times L$ matrix M_1 by a $L \times M$ matrix M_2.
k-nearest-neighbors(P, V, N, K)	47	$O(K \times N)$	Finds the K 2-D points stored in V that are closest of the 2-D point P.
rabin-karp(T, P)	46	$O(|T| \times |P|)$	Finds the first occurrence of the pattern P in the string —T—.
1d-trim(V, L, U, N)	22	$O(N)$	Given a vector V with N numbers, remove all those numbers that are outside the interval $[L, U]$.
closest-point(P, V, N)	35	$O(N)$	Finds, among the 2-D points stored in V, the one which is the closest to P.
tokenizer(S, P)	23	$O(|S| \times |P|)$	Splits the string S into substrings separated by the characters in the pattern P.
split-line(V, N, A, B)	41	$O(N)$	Separates the 2-D points stored in V into two groups, those below the line $y = Ax + b$, and those above.
string-contains-char(C, S)	13	$O(|S|)$	Tells if the string S contains the character C.

Fig. 6. Our benchmark suite. LoC: lines of JavaScript code

IonMonkey does not provide a built-in implementation of Constant Propagation. Therefore, to demonstrate the effectiveness of our implementation, we compare it with the implementation of Global Value Numbering (GVN) already available in the IonMonkey toolset. GVN is another classic compiler optimization. IonMonkey uses the algorithm first described by Alpern *et al.* [1], which relies on the SSA form to be fast and precise. Alpern *et al.* have proposed two different approaches to GVN: pessimistic and optimistic. Both are available in IonMonkey. In this section we use the pessimistic approach, because it is considerably faster when applied to our benchmarks. All the implementations that we discuss in this section are intra-procedural. None of the IonMonkey built-in optimizations are inter-procedural, given the difficulties to see the entirety of dynamically loaded programs. All the runtime numbers that we provide are the average of 1000 executions. We do not provide average errors, because they are negligible given this high quantity of executions.

Figure 7 compares our implementation of constant propagation with the implementation of global value number produced by the engineers that work in the Mozilla Foundation. The baseline of **all** charts in this section is the IonMonkey compiler running with no optimizations. The goal of figure 7 is to show that our implementation is not a straw-man: for our suite of benchmarks it produces better code than GVN, which is industrial-quality. We see in the figure that both

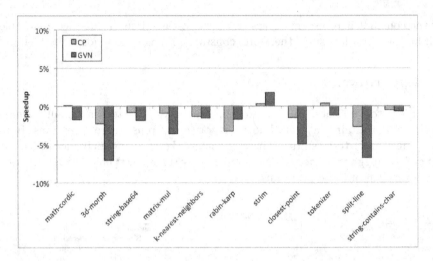

Fig. 7. Speedup of the original version of Constant Propagation and Global Value Numbering

optimizations slowdown the benchmarks. This slowdown happens because the total execution time includes the time to optimize the program, and the time that the program spends executing. Neither optimization, constant propagation or global value numbering, finds many opportunities to improve the target code in a way to pay for the optimization overhead. On the other hand, they all add an overhead on top of the just-in-time engine. However, the overhead imposed by constant propagation, a simpler optimization, is much smaller than the overhead imposed by global value numbering, as it is evident from the bars in Figure 7.

Figure 8 compares our implementation of constant propagation, with and without parameter specialization. We see that traditional constant propagation in fact slows down many of our benchmarks. Our implementation of the classic Rabin-Karp algorithm, for instance, suffers a 4% slowdown. Traditional constant propagation does not find many opportunities to remove instructions, given the very small number of constants in the program code, and given the fact that it runs intra-procedurally. On the other hand, the argument based implementation fares much better. It naturally gives us constants to propagate in all the benchmarks, and it also allows us to replace boxed values by constants. The algorithm of highest asymptotic complexity, matrix multiplication, experiments a speedup of almost 25%, for instance.

Figure 9 compares the implementation of global value numbering with and without parameter based specialization. Contrary to constant propagation, global value numbering does not benefit much from the presence of more constants in the program text. We see, for instance, that the SunSpider's `string-based64` benchmark suffers a slowdown of over 30%. This slowdown happens because of the time spent to load and propagate the values of the arguments. None of these arguments are used inside loops - although expressions derived from them are - and thus GVN cannot improve the quality of these

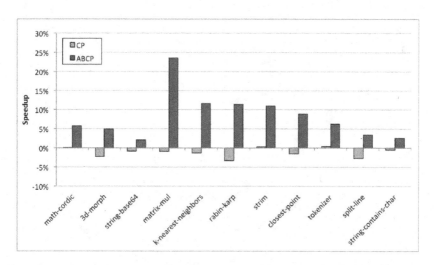

Fig. 8. Speedup of the original and parameter based version of Constant Propagation

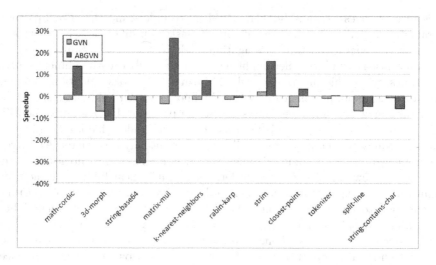

Fig. 9. Speedup of the original and parameter based version of Global Value Numbering

loops. On the other hand, again we observe a speed up in matrix multiplication. This speedup does not come from GVN directly. Rather, it is due to the fact that our constification replaces the loop boundaries by integer values, as a result of the initial value propagation that we perform upon reading values from the interpreter stack. Figure 10 compares constant propagation and global value numbering when preceded by parameter based value specialization. On the average the argument based constant propagation delivers almost 25% more speedup than argument based global value numbering.

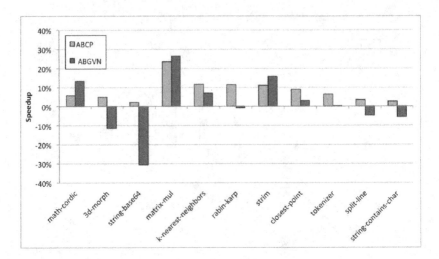

Fig. 10. Speedup of the parameter based versions of Constant Propagation and Global Value Numbering

Figure 11 gives us some further subsidies to understand the speedups that parameter specialization delivers on top of constant propagation. First, we notice that in general constant propagation leads to less code recompilation. In general a just-in-time compiler might have to re-compile the same function several times, while this function is still executing. These recompilations happen because some assumptions made by the JIT may no longer hold during program execution, or it may infer new facts about the program. For instance, the JIT may discover that a reference is used as an integer inside a loop, and this new knowledge may trigger another compilation. If, eventually this reference receives a non-integer value, or some arithmetic operation causes this integer to overflow, then a new compilation is in order. Second, it is clear from the table that argument based specialization considerably improves the capacity of constant propagation to eliminate instructions. When an instruction is eliminated because all the variables that it uses are constants, we say that the instruction has been *folded*. At least in our benchmark suite, traditional constant propagation does not find many opportunities to fold instructions. However, once we replace parameters by constants, it produces remarkably good results. In some cases, as in the function `string-contains-char`, it can eliminate almost one fourth of all the native instructions generated.

4 Related Work

The dispute for market share among Microsoft, Google, Mozilla and Apple has been known in recent years as the "browser war" [17]. Performance is a key factor in this competition. Given that the performance of a browser is strongly connected to its capacity to execute JavaScript efficiently, today we watch the development of increasingly more reliable and efficient JavaScript engines.

Benchmark	CP				ABCP			
	R	I	F	% F	R	I	F	% F
math-cordic	1	287	0	0%	1	295	22	7%
3d-morph	2	582	0	0%	2	600	63	11%
string-base64	3	1503	30	2%	3	1519	58	4%
matrix-mul	8	1574	0	0%	3	558	84	15%
k-nearest-neighbors	2	530	4	1%	1	432	46	11%
rabin-karp	2	583	9	2%	2	595	57	10%
strim	1	154	0	0%	0	82	13	16%
closest-point	1	228	0	0%	0	142	13	9%
tokenizer	2	296	3	1%	2	308	39	13%
split-line	2	390	0	0%	1	300	26	9%
string-contains-char	0	58	0	0%	0	64	15	23%

Fig. 11. A comparison, in numbers, between constant propagation, and argument based constant propagation. R: number of recompilations. I: total number of instructions produced by the JIT compiler. F: number of instructions removed (folded) due to constant propagation. %F: percentage of folded instructions.

The first just-in-time compilers were method based [2]. This approach to just-in-time compilation is still used today with very good results. Google's V8[4] and Mozilla's JaegerMonkey[5], are method-based JIT compilers. Method based compilation is popular for a number of reasons. It can be easily combined with many classical compiler optimization, such as Value Numbering and Loop Invariant Code Motion. It also capitalizes on decades of evolution of JIT technology, and can use old ideas such as Self's style type specialization [6]. Furthermore, this technique supports well profiling guided optimizations [8], such as Zhou's dynamic elimination of partial redundancies [22] and Bodik's array bounds checks elimination [4]. IonMonkey, the compiler that we have adopted as a baseline in this paper, is an method-based JIT compiler, that resorts to hybrid type inference [14] in order to produce better native code.

A more recent, and substantially different JIT technique is trace compilation [3]. This approach only compiles linear sequences of code from hot loops, based on the assumption that programs spend most of their execution time in a few parts of a function. Trace compilation is used in compilers such as Tamarimtrace [7], HotpathVM [12], Yeti [21] and TraceMonkey [11]. There exist code optimization techniques tailored for trace compilation, such as Sol et al.'s [18] algorithm to eliminate redundant overflow tests. There are also theoretical works that describe the semantics of trace compilers [20].

5   Conclusion

In this paper we have introduced the notion of *parameter based code specialization*. We have shown how this technique can be used to speedup the code

---

[4] http://code.google.com/p/v8/
[5] https://wiki.mozilla.org/JaegerMonkey

produced by IonMonkey, an industrial-strength just-in-time compiler that is scheduled to be used in the Mozilla Firefox browser. Parameter based specialization has some resemblance to partial evaluation; however, we do not pre-execute the code in order to improve it. On the contrary, we transform it using static compiler optimizations, such as constant propagation for instance. Our entire implementation plus the benchmarks that we have used in this paper are completely available at `http://code.google.com/p/im-abcp/`.

We believe that parameter based code specialization opens up many different ways to enhance just-in-time compilers. In this paper we have only scratched the tip of these possibilities, and much work is still left to be done. In particular, we would like to explore how different compiler optimizations fare in face of parameter specialization. From our preliminary experiments we know that some optimizations such as constant propagation do well in this new world; however, optimizations such as global value numbering cannot benefit much from it. We have already a small list of optimizations that we believe could benefit from our ideas. Promising candidates include loop inversion, loop unrolling and dead code elimination.

Even though we could add non-trivial speedups on top of Mozilla's JavaScript engine, our current implementation of parameter based code specialization is still research-quality. We are actively working to make it more robust. Priorities in our to-do list include to specialize functions that are compiled more than once, and to cache the values of the specialized parameters, so that future function calls can use this code. Nevertheless, the preliminary results seem to be encouraging.

References

1. Alpern, B., Wegman, M.N., Zadeck, F.K.: Detecting equality of variables in programs. In: POPL, pp. 1–11. ACM (1988)
2. Aycock, J.: A brief history of just-in-time. ACM Computing Surveys 35(2), 97–113 (2003)
3. Bala, V., Duesterwald, E., Banerjia, S.: Dynamo: A transparent dynamic optimization system. In: PLDI, pp. 1–12. ACM (2000)
4. Bodik, R., Gupta, R., Sarkar, V.: ABCD: Eliminating array bounds checks on demand. In: PLDI, pp. 321–333. ACM (2000)
5. Chaganti, P.: Google Web Toolkit GWT Java AJAX Programming, 1st edn. PACKT (2007)
6. Chambers, C., Ungar, D.: Customization: Optimizing compiler technology for SELF, a dynamically-typed object-oriented programming language. SIGPLAN Not. 24(7), 146–160 (1989)
7. Chang, M., Smith, E., Reitmaier, R., Bebenita, M., Gal, A., Wimmer, C., Eich, B., Franz, M.: Tracing for web 3.0: Trace compilation for the next generation web applications. In: VEE, pp. 71–80. ACM (2009)
8. Chang, P.P., Mahlke, S.A., Hwu, W.-M.W.: Using profile information to assist classic code optimizations. Software Practice and Experience 21(12), 1301–1321 (1991)
9. Cytron, R., Ferrante, J., Rosen, B.K., Wegman, M.N., Zadeck, F.K.: Efficiently computing static single assignment form and the control dependence graph. TOPLAS 13(4), 451–490 (1991)

10. Richards, G., Lebresne, S., Burg, B., Vitek, J.: An analysis of the dynamic behavior of JavaScript programs. In: PLDI, pp. 1–12 (2010)
11. Gal, A., Eich, B., Shaver, M., Anderson, D., Kaplan, B., Hoare, G., Mandelin, D., Zbarsky, B., Orendorff, J., Ruderman, J., Smith, E., Reitmair, R., Haghighat, M.R., Bebenita, M., Change, M., Franz, M.: Trace-based just-in-time type specialization for dynamic languages. In: PLDI, pp. 465–478. ACM (2009)
12. Gal, A., Probst, C.W., Franz, M.: HotpathVM: An effective JIT compiler for resource-constrained devices. In: VEE, pp. 144–153 (2006)
13. Gardner, P., Maffeis, S., Smith, G.D.: Towards a program logic for JavaScript. In: POPL, pp. 31–44. ACM (2012)
14. Hackett, B., Guo, S.Y.: Fast and precise hybrid type inference for JavaScript. In: PLDI. ACM (2012)
15. Muchnick, S.S.: Advanced Compiler Design and Implementation. Morgan Kaufmann (1997)
16. Patterson, J.R.C.: Accurate static branch prediction by value range propagation. In: PLDI, pp. 67–78. ACM (1995)
17. Shankland, S.: How JavaScript became a browser-war battleground (2009), http://www2.galcit.caltech.edu/~jeshep/GraphicsBib/NatBib/node3.html (accessed in April 30, 2012)
18. Sol, R., Guillon, C., Pereira, F.M.Q., Bigonha, M.A.S.: Dynamic Elimination of Overflow Tests in a Trace Compiler. In: Knoop, J. (ed.) CC 2011. LNCS, vol. 6601, pp. 2–21. Springer, Heidelberg (2011)
19. Wegman, M.N., Zadeck, F.K.: Constant propagation with conditional branches. TOPLAS 13(2) (1991)
20. Guo, S.Y., Palsberg, J.: The essence of compiling with traces. In: POPL, page to appear. ACM (2011)
21. Zaleski, M.: YETI: A Gradually Extensible Trace Interpreter. PhD thesis, University of Toronto (2007)
22. Zhou, H., Chen, W., Chow, F.C.: An SSA-based algorithm for optimal speculative code motion under an execution profile. In: PLDI, pp. 98–108. ACM (2011)

Adaptable Parsing Expression Grammars

Leonardo Vieira dos Santos Reis[1], Roberto da Silva Bigonha[1],
Vladimir Oliveira Di Iorio[2], and Luis Eduardo de Souza Amorim[2]

[1] Departamento de Ciência da Computação, Universidade Federal de Minas Gerais
{leo,bigonha}@dcc.ufmg.br
[2] Departamento de Informática, Universidade Federal de Viçosa
vladimir@dpi.ufv.br, luis.amorim@ufv.br

Abstract. The term "extensible language" is especially used when a
language allows the extension of its own concrete syntax and the definition of the semantics of new constructs. Most popular tools designed for
automatic generation of syntactic analyzers do not offer any desirable
resources for the specification of extensible languages. When used in the
implementation of features like syntax macro definitions, these tools usually impose severe restrictions. We claim that one of the main reasons
for these limitations is the lack of formal models that are appropriate for
the definition of the syntax of extensible languages.

This paper presents the design and formal definition for *Adaptable
Parsing Expression Grammars (APEG)*, an extension to the PEG model
that allows the manipulation of its own production rules during the analysis of an input string. It is shown that the proposed model may compare
favorably with similar approaches for the definition of the syntax of extensible languages.

Keywords: extensible languages, adaptable grammars, PEG.

1 Introduction

In recent years, we have witnessed important advances in parsing theory. For
example, Ford created *Parsing Expression Grammars (PEG)* [13], an alternative formal foundation for describing syntax, and packrat parsers [12], top-down
parsers with backtracking that guarantee unlimited lookahead and a linear parsing time. Parr has devised a new parsing strategy called LL(*) for the ANTLR
tool, that allows arbitrary lookahead and recognizes some context-sensitive languages [20]. The parser generator YAKKER presents new facilities for applications that operate over binary data [16]. These advances do not include important
features for the definition of extensible languages, although the importance of
extensible languages and the motivation for using it have been vastly discussed
in recent literature [1,10,11,25].

As a simple example of desirable features for the implementation of extensible
languages, Figure 1 shows an excerpt from a program written in the Fortress
language [1]. Initially, a new syntax for loops is defined, and then the new syntax
is used in the same program. Standard tools for the definition of the syntax of

F.H. de Carvalho Junior and L.S. Barbosa (Eds.): SBLP 2012, LNCS 7554, pp. 72–86, 2012.

programming languages are not well suited for this type of extension, because the syntax of the language is modified while the program is processed. A Fortress interpreter, written with the tool Rats! [14], uses the following method: it collects only the macro (extension) definitions in a first pass, processes the necessary modifications to the grammar, and then parses the rest of the program in a second pass [21]. Another solution for similar problems, used in a compiler for the extensible language OCamL [19], is to require that macro definitions and their usage always reside in different files [15].

```
grammar ForLoop extends {Expression, Identifier}
  Expr | :=
    for {i:Id ← e:Expr, ?Space}* do block:Expr end ⇒
      // ... define translation to pure Fortress code
  end
  ...
  // Using the new construct
  g₁ = < 1, 2, 3, 4, 5 >
  g₂ = < 6, 7, 8, 9, 10 >
  for i ← g₁, j ← g₂ do println "(" i "," j ")" end
```

Fig. 1. A Fortress program with a syntax macro

A tool that is able to parse the program in Figure 1 in one pass must be based in a model that allows syntax extensions. We propose *Adaptable Parsing Expression Grammars (APEG)*, a model that combines the ideas of *Extended Attribute Grammars*, *Adaptable Grammars* and *Parsing Expression Grammars*. The main goals that the model has to achieve are: legibility and simplicity for syntactic extension, otherwise it would be restricted to a very small set of users; and it must be suitable for automatic generation of syntactic analyzers.

1.1   From Context-Free to Adaptable Grammars

Context Free Grammars (CFGs) are a formalism widely used for the description of the syntax of programming languages. However, it is not powerful enough to describe context dependent aspects of any interesting programming language, let alone languages with extensible syntax. In order to deal with context dependency, several augmentations to the CFG model have been proposed, and the most commonly used is *Attribute Grammars* (AGs) [17]. In AGs, *evaluation rules* define the values for attributes associated to symbols on production rules, and *constraints* are predicates that must be satisfied by the attributes.

Authors like Christiansen [7] and Shutt [22] argue that, in AG and other extensions for CFGs, the clarity of the original base CFG model is undermined by the power of the extending facilities. Christiansen gives as an example an attribute grammar for ADA, in which a single rule representing function calls has two and a half pages associated to it, to describe the context conditions. He proposes an approach called *Adaptable Grammars* [8], explicitly providing mechanisms within the formalism to allow the production rules to be manipulated.

In an adaptable grammar, the task of checking whether a variable used in an expression has been previously defined may be performed as follows. Instead of having a general rule like `variable -> identifier`, each variable declaration may add a new rule to the grammar. For example, the declaration of a variable with name x adds the following production rule: `variable -> "x"`. The nonterminal *variable* will then generate only the declared variables, and not a general identifier. There is no need to use an auxiliary symbol table and additional code to manipulate it.

Adaptable grammars are powerful enough even for the definition of advanced extensibility mechanisms of programming languages, like the one presented in Figure 1. However, as the model is based on CFG, undesirable ambiguities may arise when the set of production rules is modified. There are also problems when using the model for defining some context sensitive dependencies. For example, it is hard to build context free rules that define that an identifier cannot be declared twice in a same environment [22], although this task can be easily accomplished using attribute grammars and a symbol table.

1.2   From Adaptable Grammars to Adaptable PEGs

We propose an adaptable model that is based on *Parsing Expression Grammars* (PEGs) [13]. Similarly to *Extended Attribute Grammars* (EAGs) [26], attributes are associated to the symbols of production rules. And similarly to *Adaptable Grammars* [8], the first attribute of every nonterminal symbol represents the current valid grammar. Every time a nonterminal is rewritten, the production rule is fetched from the grammar in its own attribute, and not from a global static grammar, as in a standard CFG. Different grammars may be built and passed to other nonterminal symbols.

A fundamental difference between CFGs and PEGs is that the choice operator in PEG is ordered, giving more control of which alternative will be used and eliminating ambiguity. PEG also defines operators that can check an arbitrarily long prefix of the input, without consuming it. We will show that this feature may allow for a simple solution for specifying the constraint that an identifier cannot be defined twice in a same environment.

The main contributions of this paper are: 1) the design of an adaptable model based on PEG for definition of the syntax of extensible languages; 2) a careful formalization for the model; 3) a comparison with adaptable models based on CFG, that exhibits the advantages of the proposal.

The rest of the paper is organized as follows. In Section 2, we present works related to ours. Section 3 contains the formalization of Adaptable PEG. Examples of usage are presented in Section 4. Conclusions and future works are discussed in Section 5.

2   Related Work

It seems that Wegbreit was the first to formalize the idea of grammars that allow for the manipulation of their own set of rules [27], so the idea has been around for at least 40 years. Wegbreit proposed *Extensible Context Free Grammars* (ECFGs), consisting of a context free grammar together with a finite state transducer. The instructions for the transducer allow the insertion of a new production rule on the grammar or the removal of an existing rule.

In his survey of approaches for extensible or adaptable grammar formalisms, Christiansen proposes the term *Adaptable Grammar* [8]. In previous works, he had used the term *Generative Grammar* [7]. Although Shutt has designated his own model as *Recursive Adaptable Grammar* [22], he has later used the term *Adaptive Grammar* [23]. The lack of uniformity of the terms may be one of the reasons for some authors to publish works that are completely unaware of important previous contributions. A recent example is [24], where the authors propose a new term *Reflective Grammar* and a new formalism that has no reference to the works of Christiansen, Shutt and other important similar models.

In [22], Shutt classifies adaptable models as *imperative* or *declarative*, depending on the way the set of rules is manipulated. Imperative models are inherently dependent on the parsing algorithm. The set of rules is treated as a global entity that is modified while derivations are processed. So the grammar designer must know exactly the order of decisions made by the parser. One example is the ECFG model mentioned above.

The following works may also be classified as imperative approaches. Burshteyn proposes *Modifiable Grammars* [4], using the model in the tool USSA [5]. A Modifiable Grammar consists of a CFG and a Turing transducer, with instructions that may define a list of rules to be added, and another to be deleted. Because of the dependency on the parser algorithm, Burshteyn presents two different formalisms, one for bottom-up and another one for top-down parsing. Cabasino and Todesco [6] propose *Dynamic Parsers and Evolving Grammars*. Instead of a transducer, as works mentioned above, each production of a CFG may have an associated rule that creates new nonterminals and productions. The derivations must be rightmost and the associated parser must be bottom-up. Boullier's *Dynamic Grammars* [2] is another example that forces the grammar designer to be aware that derivations are rightmost and the associated parser is bottom-up.

One advantage of declarative adaptable models is the relative independency from the parsing algorithm. Christiansen's *Adaptable Grammars*, mentioned above, is an example of a declarative model. Here we refer to the first formalization presented by Christiansen – later, he proposed an equivalent approach, using definite clause grammars [9]. It is essentially an Extended Attribute Grammar where the first attribute of every non terminal symbol is inherited and represents the *language attribute*, which contains the set of production rules allowed in each derivation. The initial grammar works as the language attribute for the root node of the parse tree, and new language attributes may be built and used in different nodes. Each grammar adaptation is restricted to a specific branch of the parse tree. One advantage of this approach is that it is easy to define statically scope dependent relations, such as the block structure declarations of several programming languages.

Shutt observes that Christiansen's *Adaptable Grammars* inherits the non orthogonality of attribute grammars, with two different models competing. The CFG kernel is simple, generative, but computationally weak. The augmenting facility is obscure and computationally strong. He proposes *Recursive Adaptable Grammars* [22], where a single domain combines the syntactic elements (terminals), meta-syntactic (nonterminals and the language attribute) and semantic values (all other attributes).

Our work is inspired on *Adaptable Grammars*. The main difference is that, instead of a CFG as the base model, we use PEG. Defining a special inherited attribute as the language attribute, our model keeps the advantage of easy definitions for block structured scope. The use of PEG brings additional advantages, such as coping with ambiguities when modifying the set of rules and more powerful operators that provide arbitrary lookahead. With these operators is easy, for example, to define constraints that prevent multiple declarations, a problem that is difficult to solve in other adaptable models.

Our model has some similarities also with the imperative approaches. PEG may be viewed as a formal description of a top-down parser, so the order the productions are used is important to determine the adaptations our model performs. But we believe that it is not a disadvantage as it is for imperative adaptable models based on CFG. Even for standard PEG (non adaptable), designers must be aware of the top-down nature of model, so adaptability is not a significant increase on the complexity of the model.

We believe that problems regarding efficient implementation are one of the reasons that adaptable models are not used yet in important tools for automatic parser generation. Evidence comes from recent works like *Sugar Libraries* [11], that provide developers with tools for importing syntax extensions and their desugaring as libraries. The authors use SDF and Stratego [3] for the implementation. They mention that adaptable grammars could be an alternative that would simplify the parsing procedures, but indicate that their efficiency is questionable. One goal of our work is to develop an implementation for our model that will cope with the efficiency demands of parser generators.

3   Definition of the Model

The adaptability of Adaptable PEGs is achieved by means of an attribute associated with every nonterminal to represent the current grammar. In order to understand the formal definition of the model, it is necessary to know how attributes are evaluated and how constraints over them can be defined. In this section, we discuss our design decisions on how to combine PEG and attributes (*Attribute PEGs*), and then present a formal definition for *Adaptable PEG*. Basic knowledge about Extended Attribute Grammars and Parsing Expression Grammars is desirable – we recommend [26] and [13].

3.1   PEG with Attributes

Extended Attribute Grammar (EAG) is a model for formalizing context sensitive features of programming languages, proposed by Watt and Madsen [26]. Compared to *Attribute Grammar* (AG) [17] and *Affix Grammar* [18], EAG is more readable and generative in nature [26].

Figure 2 shows an example of a EAG that generates a binary numeral and calculates its value. Inherited attributes are represented by a down arrow symbol, and synthesized attributes are represented by an up arrow symbol. Inherited attributes on the left side and synthesized attributes on the right side of a rule are called *defining positions*. Synthesized attributes on the left side and inherited attributes on the right side of a rule are called *applying positions*.

$$
\begin{array}{ll}
\langle S \uparrow x_1 \rangle & \rightarrow \ \langle T \downarrow 0 \uparrow x_1 \rangle \\
\langle T \downarrow x_0 \uparrow x_2 \rangle & \rightarrow \ \langle B \uparrow x_1 \rangle \ \langle T \downarrow 2 * x_0 + x_1 \uparrow x_2 \rangle \\
\langle T \downarrow x_0 \uparrow 2 * x_0 + x_1 \rangle & \rightarrow \ \langle B \uparrow x_1 \rangle \\
\langle B \uparrow 0 \rangle & \rightarrow \ \mathbf{0} \\
\langle B \uparrow 1 \rangle & \rightarrow \ \mathbf{1}
\end{array}
$$

Fig. 2. An example of an EAG that generates binary numerals

A reader not familiar with the EAG notation can use the following association with procedure calls of an imperative programming language, at least for the examples presented in this paper. The left side of a rule may be compared to a procedure signature, with the inherited attributes representing the names of the formal parameters and the synthesized attributes representing expressions that define the values returned (it is possible to return more than one value). For example, $\langle T \downarrow x_0 \uparrow 2 * x_0 + x_1 \rangle$ (third line of Figure 2) would represent the signature of a procedure with name T having x_0 as formal parameter, and returning the value $2 * x_0 + x_1$, an expression that involves another variable x_1 defined in the right side of the rule. The right side of a rule may be compared to the body of a procedure, with every symbol being a new procedure call. Now inherited attributes represent expressions that define the values for the arguments, and synthesized attributes are variables that store the resulting values. For example, $\langle T \downarrow 2 * x_0 + x_1 \uparrow x_2 \rangle$ (second line of Figure 2) would represent a call to procedure T having the value of $2 * x_0 + x_1$ as argument, and storing the result in variable x_2.

One of the improvements introduced by EAG is the use of *attribute expressions* in applying positions, allowing a more concise specification of AG *evaluation rules*. For example, the rules with B as left side indicate that the synthesized attribute is evaluated as either 0 or 1. Without the improvement proposed by EAG, it would be necessary to choose a name for an attribute variable and to add an explicit evaluation rule defining the value for this variable.

We define *Attribute PEGs* as an extension to PEGs, including attribute manipulation. Attribute expressions are not powerful enough to replace all uses of explicit evaluation rules in PEGs, so we propose that Attribute PEGs combine attribute expressions and explicit evaluation rules. In PEGs, the use of recursion is frequently replaced by the use of the *repetition* operator "*", giving definitions more related to an imperative model. So we propose that evaluation rules in Attribute PEGs may update the values of the attribute variables, treating them as variables of an imperative language.

Figure 3 shows an Attribute PEG equivalent to the EAG presented in Figure 2. Expressions in brackets are explicit evaluation rules. In the third line, each of the options of the ordered choice has its own evaluation rule, defining that the value of the variable x_1 is either 0 (if the input is "0") or 1 (if the input is "1"). It is not possible to replace these evaluation rules with attribute expressions because the options are defined in a single parsing expression. In the second line, the value of variable x_0 is initially defined on the first use of the nonterminal B. Then it is cumulatively updated by the evaluation rule $[x_0 := 2 * x_0 + x_1]$.

$$
\begin{aligned}
\langle S \uparrow x_0 \rangle &\leftarrow \langle T \uparrow x_0 \rangle \\
\langle T \uparrow x_0 \rangle &\leftarrow \langle B \uparrow x_0 \rangle \ (\langle B \uparrow x_1 \rangle [x_0 := 2 * x_0 + x_1]) * \\
\langle B \uparrow x_1 \rangle &\leftarrow (\mathbf{0} \ [x_1 := 0]) \quad / \quad (\mathbf{1} \ [x_1 := 1])
\end{aligned}
$$

Fig. 3. An example of an attribute PEG

Besides explicit evaluation rules, AGs augment context-free production rules with *constraints*, predicates which must be satisfied by the attributes in each application of the rules. In Attribute PEGs, we allow also the use of constraints, as predicates defined in any position on the right side of a rule. If a predicate fails, the evaluation of the parsing expression also fails. The use of attributes as variables of an imperative language and predicate evaluation are similar to the approach adopted for the formal definition of YAKKER in [16].

Another improvement provided by EAG is the possibility of using the same attribute variable in more than one defining rule position. It defines an implicit constraint, requiring the variable to have the same value in all instances. In our proposition for Attribute PEG, we do not adopt this last improvement of EAG, because it would not be consistent with our design decision of allowing attributes to be updated as variables of an imperative language.

3.2   Formal Definition of Attribute PEG

We extend the definition of PEG presented in [13] and define Attribute PEG as a 6-tuple (V_N, V_T, A, R, S, F), where V_N and V_T are finite sets of nonterminals and terminals, respectively. $A : V_N \rightarrow \mathcal{P}(\mathbb{Z}^+ \times \{\uparrow, \downarrow\})$ is an attribute function that maps every nonterminal to a set of attributes. Each attribute is represented by a pair (n, t), where n is a distinct attribute position number and t is an element of the set $\{\uparrow, \downarrow\}$. The use of positions instead of names makes definitions shorter [26]. The symbol $\uparrow$ represents an inherited attribute and $\downarrow$ represents a synthesized attribute. $R : V_N \rightarrow \mathcal{P}_e$ is a total rule function which maps every nonterminal to a *parsing expression* and $S \in V_N$ is an initial *parsing expression*.

F is a finite set of functions that operate over the domain of attributes, used in attribute expressions. We assume a simple, untyped language of attribute expressions that include variables, boolean, integer and string values. If $f \in F$ is a function of arity n and $e_1, \ldots, e_n$ are attribute expressions, then $f(e_1, \ldots, e_n)$ is also an attribute expression.

Suppose that e, e_1 and e_2 are *attribute parsing expressions*. The set of valid *attribute parsing expressions* $(\mathcal{P}_e)$ can be recursively defined as:

$$\lambda \in \mathcal{P}_e \quad \text{(empty expression)}$$
$$a \in \mathcal{P}_e, \text{ for every } a \in V_T \quad \text{(terminal expression)}$$
$$A \in \mathcal{P}_e, \text{ for every } A \in V_N \quad \text{(nonterminal expression)}$$
$$e_1 e_2 \in \mathcal{P}_e \quad \text{(sequence expression)}$$
$$e_1/e_2 \in \mathcal{P}_e \quad \text{(ordered choice expression)}$$
$$e^* \in \mathcal{P}_e \quad \text{(zero-or-more repetition expression)}$$
$$!e \in \mathcal{P}_e \quad \text{(not-predicate expression)}$$
$$[v := exp] \in \mathcal{P}_e \quad \text{(update expression)}$$
$$[exp] \in \mathcal{P}_e \quad \text{(constraint expression)}$$

To the set of standard *parsing expressions*, we add two new types of expressions. *Update expressions* have the format $[v := exp]$, where v is a variable name and exp is an attribute expression, using functions from F. They are used to update the value of variables in an environment. *Constraint expresssions* with the format $[exp]$, where exp is an attribute expression that evaluates to a boolean value, are used to test for predicates over the attributes.

Nonterminal expressions are nonterminals symbols with attribute expressions. Without losing generality, we will assume that all inherited attributes are represented in a nonterminal before its synthesized attributes. So, suppose that $e \in R(A)$ is the parsing expression associated with nonterminal A, p is its number of inherited attributes and q the number of synthesized attributes. Then $\langle A \downarrow a_1 \downarrow a_2 \ldots \downarrow a_p \uparrow b_1 \uparrow \ldots \uparrow b_q \rangle \leftarrow e$ represents the rule for A and its attributes. We will also assume that the attribute expressions in defining positions of nonterminals are always represented by a single variable.

The example of Figure 3 can be expressed formally as $G = (\{S, T, B\}, \{0, 1\}, \{(S, \{(1, \uparrow)\}), (T, \{(1, \uparrow)\}), (B, \{(1, \uparrow)\})\}, R, S, \{+, *\})$, where R represents the rules described in Figure 3.

3.3   Semantics of Adaptable PEG

An Adaptable PEG is an Attribute PEG whose first attribute of all nonterminals is inherited and represents the language attribute. Figure 4 presents the semantics of an Adaptable PEG. Almost all the formalization is related to PEG with attributes. Only the last equation defines adaptability.

An environment maps variables to values, with the following notation: . (a dot) represents an empty environment, i.e., all variables map to the *unbound* value; $[x_1/v_1, \ldots, x_n/v_n]$ maps x_i to v_i, $1 \leq i \leq n$; $E[x_1/v_1, \ldots, x_n/v_n]$ is an environment which is equal to E, except for the values of x_i that map to v_i,

$1 \leq i \leq n$. We write $E[\![e]\!]$ to indicate the value of the expression e evaluated in the environment E.

Figure 4 defines the judgement $E \vdash (e, x) \Rightarrow (n, o) \vdash E'$, which says that the interpretation of the parsing expression e, for the input string x, in an environment E, results in (n, o), and produces a new environment E'. In the pair (n, o), n indicates the number of steps for the interpretation and $o \in V_T^* \cup \{f\}$ indicates the prefix of x that is consumed, if the expression succeeds, or $f \notin V_T^*$, if it fails.

Note that the changes in an environment are discarded when an expression fails. For example, in a sequence expression, a new environment is computed when it succeeds, a situation represented by rule **Seq**. If the first or the second subexpression of a sequence expression fails, the changes are discarded and the environment used is the one before the sequence expression. These situations are represented by rules $\neg$**Seq**$_1$ and $\neg$**Seq**$_2$. A similar behaviour is defined for $\neg$**Term**$_1$ and $\neg$**Term**$_2$, when a terminal expression fails, and for $\neg$**Rep**, when a repetition fails.

Rules **Neg** and $\neg$**Neg** show that the environment changes computed inside a not-predicate expression are not considered in the outer level, allowing arbitrary lookahead without colateral effects. Rules **Atrib** and $\neg$**Atrib** define the behaviour for update expression, and rules **True** and **False** represent predicate evaluation in constraint expressions.

The most interesting rule is **Adapt**. It defines how nonterminal expressions are evaluated. Attribute values are associated with variables using an approach similar to EAG, but in a way more operational; it is also similar to *parameterized nonterminals* described in [16], but allowing several return values instead of just one. When a nonterminal is processed, the values of its inherited attributes are calculated considering the current environment. The corresponding parsing expression is fetched from the current set of production rules, defined by the language attribute, that is always the first attribute of the symbol. It is indeed the only point in all the rules of Figure 4 associated with the property of adaptability.

Now we can define the language accepted by an Adaptable PEG as follows. Let $G = (V_N, V_T, A, R, S, F)$ be an Adaptable PEG. Then

$$L(G) = \{w \in V_T^* \mid . \vdash (\langle S \downarrow G \ldots \rangle, w) \Rightarrow (n, w') \vdash E'\}$$

The derivation process begins using an empty environment, with the starting parsing expression S matching the input string w. The original grammar G is used as the value for the inherited language attribute of S. If the process succeeds, n represents the number of steps for the derivation, w' is the prefix of w matched and E' is the resulting environment as in [13]. The language $L(G)$ is the set of words w that do not produce f (failure).

4   Empirical Results

In this section, we present three examples of usage of Adaptable PEG. The first example is a definition of context dependent constraints commonly required in binary data specification. The second illustrates the specifications of static

$$\boxed{E \vdash (e,x) \Rightarrow (n,o) \vdash E'}$$

Empty $\dfrac{x \in V_T^*}{E \vdash (\lambda,x) \Rightarrow (1,\lambda) \vdash E}$
   Term $\dfrac{a \in V_T \qquad x \in V_T^*}{E \vdash (a,ax) \Rightarrow (1,a) \vdash E}$

¬Term$_1$ $\dfrac{a,b \in V_T \qquad a \neq b \qquad x \in V_T^*}{E \vdash (a,bx) \Rightarrow (1,f) \vdash E}$
   ¬Term$_2$ $\dfrac{a \in V_T}{E \vdash (a,\lambda) \Rightarrow (1,f) \vdash E}$

Seq $\dfrac{E_1 \vdash (e_1, x_1 x_2 y) \Rightarrow (n_1, x_1) \vdash E_2 \qquad E_2 \vdash (e_2, x_2 y) \Rightarrow (n_2, x_2) \vdash E_3}{E_1 \vdash (e_1 e_2, x_1 x_2 y) \Rightarrow (n_1 + n_2 + 1, x_1 x_2) \vdash E_3}$

¬Seq$_1$ $\dfrac{E_1 \vdash (e_1, x_1 y) \Rightarrow (n_1, x_1) \vdash E_2 \qquad E_2 \vdash (e_2, y) \Rightarrow (n_2, f) \vdash E_3}{E_1 \vdash (e_1 e_2, x_1 y) \Rightarrow (n_1 + n_2 + 1, f) \vdash E_1}$

¬Seq$_2$ $\dfrac{E_1 \vdash (e_1, x) \Rightarrow (n_1, f) \vdash E_2}{E_1 \vdash (e_1 e_2, x) \Rightarrow (n_1 + 1, f) \vdash E_1}$

Choice$_1$ $\dfrac{E \vdash (e_1, x_1 y) \Rightarrow (n_1, x_1) \vdash E'}{E \vdash (e_1/e_2, x_1 y) \Rightarrow (n_1 + 1, x_1) \vdash E'}$

Choice$_2$ $\dfrac{E_1 \vdash (e_1, x) \Rightarrow (n_1, f) \vdash E_2 \qquad E_1 \vdash (e_2, x) \Rightarrow (n_2, o) \vdash E_3}{E_1 \vdash (e_1/e_2, x) \Rightarrow (n_1 + n_2 + 1, o) \vdash E_3}$

Rep $\dfrac{E_1 \vdash (e, x_1 x_2 y) \Rightarrow (n_1, x_1) \vdash E_2 \qquad E_2 \vdash (e^*, x_2 y) \Rightarrow (n_2, x_2) \vdash E_3}{E_1 \vdash (e^*, x_1 x_2 y) \Rightarrow (n_1 + n_2 + 1, x_1 x_2) \vdash E_3}$

¬Rep $\dfrac{E_1 \vdash (e, x) \Rightarrow (n_1, f) \vdash E_2}{E_1 \vdash (e^*, x) \Rightarrow (n_1 + 1, \lambda) \vdash E_1}$

Neg $\dfrac{E \vdash (e, xy) \Rightarrow (n_1, x) \vdash E'}{E \vdash (!e, xy) \Rightarrow (n_1 + 1, f) \vdash E}$
   ¬Neg $\dfrac{E \vdash (e, xy) \Rightarrow (n_1, f) \vdash E'}{E \vdash (!e, x) \Rightarrow (n_1 + 1, \lambda) \vdash E}$

Atrib $\dfrac{v = E[\![e]\!]}{E \vdash ([x := e], y) \Rightarrow (1, \lambda) \vdash E[x/v]}$
   ¬Atrib $\dfrac{unbound = E[\![e]\!]}{E \vdash ([x := e], y) \Rightarrow (1, f) \vdash E}$

True $\dfrac{true = E[\![e]\!]}{E \vdash ([e], x) \Rightarrow (1, \lambda) \vdash E}$
   False $\dfrac{false = E[\![e]\!]}{E \vdash ([e], x) \Rightarrow (1, f) \vdash E}$

$$\langle A \downarrow a_1 \downarrow \ldots \downarrow a_p \uparrow e'_1 \uparrow \ldots \uparrow e'_q \rangle \leftarrow e \in E[\![e_1]\!], \quad \text{where } E[\![e_1]\!] \equiv \text{language attribute}$$
$$v_i = E[\![e_i]\!], 1 \leq i \leq p \qquad v'_j = E_1[\![e'_j]\!], 1 \leq j \leq q$$

Adapt $\dfrac{[a_1/v_1, \ldots, a_p/v_p] \vdash (e, x) \Rightarrow (n, o) \vdash E_1}{E \vdash (\langle A \downarrow e_1 \downarrow \ldots \downarrow e_p \uparrow b_1 \uparrow \ldots \uparrow b_q \rangle, x) \Rightarrow (n + 1, o) \vdash E[b_1/v'_1, \ldots, b_q/v'_q]}$

Fig. 4. Semantics of Adaptable PEG

semantics of programming languages. And the third one shows how syntax extensibility can be expressed with Adaptable PEG.

4.1 Data Dependent Languages

As a motivating example of a context-sensitive language specification, Jim et alii [16] present a data format language in which an integer number is used to define the length of the text that follows it. Figure 5 shows how a similar language may be defined in an Attribute (non adaptable) PEG. The nonterminal *number* has a synthesized attribute, whose value is used in the constraint expression that controls the length of text to be parsed in the sequel. The terminal *CHAR* represents any single character.

$$
\begin{array}{ll}
\langle literal \rangle & \leftarrow \ \langle number \uparrow n \rangle \ \langle strN \downarrow n \rangle \\
\langle strN \downarrow n \rangle & \leftarrow \ ([n > 0] \ CHAR \ [n := n - 1])^* \ [n = 0] \\
\langle number \uparrow x_2 \rangle & \leftarrow \ \langle digit \uparrow x_2 \rangle \ (\langle digit \uparrow x_1 \rangle [x_2 := x_2 * 10 + x_1])^* \\
\langle digit \uparrow x_1 \rangle & \leftarrow \ \mathbf{0} \ [x_1 := 0] \ / \ \mathbf{1} \ [x_1 := 1] \ / \ ... / \ \mathbf{9} \ [x_1 := 9]
\end{array}
$$

Fig. 5. An example of a data dependent language

Using features from Adaptable PEG in the same language, we could replace the first two rules of Figure 5 by:

$$
\begin{array}{ll}
\langle literal \downarrow g \rangle & \leftarrow \ \langle number \downarrow g \uparrow n \rangle \\
& [g_1 = g \ \oplus \ rule("\langle strN \downarrow g \rangle \leftarrow " + rep("CHAR\ ", n))] \\
& \langle strN \downarrow g_1 \rangle
\end{array}
$$

In an Adaptable PEG, every nonterminal has the language attribute as its first inherited attribute. The attribute g of the start symbol is initialized with the original PEG, but when nonterminal *strN* is used, a new grammar g_1 is considered. The symbol "$\oplus$" represents an operator for adding rules to a grammar and function *rep* produces a string repeatedly concatenated, then g_1 will be equal to g together with a new rule that indicates that *strN* can generate a string with length n. These two functions are not formalized here for short.

4.2 Static Semantics

Figure 6 presents a PEG definition for a language where a block starts with a list of declarations of integer variables, followed by a list of update commands. For simplification, white spaces are not considered. An update command is formed by a variable on the left side and a variable on the right side.

Suppose that the context dependent constraints are: a variable cannot be used if it was not declared, and a variable cannot be declared more than once. The Adaptable PEG in Figure 7 implements these context dependent constraints.

$$
\begin{array}{ll|ll}
block & \leftarrow \ \{ \ dlist \ slist \ \} & decl & \leftarrow \ \textbf{int} \ id \ ; \\
dlist & \leftarrow \ decl \ decl^* & stmt & \leftarrow \ id = id \ ; \\
slist & \leftarrow \ stmt \ stmt^* & id & \leftarrow \ alpha \ alpha^*
\end{array}
$$

Fig. 6. Syntax of block with declaration and use of variables (simplified)

$$
\begin{aligned}
\langle block \downarrow g \rangle \quad &\leftarrow \ \{ \ \langle dlist \downarrow g \uparrow g_1 \rangle \ \langle slist \downarrow g_1 \rangle \ \} \\
\langle dlist \downarrow g \uparrow g_1 \rangle \quad &\leftarrow \ \langle decl \downarrow g \uparrow g_1 \rangle \ [g := g_1] \ (\langle decl \downarrow g \uparrow g_1 \rangle \ [g := g_1])^* \\
\langle decl \downarrow g \uparrow g_1 \rangle \quad &\leftarrow \ !(\ \textbf{int} \ \langle var \downarrow g \rangle \ ) \ \textbf{int} \ \langle id \downarrow g \uparrow n \rangle \ ; \\
& \qquad [g_1 := g \oplus rule("\langle var \downarrow g \rangle \leftarrow \#n")] \\
\langle slist \downarrow g \rangle \quad &\leftarrow \ \langle stmt \downarrow g \rangle \ \langle stmt \downarrow g \rangle^* \\
\langle stmt \downarrow g \rangle \quad &\leftarrow \ \langle var \downarrow g \rangle = \langle var \downarrow g \rangle \ ; \\
\langle id \downarrow g \uparrow n \rangle \quad &\leftarrow \ \langle alpha \downarrow g \uparrow ch_1 \rangle [n = ch_1] (\langle alpha \downarrow g \uparrow ch_2 \rangle [n = n + ch_2])^*
\end{aligned}
$$

Fig. 7. Adaptable PEG for declaration and use of variables

In the rule that defines *dlist*, the PEG synthesized by each *decl* is passed on to the next one. The rule that defines *decl* first checks whether the input matches a declaration generated by the current PEG g. If so, it is an indication that the variable has already been declared. Using the PEG operator "!", it is possible to perform this checking without consuming the input and indicating a failure, in case of repeated declaration. Next, a new declaration is processed and the name of the identifier is collected in n. Finally, a new PEG is built, adding a rule that states that the nonterminal *var* may derive the name n. The symbol "#" indicates that the string n must be treated as a variable.

The use of the PEG operator "!" on rule for *decl* prevents multiple declarations, a problem reported as very difficult to solve when using adaptable models based on CFG. The new rule added to the current PEG ensures that a variable may be used only if it was previously declared. The symbol *block* may be part of a larger PEG, with the declarations restricted to the static scope defined by the block.

4.3 Fortress Language

In Figure 8, we show how extensions defined to Fortress could be integrated into the language base grammar using Adaptable PEG. It is an adapted version of the original grammar proposed in the open source Fortress project, considering only the parts related to syntax extension. The rules can derive grammar definitions as the one presented in Figure 1.

Nonterminal *gram* defines a grammar which has a name specified by nonterminal *Id*, a list of extended grammars (*extends*) and a list of definitions. The grammar declared is located in the synthesized attribute t_2, which is a map of names to grammars. Note that language attribute is not changed, because the nonterminal *gram* only declares a new grammar that can be imported when

$$\langle gram \downarrow g \downarrow t_1 \uparrow t_2 \rangle \qquad \leftarrow \textbf{grammar} \ \langle Id \downarrow g \uparrow id \rangle \ \langle extends \downarrow g \uparrow l \rangle$$
$$(\langle nonterm \downarrow g \downarrow t_1 \downarrow l \uparrow g_1 \rangle$$
$$[t_2 := [id \ / \ t_2(id) \bigcup g_1]])^* \ \textbf{end}$$

$$\langle extends \downarrow g \uparrow l \rangle \qquad \leftarrow \textbf{extends} \ \{ \ \langle Id \downarrow g \uparrow id_1 \rangle \ [l := [id_1]]$$
$$(, \ \langle Id \downarrow g \uparrow id_2 \rangle \ [l := l : [id_2]])^* \ \}$$
$$/ \ \lambda \ [l := []]$$

$$\langle nonterm \downarrow g \downarrow t_1 \downarrow l \uparrow g_1 \rangle \leftarrow \langle Id \downarrow g \uparrow id_1 \rangle \ |:= \langle syntax \downarrow g \uparrow e_1 \rangle$$
$$[g_1 := \{id_1 \leftarrow \otimes(t_1, l, id_1, e_1)\}]$$
$$/ \ \langle Id \downarrow g \uparrow id_2 \rangle \ ::= \langle syntax \downarrow g \uparrow e_2 \rangle \ [g_1 := \{id_2 \leftarrow e_2\}]$$

$$\langle syntax \downarrow g \uparrow e \rangle \qquad \leftarrow ((\langle part \downarrow g \uparrow e_1 \rangle \ [e := e \ e_1])^* \Rightarrow \langle sem \downarrow g \rangle$$
$$(| \ (\langle part \downarrow g \uparrow e_2 \rangle \ [x := x \ e_2])^*$$
$$[e := e \ / \ x] \Rightarrow \langle sem \downarrow g \rangle))^*$$

$$\langle part \downarrow g \uparrow e \rangle \qquad \leftarrow \langle single \downarrow g \uparrow e_1 \rangle ? \ [e \leftarrow e_1 \ / \ \lambda]$$
$$/ \ \langle single \downarrow g \uparrow e_2 \rangle * \ [e := e_2^*]$$
$$/ \ \langle single \downarrow g \uparrow e_3 \rangle + \ [e := e_3 \ e_3^*]$$
$$/ \ \langle single \downarrow g \uparrow e_4 \rangle \ [e := e_4]$$
$$/ \ \neg \langle single \downarrow g \uparrow e_5 \rangle * \ [e := !e_5]$$
$$/ \ \wedge \langle single \downarrow g \uparrow e_6 \rangle \ [e := !(!e_6)]$$
$$/ \ \{ \ (\langle part \downarrow g \uparrow e_7 \rangle [x := x \ e_7])^* \ \} \ [e := (x)]$$

$$\langle single \downarrow g \uparrow e \rangle \qquad \leftarrow \langle Id \downarrow g \uparrow id \rangle : \langle Base \downarrow g \uparrow e \rangle$$
$$/ \ \langle Base \downarrow g \uparrow e \rangle$$

Fig. 8. Fortress syntax grammar

needed. The attribute t_1 is also a map, and it is used for looking up available grammars.

Nonterminal *extends* defines a list of grammars that can be used in the definition of the new grammar. Every nonterminal of the imported grammar can be extended or used in new nonterminals definitions. Nonterminal *nonterm* defines a rule for extending the grammar, either extending the definition of a nonterminal or declaring a new one, depending whether the symbol used is |:= or ::=. If the definition of a nonterminal is extended, the function $\otimes$ is used to together the original rule and the new expression defined. Otherwise, a grammar that has only one rule is created and stored in attribute g_1.

The rule of the nonterminal *syntax* has two parts: one is a parsing expression of a nonterminal (sequence of *part*) and the other is a transformation rule. A transformation rule defines the semantics of an extension, which is specified by nonterminal *sem*. Nonterminal *part* defines the elements that can be used in a parsing expression with addition that nonterminal can have aliases. Nonterminal *Base* generates nonterminal names, terminals and strings.

The rules in Figure 8 do not change the Fortress grammar directly; the extensions are only accomplished when an import statement is used.

5   Conclusion and Future Work

The main goals for the model proposed in this work, as stated in Section 1, are: legibility and simplicity; and it must be suitable for automatic generation of syntactic analyzers. We have no proofs that these goals have been attained, however we believe that we have presented enough evidence for the first goal. Our model has a syntax as clear as Christiansen's Adaptable Grammars, since the same principles are used. In order to explore the full power of the model, it is enough for a developer to be familiar with Extended Attribute Grammars and Parsing Expression Grammars.

We keep some of the most important advantages of declarative models, such as an easy definition of context dependent aspects associated to static scope and nested blocks. We showed that the use of PEG as the basis for the model allowed a very simple solution for the problem of checking for multiple declarations of an identifier. This problem is reported as very difficult to solve with adaptable models based on CFG.

When defining the syntax of extensible languages, the use of PEG has at least two important advantages. The production rules can be freely manipulated without the insertion of undesirable ambiguities, since it is not possible to express ambiguity with PEG. Extending a language specification may require the extension of the set of its lexemes. PEGs is scannerless, so the extension of the set of lexemes in a language is performed with the same features used for the extension of the syntax of the language.

In order to know exactly the adaptations performed by an Adaptable PEG, a developer must be aware that it works as a top down parser. It could be considered as a disadvantage when compared to declarative models, but any PEG developer is already prepared to deal with this feature, since PEG is, by definition, a description of a top down parser.

We have not developed yet any proof that our model is suitable for automatic generation of syntactic analyzers. So the immediate next step of our work is to develop an efficient implementation for Adaptable PEG, considering frequent modifications on the set of production rules. In this implementation, we must offer an appropriate set of operations to manipulate the grammar. Grimm proposes an interesting mechanism for the tool Rats! [14], inserting labels in places that the rules may be modified. We may use a similar approach in our future implementation.

References

1. Allen, E., Culpepper, R., Nielsen, J.D., Rafkind, J., Ryu, S.: Growing a syntax. In: Proceedings of FOOL 2009 (2009)
2. Boullier, P.: Dynamic grammars and semantic analysis. Rapport de recherche RR-2322, INRIA. Projet CHLOE (1994)
3. Bravenboer, M., Kalleberg, K.T., Vermaas, R., Visser, E.: Stratego/XT 0.17. A language and toolset for program transformation. Sci. Comput. Program. 72(1-2), 52–70 (2008)

4. Burshteyn, B.: Generation and recognition of formal languages by modifiable grammars. SIGPLAN Not. 25, 45–53 (1990)
5. Burshteyn, B.: Ussa – universal syntax and semantics analyzer. SIGPLAN Not. 27, 42–60 (1992)
6. Cabasino, S., Paolucci, P.S., Todesco, G.M.: Dynamic parsers and evolving grammars. SIGPLAN Not. 27, 39–48 (1992)
7. Christiansen, H.: The Syntax and Semantics of Extensible Languages. Roskilde datalogiske skrifter. Computer Science, Roskilde University Centre (1987)
8. Christiansen, H.: A survey of adaptable grammars. SIGPLAN Not. 25, 35–44 (1990)
9. Christiansen, H.: Adaptable Grammars for Non-Context-Free Languages. In: Cabestany, J., Sandoval, F., Prieto, A., Corchado, J.M. (eds.) IWANN 2009, Part I. LNCS, vol. 5517, pp. 488–495. Springer, Heidelberg (2009)
10. Dinkelaker, T., Eichberg, M., Mezini, M.: Incremental concrete syntax for embedded languages. In: Proceedings of the 2011 ACM Symposium on Applied Computing, SAC 2011, pp. 1309–1316. ACM, New York (2011)
11. Erdweg, S., Rendel, T., Kästner, C., Ostermann, K.: Sugarj: library-based syntactic language extensibility. In: Proceedings of OOPSLA 2011, pp. 391–406. ACM, New York (2011)
12. Ford, B.: Packrat parsing: simple, powerful, lazy, linear time, functional pearl. SIGPLAN Not. 37(9), 36–47 (2002)
13. Ford, B.: Parsing expression grammars: a recognition-based syntactic foundation. SIGPLAN Not. 39(1), 111–122 (2004)
14. Grimm, R.: Better extensibility through modular syntax. SIGPLAN Not. 41(6), 38–51 (2006)
15. Jambon, M.: How to customize the syntax of ocaml, using camlp5 (2011), http://mjambon.com/extend-ocaml-syntax.html
16. Jim, T., Mandelbaum, Y., Walker, D.: Semantics and algorithms for data-dependent grammars. SIGPLAN Not. 45, 417–430 (2010)
17. Knuth, D.E.: Semantics of Context-Free Languages. Mathematical Systems Theory 2(2), 127–145 (1968)
18. Koster, C.H.A.: Affix grammars. In: Algol 68 Implementation, pp. 95–109. North-Holland (1971)
19. Minsky, Y.: Ocaml for the masses. Commun. ACM 54(11), 53–58 (2011)
20. Parr, T., Fisher, K.: LL(*): the foundation of the ANTLR parser generator. SIGPLAN Not. 46(6), 425–436 (2011)
21. Ryu, S.: Parsing fortress syntax. In: Proceedings of PPPJ 2009, pp. 76–84. ACM, New York (2009)
22. Shutt, J.N.: Recursive adaptable grammars. Master's thesis, Worchester Polytechnic Institute (1998)
23. Shutt, J.N.: What is an adaptive grammar? (2001), http://www.cs.wpi.edu/~jshutt/adapt/adapt.html
24. Stansifer, P., Wand, M.: Parsing reflective grammars. In: Proceedings of LDTA 2011, pp. 10:1–10:7. ACM, New York (2011)
25. Steele Jr., G.L.: Growing a language. In: Addendum to OOPSLA 1998, pp. 0.01–A1. ACM, New York (1998)
26. Watt, D.A., Madsen, O.L.: Extended attribute grammars. Comput. J. 26(2), 142–153 (1983)
27. Wegbreit, B.: Studies in Extensible Programming Languages. Outstanding Dissertations in the Computer Sciences. Garland Publishing, New York (1970)

Optimizing a Geomodeling Domain Specific Language

Bruno Morais Ferreira, Fernando Magno Quintão Pereira,
Hermann Rodrigues, and Britaldo Silveira Soares-Filho

Departamento de Ciência da Computação – UFMG
Av. Antônio Carlos, 6627 – 31.270-010 – Belo Horizonte – MG – Brazil
{brunomf,fernando}@dcc.ufmg.br, {hermann,britaldo}@csr.ufmg.br

Abstract. In this paper we describe Dinamica EGO, a domain specific languages (DSL) for geomodeling. Dinamica EGO provides users with a rich suite of operators available in a script language and in a graphical interface, which they can use to process information extracted from geographic entities, such as maps and tables. We analyze this language through the lens of compiler writers. Under this perspective we describe a key optimization that we have implemented on top of the Dinamica EGO execution environment. This optimization consists in the systematic elimination of memory copies that Dinamica EGO uses to ensure referential transparency. Our algorithm is currently part of the official distribution of this framework. We show, via a real-life case study, that our optimization can speedup geomodeling applications by almost 100x.

1 Introduction

Domain Specific Languages (DSLs) are used in the most varied domains, and have been shown to be effective to increase the productivity of programmers [10]. In particular, DSLs enjoy remarkable success in the geomodeling domain [2]. In this case, DSLs help non-professional programmers to extract information from maps, to blend and modify this information in different ways, and to infer new knowledge from this processing. A tool that stands out in this area is *Dinamica EGO* [11,14,13,15]. This application, a Brazilian home-brew created in the Centro de Sensoriamento Remoto of the Federal University of Minas Gerais (UFMG), today enjoys international recognition as an effective and useful framework for geographic modeling. Applications of it include, for instance, carbon emissions and deforestation [3], assessment of biodiversity loss [12], urbanization and climate change [9], emission reduction(REDD) [8] and urban growth [17].

Users interact with this framework via a graphical programming language which allows them to describe how information is extracted from maps, possibly modified, and written back into the knowledge base. Henceforth we will use the term EGO Script to describe the graphical programming language that is used as the scripting language in the Dinamica EGO framework. This language, and its underlying execution environment, has been designed to fulfill two main

F.H. de Carvalho Junior and L.S. Barbosa (Eds.): SBLP 2012, LNCS 7554, pp. 87–101, 2012.

goals. Firstly, it must be easy to use; hence, requiring a minimum of programming skill. Users manipulate maps and other geographic entities via graphical symbols which can be connected through different data-flow channels to build patterns for branches and loops. Secondly, it must be efficient. To achieve this goal, it provides a 64-bit native version written in C++ and java with multi-threading and dynamic compilation. Being a dynamic execution environment, EGO Script relies heavily on Just-in-time compilation to achieve the much necessary speed.

Dinamica's current success is the result of a long development process, which includes engineering decisions that have not been formally documented. In this paper we partially rectify this omission, describing a key compiler optimization that has been implemented in the Dinamica EGO execution environment. In order to provide users with a high-level programming environment, one of the key aspects of Dinamica's semantics is referential transparency, as we explain in Section 3. Scripts are formed by components, and these components must not modify the data that they receive as inputs. This semantics imposes on the tool a heavy burden, because tables containing data to be processed must be copied before been passed from one component to the other. Removing these copies is a non-trivial endeavor, inasmuch as minimizing such copies is a NP-complete problem, as we show in Section 3. Because this problem is NP-complete, we must recourse to heuristics to eliminate redundant copies. We discuss these heuristics in Section 4. Although we have discussed this algorithm in the context of Dinamica EGO, we believe that it can also be applied in other data-flow based systems, such as programs built on top of the filter-stream paradigm [16].

We provide empirical evidence that supports our design decisions in Section 5, by analyzing the runtime behavior of a complex application in face of our optimization. This application divides an altitude map into slices of same height. In order to get more precise ground information, we must decrease the height of each slice; hence, increasing the amount of slices in the overall database. In this case, for highly accurate simulations our copy elimination algorithm boosts the performance of Dinamica EGO by almost 100x.

2   A Bird's Eye View of Dinamica EGO

We illustrate EGO Script through an example that, although artificial, contains some of the key elements that we will discuss in the rest of this paper. Consider the following problem: "what is the mean slope of the cities from a given region?" We can answer this query by combining data from two maps encompassing the same geographic area. The first map contains the slope of each area. We can assume that each cell of this matrix represents a region of a few hectares, and that the value stored in it is the average inclination of that region. The second map is a matrix that associates with each region a number that identifies the municipality where that region is located. Regions that are part of the same city jurisdiction have the same identifier. The EGO script that solves this problem is shown in Figure 1. An EGO Script program is an ensemble of components,

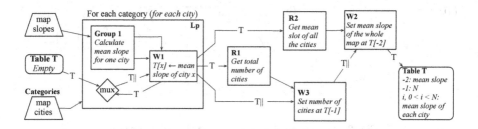

Fig. 1. An EGO Script program that finds the average slope of the cities that form a certain region. The parallel bars (||) denote places where the original implementation of Dinamica EGO replicates the table T.

which are linked together by data channels. Some components encode data, others computation. Components in this last category are called *functors*. The order in which functors must execute is determined by the runtime environment, and should obey the dependencies created by the data channels.

EGO Script uses the trapezoid symbol to describe data to be processed, which is usually loaded from files. In our example, this data are the two maps. We call the map of cities a *categorical* map, as it divides a matrix into equivalence classes. Each equivalence class contains the cells that belong to the same city administration. The large rectangle named **Lp** with smaller components inside it is a *container*, which represents a loop. It will cause some processing to be executed for each different category in the map of cities. The results produced by this script will be accumulated in the table T. Some functors can write into T. We use names starting with **W** to refer to them. Others only read the table. Their names start with **R**. In our example, the positive indices of T represent city entries. Once the script terminates, T will map each city to its slope. Additionally, this accumulator will have in its -1 index the total number of cities that have been processed, and in its -2 index the average slope of the entire map of slopes.

The functor called **W1** is responsible for filling the table with the results obtained for each city. The element called mux works as a loop header: it passes the empty accumulator to the loop, and after the first iteration, it is in charge of merging the newly produced data with the old accumulator. **W1** always copies the table before updating it. We denote this copy by the double pipes after the table name in the input channel, e.g., T||. The attentive reader must be wondering: why is this copy necessary? Even more if we consider that it is performed inside a loop? The answer is pragmatic: before we had implemented the optimization described in this paper, each component that could update data should replicate this data. In this way, any component could be reused as a black box, without compromising the referential transparency that is a key characteristics of the language. We have departed from this original model by moving data replication to the channels, instead of the components, and using a whole program analysis to eliminate unnecessary copies.

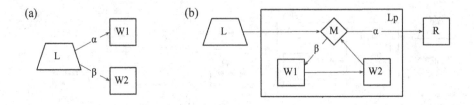

Fig. 2. Two examples in which copies are necessary

The functor called **R1** counts the number of cities in the map, and gives this information to **W3**, which writes it in the index -1 of the table. Functor **R2** computes the mean slope of the entire map. This information is inserted into the index -2 of the table by **W2**. Even though the updates happen in different locations of T, the components still perform data replication to preserve referential transparency. The running example cannot trivially discover that updates happen at different locations of the data-structure. In this simple example, each of these indices, -1 and -2, are different constants. However, the locations to be written could have been derived, instead, from much more complicated expressions whose values could only be known at execution time.

As we will show later in this paper, we can remove all the three copies in the script from Figure 1. However, there are situations in which copies are necessary. Figure 2 provides two such examples. A copy is necessary in Figure 2(a), either in channel α or in channel β – but not in both – because of a write-write hazard. Both functors, **W1** and **W2** need to process the original data that comes out of the loader **L**. Without the copy, one of them would read a stained value. Data replication is necessary in Figure 2(b), either in channel α or β, because there is a read-write hazard between **R** and **W1**, and it is not possible to schedule **R** to run before **W1**. **W1** is part of a container, **Lp**, that precedes **R** in any scheduling, i.e., a topological ordering, of the script.

3   The Core Semantics

In order to formally state the copy minimization problem that we are interested, we will define a core language, which we call μ-EGO. A μ-EGO program is defined by a tuple (S, T, Σ), where S, a *scheduling*, is a list of processing elements to be evaluated, T is an output table, and Σ is a storage memory. Each processing element is either a *functor* or a *container*. Functors are three element tuples (N, I, P), where N is this component's unique identifier in T, I is the index of the storage area that the component owns inside Σ, and P is the list of *predecessors* of the component. We let $T : N \mapsto \mathbb{N}$, and $\Sigma : I \mapsto \mathbb{N}$. A container is a pair $(\mathbb{N}, S)$, where S is a scheduling of processing elements.

Figure 3 describes the operational semantics of μ-EGO. Rule CONT defines the evaluation of a container. Containers work like loops: the evaluation of (N, S_l)

[NULL] $$([], T, \Sigma) \rightarrow (T, \Sigma)$$

[CONT]
$$\frac{S' = S_l^K @ S \quad (S', T, \Sigma) \rightarrow (T', \Sigma')}{((K, S_l) :: S, T, \Sigma) \rightarrow (T', \Sigma')}$$

[FUNC]
$$\frac{\Sigma' = \Sigma \setminus [I \mapsto V + 1] \quad \begin{array}{c} V = \max(P, \Sigma) \\ T' = T \setminus [N \mapsto V + 1] \end{array} \quad (S, T', \Sigma') \rightarrow (T'', \Sigma'')}{((N, I, P) :: S, T, \Sigma) \rightarrow (T'', \Sigma'')}$$

Fig. 3. The operational semantics of μ-EGO

consists in evaluating sequentially N copies of the scheduling S_l. We let the symbol @ denote list concatenation, like in the ML programming language. The expression $S_l^K @ S$ denotes the concatenation of K copies of the list S_l in front of the list S. Rule FUNC describes the evaluation of functors. Each functor (N, I, P) produces a value V. If we let V_m be the maximum value produced by any predecessor of the component, i.e., some node in P, then $V = V_m + 1$. When processing the component (N, I, P), our interpreter binds V to N in T, and binds V to I in Σ.

Figure 4 illustrates the evaluation of a simple μ-EGO program. The digraph in Figure 4(a) denotes a program with five functors and a container. We represent each functor as a box, with a natural number on its upper-right corner, and a letter on its lower-left corner. The number is the component's name N, and the letter is its index I in the store. The edges in Figure 4(a) determine the predecessor relations among the components. Figure 4(b) shows the scheduling that we are using to evaluate this program. We use the notation $(p_1, \ldots, p_n)^k$ to denote a container with k iterations over the processing elements $p_1, \ldots, p_n$. Figure 4(c) shows the store Σ, and Figure 4(d) shows the output table T, after each time the Rule FUNC is evaluated. In this example, Σ and T have the same number of indices. Whenever this is the case, these two tables will contain the same data, as one can check in Rule FUNC. We use gray boxes to mark the value that is updated at each iteration of the interpreter. These boxes, in Figure 5(d), also identify which component is been evaluated at each iteration.

We say that a μ-EGO program is *canonical* if it assigns a unique index I in the domain of Σ to each component. We call the evaluation of such a program a *canonical evaluation*. The canonical evaluation provides an upper bound on the number of storage cells that a μ-EGO program requires to execute correctly. Given that each component has its own storage area, data is copied whenever it reaches a new component. In this case, there is no possibility of data races. However, there is a clear waste of memory in a canonical evaluation. It is possible to re-use storage indices, and still to reach the same final configuration of the output table. This observation brings us to Definition 1, which formally states the storage minimization problem.

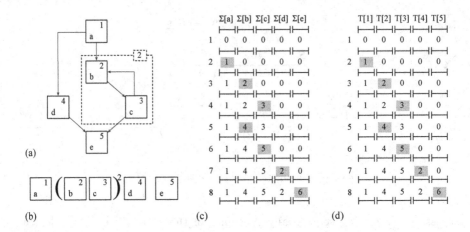

Fig. 4. Canonical evaluation of an μ-EGO program. (a) The graph formed by the components. (b) The scheduling. (c) The final configuration of Σ. (d) The final configuration of T.

Definition 1. STORAGE MINIMIZATION WITH FIXED SCHEDULING [SMFS]

Instance: a scheduling S of the components in a μ-EGO program, plus a natural K, the number of storage cells that any evaluation can use.

Problem: find an assignment of storage indices to the components in S with K or less indices that produces the same T as a canonical evaluation of S.

For instance, the program in Figure 5 produces the same result as the canonical evaluation given in Figure 4; however, it uses only 3 storage cells. In this example, the smallest number of storage indices that we can use to simulate a canonical evaluation is three. Figure 6 illustrates an evaluation that does not lead to a canonical result. In this case, we are using only two storage cells to keep the values of the components. In order to obtain a canonical result, when evaluating component 4 we need to remember the value of components 2 and 3. However, this is not possible in the configuration seen in Figure 6, because these two different components reuse the same storage unit.

3.1 SMFS Has Polynomial Solution for Schedulings with No Back-Edges

If a scheduling S has a component c'' scheduled to execute after a component $c' = (N, I, P)$, and $c'' \in P$, then we say that the scheduling has a back-edge $\overrightarrow{c''c'}$. SMFS has a polynomial time - exact - solution for programs without back-edges, even if they contain loops. We solve instances of SMFS that have this restriction by reducing them to interval graph coloring. Interval graph coloring has an $O(N)$ exact solution, where N is the number of lines in the interval [7]. The reduction

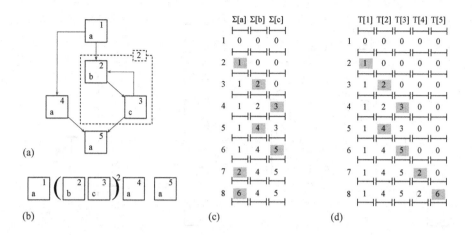

Fig. 5. Evaluation of an optimized μ-EGO program

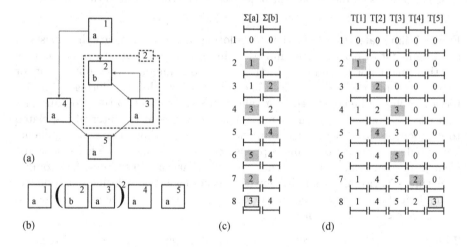

Fig. 6. Evaluation of an μ-EGO program that does not produce a canonical result

is as follows: given a scheduling S, let s_c be the order of component c in S; that is, if component c appears after $n - 1$ other components in S, then $s_c = n$. For each component c we create an interval that starts at s_c and ends at s_x, where s_x is the greatest element among:

- s'_c, where c' is a successor of c.
- s_{c_f}, where c_f is the first component after any component in a loop that contains a successor of c.

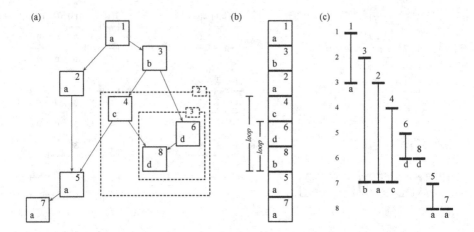

Fig. 7. Reducing SMFS to interval graph coloring for schedulings without back-edges. (a) The input μ-EGO program. (b) The input scheduling. (c) The corresponding intervals. The integers on the left are the orderings of each component in the scheduling.

Figure 7 illustrates this reduction. A coloring of the interval graph consists of an assignment of colors to the intervals, in such a way that two intervals may get the same color if, and only if, they have no common overlapping point, or they share only their extremities. Theorem 1 shows that a coloring of the interval graph can be converted to a valid index assignment to the program, and that this assignment is optimal. In the figure, notice that the interval associated to component three goes until component five, even though these components have no direct connection. This happens because component five is the leftmost element after any component in the two loops that contain successors of component three. Notice also that, by our definition of interval coloring, components six and eight, or five and seven, can be assigned the same colors, even though they have common extremities.

Theorem 1. *A tight coloring of the interval graph provides a tight index assignment in the μ-EGO program.*

proof: See [4].   □

3.2   SMFS Is NP-Complete for General Programs with Fixed Scheduling

We show that SMFS is NP-complete for general programs with fixed schedulings by reducing this problem to the coloring of Circular-Arc graphs. A circular-arc graph is the intersection graph formed by arcs on a circle. The problem of finding a minimum coloring of such graphs is NP-complete, as proved by Garey *et al* [6]. Notice that if the number of colors k is fixed, then this problem has an exact solution in $O(n \times k! \times k \times \ln k)$, where n is the number of arcs [5].

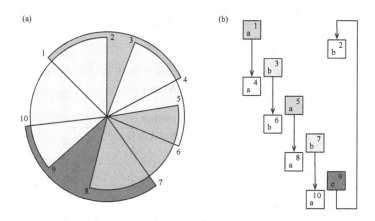

Fig. 8. Reducing SMFS to circular-arc graph coloring for general schedulings. (a) The input arcs. (b) The corresponding μ-EGO program.

We define a reduction R, such that, given an instance P_g of the coloring of arc-graphs, $R(P_g)$ produces an equivalent instance P_s of SMFS as follows: firstly, we associate an increasing sequence of integer number with each end point of an arc, in clockwise order, starting from any arc. If i and j are the integers associated with a given arc, then we create two functors, c_i and c_j. We let c_i be the single element in the predecessor set of c_j, and we let the predecessor set of c_i be empty. We define a fixed scheduling S that contains these components in the same order their corresponding integers appear in the input set of arcs. Figure 8 illustrates this reduction. We claim that solving SMFS to this μ-EGO program is equivalent to coloring the input graph.

Theorem 2. *Let P_s be an instance of SMFS produced by $R(P_g)$. P_s can be allocated with K indices, if, and only if, P_g can be colored with K colors.*

proof: See [4]. □

4   Copy Minimization

Data-Flow Analysis: We start the process of copy pruning with a backward-must data-flow analysis that determines which channels can lead to places where data is written. Our data-flow analysis is similar to the well-known *liveness analysis* used in compilers [1, p.608]. Figure 9 defines this data-flow analysis via four inference rules. If (N, I, P) is a component, and $N' \in P$, then the relation channel(N', N) is true. If N is a component that writes data, then the relation write(N) is true. Contrary to the original semantics of μ-EGO, given in Figure 3, we also consider, for the sake of completeness, the existence of functors that only read the data. If N is such a functor, than the predicate read(N) is true. This

$$[\text{D\textsc{f}1}] \quad \frac{\text{channel}(N_1, N_2) \qquad \text{write}(N_2)}{\text{abs}(N_1, N_2, \{N_2\})} \qquad\qquad [\text{D\textsc{f}2}] \quad \frac{\text{abs}(N_1, N_2, A') \qquad \text{out}(N_1, A)}{A' \subseteq A}$$

$$[\text{D\textsc{f}3}] \quad \frac{\text{channel}(N_1, N_2) \qquad \neg\text{write}(N_2) \qquad \text{out}(N_2, A)}{\text{abs}(N_1, N_2, A)}$$

$$[\text{D\textsc{f}4}] \quad \frac{\text{channel}(N_1, N_2) \qquad \text{read}(N_2) \qquad \text{out}(N_2, A)}{\text{abs}(N_1, N_2, A \cup \{r\})}$$

Fig. 9. Inference rules that define our data-flow analysis

analysis uses the lattice constituted by the power-set of functor names, plus a special name "r", that is different from any functor name. We define the abstract state of each channel by the predicate $\text{abs}(N_1, N_2, P)$, which is true if P is the set of functors that can write data along any path that starts in the channel (N_1, N_2), or $P = \{r\}$. Rule D\textsc{f}1 states that if a functor N_2 updates the data, then the abstract state of any channel ending at N_2 is a singleton that contains only the name of this functor. We associate with each functor N a set (out) of all the functor names present in abstract states of channels that leave N. This set is defined by Rule D\textsc{f}2. According to Rule D\textsc{f}3, if a functor N does not write data, the abstract state of any channel that ends at N is formed by N's out set. Finally, Rule D\textsc{f}4 back propagates the information that a functor reads data.

Figure 10 shows the result of applying our data-flow analysis onto the example from Section 2. The channels that lead to functors where table T can be read or written have been labeled with the abstract states that the data-flow analysis computes, i.e., sets of functor names. In this example each of these sets is a singleton. There is no information on the dashed-channels, because T is not transmitted through them. Notice that we must run one data-flow analysis for each data whose copies we want to eliminate. In this sense, our data-flow problem is a *partitioned variable problem*, following Zadeck's taxonomy [18]. A partitioned variable problem can be decomposed into a set of data-flow problems – usually one per variable – each independent on the other.

Criteria to Eliminate Copies: Once we are done with the data-flow analysis, we proceed to determine which data copies are necessary, and which can be eliminated without compromising the semantics of the script. Figure 11 shows the two rules that we use to eliminate copies: (C\textsc{p}1) write-write race, and (C\textsc{p}2) write-read race. Before explaining each of these rules, we introduce a number of relations used in Figure 11. The rules P\textsc{t}1 and P\textsc{t}2 denote a path between two components. Rule D\textsc{om} defines a predicate $\text{dom}(C, N)$, which is true whenever the component N names a functor that is scheduled to execute inside a container C. We say that C *dominates* N, because N will be evaluated if, and only if, C

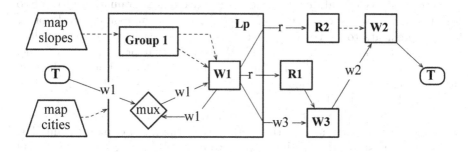

Fig. 10. The result of the data-flow analysis on the program seen in Figure 1

[PT1] $\dfrac{\text{channel}(N_1, N_2)}{\text{path}(N_1, N_2)}$

[PT2] $\dfrac{\text{channel}(N_1, N) \qquad \text{path}(N, N_2)}{\text{path}(N_1, N_2)}$

[DOM] $\dfrac{C = (\mathbb{N}, S) \qquad N \in S}{\text{dom}(C, N)}$

[ORI] $\dfrac{\text{channel}(N, N_1) \qquad \text{channel}(N, N_2) \qquad N_1 \neq N_2}{\text{orig}(N, N_1, N_2)}$

[DP1] $\dfrac{\text{path}(N_1, N_2)}{\text{dep}(N_1, N_2)}$

[DP2] $\dfrac{\text{path}(N_1, N) \qquad \text{dom}(N_2, N)}{\text{dep}(N_1, N_2)}$

[DP3] $\dfrac{\text{dom}(N_1, N) \qquad \text{path}(N, N_2)}{\text{dep}(N_1, N_2)}$

[DP4] $\dfrac{\text{dom}(N_1, N_1') \qquad \text{dom}(N_2, N_2') \qquad \text{path}(N_1', N_2')}{\text{dep}(N_1, N_2)}$

[LCD] $\dfrac{\text{dom}(N, N_1) \qquad \text{dom}(N, N_2) \qquad \nexists N', \text{dom}(N', N_1), \text{dom}(N', N_2), \text{dom}(N, N')}{\text{lcd}(N_1, N_2, N)}$

[PRD] $\dfrac{\text{orig}(O, N_1, N_2) \qquad \text{lcd}(N_1, N_2, D) \qquad \text{dom}(D, O) \qquad \neg \text{dep}(N_2, N_1)}{\text{pred}(N_1, N_2)}$

[CP1] $\dfrac{\text{orig}(N, N_1, N_2) \qquad \text{out}(N_1, \{\dots, f_1, \dots, \}) \qquad \text{out}(N_2, \{\dots, f_2, \dots\}) \qquad f_1 \neq f_2 \neq N}{\text{need\_copy}(N, N_1)}$

[CP2] $\dfrac{\text{orig}(N, N_1, N_2) \qquad \text{out}(N_1, \{\dots, f_1, \dots\}) \qquad \text{out}(N_2, \{r\}) \qquad f_1 \neq N \qquad \neg \text{pred}(N_2, N_1)}{\text{need\_copy}(N, N_1)}$

Fig. 11. Criteria to replicate data in Ego Script programs

is evaluated. Rule LCD defines the concept of *least common dominator*. The predicate $\text{lcd}(N_1, N_2, N)$ is true if N dominates both N_1 and N_2, and for any other component N' that also dominates these two components, we have that N' dominates N. The relation $\text{orig}(N, N_1, N_2)$ is true whenever the functor N is linked through channels to two different components N_1 and N_2. As an example, in Figure 7(a) we have $\text{orig}(3, 4, 6)$.

Rules DP1 through DP4 define the concept of *data dependence* between components. A component N_2 depends on a component N_1 if a canonical evaluation of the script requires N_1 to be evaluated before N_2. The relation $\text{pred}(N_1, N_2)$

indicates that N_1 can always precede N_2 in a canonical evaluation of the Ego Script program, where components N_1 and N_2 have a common origin. In order for this predicate to be true, N_1 and N_2 cannot be part of a loop that does not contain O. Going back to Figure 7(a), we have that $\mathrm{pred}(4,6)$ is not true, because 3, the common origin of components 4 and 6, is located outside the loop that dominates these two components. Furthermore, N_1 should not depend on N_2 for $\mathrm{pred}(N_1, N_2)$ to be true.

By using the predicates that we have introduced, we can determine which copies need to be performed in the flow chart of the Ego Script program. The first rule, CP1, states that if there exist two channels leaving a functor f, and these channels lead to other functors different than f where the data can be overwritten, then it is necessary to replicate the data in one of these channels. Going back to the example in Figure 10, we do not need a copy between the components **W1** and mux, because this channel is bound to the name of **W1** itself. This saving is possible because any path from mux to all the other functors that can update the data must go across **W1**. Otherwise, we would have also the names of these functors along the **W1**-mux channel. On the other hand, by this very Rule CP1, a copy is necessary between one of the channels that leave **L** in Figure 2(a). The second rule, CP2, is more elaborated. If two components, N_1 and N_2 are reached from a common component N, N_2 only reads data, and N_1 writes it, it might be possible to avoid the data replication. This saving is legal if it is possible to schedule N_2 to be executed before N_1. In this case, once the data is written by N_1, it will have already been read by N_2. If that is not the case, e.g., $\mathrm{pred}(N_2, N_1)$ is false, then a copy is necessary along one of the channels that leave out N. This rule lets us avoid the data replication in the channel that links **W1** and **W3** in Figure 1. In this case, there is no data-hazard between **W3** and either **R1** or **R2**. These components that only read data can be scheduled to execute before **W3**.

4.1   Correctness

In order to show that the rules in Figure 11 correctly determine the copies that must be performed in the program, we define a correctness criterion in Theorem 3. A μ-EGO program is correct if its evaluation produces the same output table as a canonical evaluation. The condition in Theorem 3 provides us with a practical way to check if the execution of a program is canonical. Given a scheduling of components S, we define a *dynamic scheduling* $\boldsymbol{S}$ as the complete trace of component names observed in an execution of S. For instance, in Figure 5, we have $S = 1, (2, 3)^2, 4, 5$, and we have $\boldsymbol{S} = 1, 2, 3, 2, 3, 4, 5$. We let $\boldsymbol{S}[i]$ be the i-th functor in the trace $\boldsymbol{S}$, and we let $|\boldsymbol{S}|$ be the number of elements in this trace. In our example, we have $\boldsymbol{S}[1] = 1$, $\boldsymbol{S}[7] = 5$, and $|\boldsymbol{S}| = 7$. Finally, if $p = \boldsymbol{S}[j]$ is a predecessor of the functor $\boldsymbol{S}[i]$, and for any $k, j < k < i$, we have that $\boldsymbol{S}[k] \neq \boldsymbol{S}[j]$, then we say that $\boldsymbol{S}[j]$ is an immediate dynamic predecessor of $\boldsymbol{S}[i]$.

Theorem 3. *The execution of an μ-EGO program (S, T, Σ) is canonical if, for any $n, 1 \leq n \leq |S|$, we have that, for any predecessor p of $S[n]$, if $S[i] = p$ and $i, 1 \leq i < n$ is an immediate dynamic predecessor of $S[i]$, then for any $j, i < j < n$, we have that $\Sigma[S[j]] \neq \Sigma[p]$.*

proof: See [4]. □

We prove that the algorithm to place copies is correct by showing that each copy that it eliminates preserves the condition in Theorem 3. There is a technical inconvenient that must be circumvented: the Rules CP1 and CP2 from Figure 11 determine which copies *cannot* be eliminated. We want to show that the *elimination* of a copy is safe. Thus, we proceed by negating the conditions in each of these rules, and deriving the correctness criterion from Theorem 3.

Theorem 4. *The elimination of copies via the algorithm in Figure 11 preserves the correctness criterion from Theorem 3.*

proof: See [4]. □

5   Experiments

We show how our optimization speeds up Dinamica EGO via a case study. This case study comes from a model used to detect hilltops in protected areas, which is available in Dinamica's webpage. Figure 12 gives a visual overview of this application. This model receives two inputs: an elevation map and a vertical resolution value. The EGO script divides the elevation map vertically into slices of equal height. This height is defined by the vertical resolution. Then the map is normalized and divided in discrete regions, as we see in Figure 12(b) and (c). Before running the functor that finds hilltops, this script performs other analyses to calculate average slopes, to compute the area of each region and to find the average elevation of each region. The model outputs relative height, plateau identifiers, hilltops, plus coordinates of local minima and local maxima. This EGO script uses tables intensively; hence, data replication was a bottleneck serious enough to prevent it from scaling to higher resolutions before the deployment of our optimization.

Figure 13 shows the speedup that we obtain via our copy elimination algorithm. These numbers were obtained in an Intel Core2Duo with a 3.00 GHz processor and 4.00 GB RAM. We have run this model for several different vertical resolution values. The smaller this value, more slices the map will have and, therefore more regions and more table inputs. This model has three operators that perform data replication, but given that they happen inside loops, the dynamic number of copies is much greater. Figure 13 shows the number of *dynamic copies* in the unoptimized program. High resolution, plus the excessive number of copies, hinders scalability, as we can deduce from the execution times given in Figure 13. This model has three components that copy data, and our optimization has been able to eliminate all of them. The end result is an improvement of almost 100x in execution speed, as we observe in the fourth column of Figure 13.

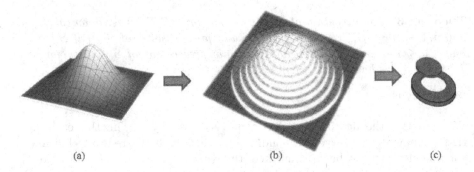

(a)   (b)   (c)

Fig. 12. Hilltop detection. (a) Height map. (b) Normalized map. (c) Extracted discrete regions.

V	D	T_u	T_o	R
20	1,956	20	20	1
15	2,676	28	26	1.0769
13	3,270	30	29	1.0344
11	4,677	32	32	1
10	6,126	36	36	1
9	9,129	39	36	1.08333
8	15,150	49	39	1.25641
7	29,982	87	50	1.74
5	137,745	995	76	13.0921
4	279,495	4,817	116	41.5258
3	518,526	18,706	197	94.9543

Fig. 13. V: Vertical resolution(m). D: Number of dynamic copies without optimization. T_u: Execution time without optimization (sec). T_o: Execution time with optimization (sec). R: Execution time ratio: (time non optimized / time optimized).

6   Conclusion

This paper has described a compiler optimization that we have implemented on top of the Dinamica EGO domain specific language for geomodeling. This optimization is, nowadays, part of the official distribution of Dinamica EGO, and is one of the key elements responsible for the high scalability of this framework. Dinamica EGO is freeware, and its use is licensed only for educational or scientific purposes. The entire software, and accompanying documentation can be found in Dinamica's website at http://www.csr.ufmg.br/dinamica/.

References

1. Aho, A.V., Lam, M.S., Sethi, R., Ullman, J.D.: Compilers: Principles, Techniques, and Tools, 2nd edn. Addison Wesley (2006)
2. Beven, K.: Towards a coherent philosophy for modelling the environment. Proceedings of the Royal Society 458, 2465–2484 (2002)

3. Carlson, K.M., Curran, L.M., Ratnasari, D., Pittman, A.M., Soares-Filho, B.S., Asner, G.P., Trigg, S.N., Gaveau, D.A., Lawrence, D., Rodrigues, H.O.: Committed carbon emissions, deforestation, and community land conversion from oil palm plantation expansion in West Kalimantan, Indonesia. Proceedings of the National Academy of Sciences (2012)
4. Ferreira, B.M., Pereira, F.M.Q., Rodrigues, H., Soares-Filho, B.S.: Optimizing a geomodeling domain specific language. Tech. Rep. LLP001/2012, Universidade Federal de Minas Gerais (2012)
5. Garey, M.R., Johnson, D.S., Miller, G.L., Papadimitriou, C.H.: The complexity of coloring circular arcs and chords. J. Algebraic Discrete Methods 1, 216–227 (1980)
6. Garey, M.R., Johnson, D.S., Sockmeyer, L.: Some simplified NP-complete problems. Theoretical Computer Science 1, 193–267 (1976)
7. Golumbic, M.C.: Algorithmic Graph Theory and Perfect Graphs, 1st edn. Elsevier (2004)
8. Hajek, F., Ventresca, M.J., Scriven, J., Castro, A.: Regime-building for redd+: Evidence from a cluster of local initiatives in south-eastern peru. Environmental Science and Policy 14(2), 201–215 (2011)
9. Huong, H.T.L., Pathirana, A.: Urbanization and climate change impacts on future urban flood risk in Can Tho city, Vietnam. Hydrology and Earth System Sciences Discussions 8(6), 10781–10824 (2011)
10. Mernik, M., Heering, J., Sloane, A.M.: When and how to develop domain-specific languages. ACM Comput. Surv. 37(4), 316–344 (2005)
11. Nepstad, D., Soares-Filho, B., Merry, F., Lima, A., Moutinho, P., Carter, J., Bowman, M., Cattaneo, A., Rodrigues, H., Schwartzman, S., McGrath, D., Stickler, C., Lubowski, R., Piris-Cabeza, P., Rivero, S., Alencar, A., Almeida, O., Stella, O.: The end of deforestation in the brazilian amazon. Science 326, 1350–1351 (2009)
12. Pérez-Vega, A., Mas, J.F., Ligmann-Zielinska, A.: Comparing two approaches to land use/cover change modeling and their implications for the assessment of biodiversity loss in a deciduous tropical forest. Environmental Modelling and Software 29(1), 11–23 (2012)
13. Soares-Filho, B., Nepstad, D., Curran, L., Cerqueira, G., Garcia, R., Ramos, C., Voll, E., McDonald, A., Lefebvre, P., Schlesinger, P.: Modelling conservation in the Amazon basin. Nature 440, 520–523 (2006)
14. Soares-Filho, B., Pennachin, C., Cerqueira, G.: Dinamica - a stochastic cellular automata model designed to simulate the landscape dynamics in an Amazonian colonization frontier. Ecological Modeling 154, 217–235 (2002)
15. Soares-Filho, B., Rodrigues, H., Costa, W.: Modeling Environmental Dynamics with Dinamica EGO. Centro de Sensoriamento Remoto, IGC/UFMG (2009)
16. Spring, J.H., Privat, J., Guerraoui, R., Vitek, J.: Streamflex: high-throughput stream programming in java. In: OOPSLA, pp. 211–228. ACM (2007)
17. Thapa, R.B., Murayama, Y.: Urban growth modeling of Kathmandu metropolitan region, Nepal. Computers, Environment and Urban Systems 35(1), 25–34 (2011)
18. Zadeck, F.K.: Incremental Data Flow Analysis in a Structured Program Editor. Ph.D. thesis, Rice University (1984)

A System for Runtime Type Introspection in C++

Maximilien de Bayser and Renato Cerqueira

Pontifcia Universidade Catlica do Rio de Janeiro, Brasil
{rcerq,mbayser}@inf.puc-rio.br
http://www.inf.puc-rio.br

Abstract. Many object-oriented languages support some kind of runtime introspection that allows programmers to navigate through metadata describing the available classes, their attributes and methods. In general, the meta-data can be used to instantiate new objects, manipulate their attributes and call their methods. The meta-programming enabled by this kind of reflection has proven itself useful in a variety of applications such as object-relational mappings and inversion-of-control containers and test automation

Motivated by the need of programmatic support for composition and configuration of software components at runtime, in this work we show how to implement a runtime reflection support for C++11, using the available runtime type information, template metaprogramming and source code analysis. We will show the capabilities of the reflection API and the memory footprint for different kinds of meta-data. The API relies on a few features introduced by C++11, the new ISO standard for C++. Our reflection system is not invasive as it requires no modifications whatsoever of the application code.

Keywords: reflection, introspection, C++.

1 Introduction

In some languages, such as Lua and Smalltalk, reflection is a direct consequence of the way object-oriented programming is implemented. In other languages, like Java, reflection is provided as a part of the standard library. C++, on the other hand, offers only a very limited form of runtime type information. C++ template meta-programming provides some introspection capabilities at compile-time but too limited to extract informations such as the number and type of the attributes defined by a class. In this work, we show how to implement a reflection library similar to Java's but respecting the language's own characteristics.

Of course we don't expect to have meta-data for all classes in an application, as it would be impossible to recover the private type definitions out of third-party libraries. The types in an application, however, can be divided into two categories: the types used for implementation and the types used as interface between modules. Because as users of a library we only need to use the types that are part of its API, a reflection support system only needs to retrieve type

F.H. de Carvalho Junior and L.S. Barbosa (Eds.): SBLP 2012, LNCS 7554, pp. 102–116, 2012.

definitions from the exported header files. With sufficiently powerful introspection support for these types, we can build tools such as an inversion of control (IoC) container for C++.

Inversion of control, also known as dependency injection, is a design pattern that enhances the re-usability of software components[1]. [1] The less assumptions a piece of code makes, the more general and the more reusable it is. If a component actively searches for resources it depends on, there is no other way but to make several assumptions about the availability of the mechanisms to do so. On the other hand, using IoC the component only assumes that there is an explicit configuration phase where all of its dependencies will be provided externally.

Reflection is useful for IoC because it allows the container implementation to be independent of the definitions of the manipulated types. It also helps to create bindings to scripting languages which can be used for the configuration phase. These languages are often better suited for this task because it can be done in a more natural declarative style. Besides, scripting has the added benefit that the applications can be reconfigured without the need for recompilation.

Reflection support and IoC containers are already common for higher-level languages like Java but some applications need flexibility, performance and low-level interaction with the operating system. For example, ReservationSuite [2] is an application monitor that tries to guarantee quality of services levels for specific processes by manipulating operating system priorities. It runs as a high-priority process and needs to respond to changes in system load with the lowest possible latency. It also must run very fast to reduce the CPU usage overhead. It has components for CPU time, disk I/O rate and network I/O rate. Some components support several scheduling policies that can be changed at runtime. The user can even write components implementing new policies and load them into the monitor. With a good IoC container the user of this application could select the components he needs and add components he implemented himself.

The main contribution of this work is to show how C++'s new feature of variadic macros can be used to implement a method call mechanism that shields the application code from the type definitions of the object, the return value and the parameters. Our solution is type-safe and by construction there are no restrictions on the number of parameters of reflected methods. It is very flexible because it makes implicit type conversions that the compiler would automatically apply such as conversions between arithmetic types or from a derived class to a more abstract class. Our solution is also standards conforming and is not invasive as it can be used with third-party components without requiring their modification.

The remainder of this text is organized as follows. Section 2 presents our goal which is the reflection API and its properties. Section 3 presents the features of C++ that are relevant to the implementation and in section 4 we show how we can combine them to build an effective method call mechanism. Section 5 analyzes the overhead of meta-data. Section 6 list a few related works and in section 7 we present our conclusions about this work and the possibilities of extending it.

---

[1] In this text, we adopt a loose definition of software components. It is anything that can be seen as a building block of applications, in binary form or as source code.

2 Proposed Reflection API

In short, this work's objective is to create an introspection API with the following features:

1. Listing of reflected classes and functions
2. Listing of the relevant characteristics of classes: accessible attributes, methods, constructors and super classes.
3. Invocation of functions, methods and constructors.
4. Compile-time independence of reflected types.

In listing 1 we present a simplified view of the API we want to implement. We have omitted many methods and classes for attributes and functions, but the essential parts are there. Basically, the user can obtain a Class meta-data object by name (line 7) and, from there, locate its methods and attributes. The Method class at line 10 gives basic informations about the corresponding method including name, number of parameters and their types, among other features. The sequences of three dots are part of C++11's notation for templates that accept an unknown number of arguments.

We can divide the reflection API in two parts: a descriptive one comprised of read-only information and an active one supporting the invocation of callable entities and modification of attributes. The descriptive part has been covered by other authors so we will not enter into much detail here ([3], [4]). The active part is represented here by the call and callArgArray methods at lines 16 and 17 respectivly. The VariantValue type that appears in their signature is a wrapper class for unknown types that will be described in section 4.1. The template method call is only provided as syntactic sugar that captures the arguments, wraps them in variants and calls callArgArray.

As we want to manipulate binary components, we don't reflect compile-time entities such as *typedefs* and templates (we do represent template *instantiations*).

Listing 1. The simplified interface for Class and Method introspection objects

```
1   class Class {
2     string name();
3     Class superclasses();
4     MethodList methods();
5     AttributesList attributes();
6     ConstructorList constructors();
7     static Class forName(string name);
8   };
9
10  class Method {
11    string name();
12    string returnTypeSpelling();
13    list<string> returnArgumentSpellings();
14
15    template<class... Args>
16    VariantValue call(VariantValue& object, Args... args) { //impl }
17    VariantValue callArgArray(VariantValue& object, vector<
          VariantValue>& args);
18  };
```

Because we want the `API` to be as natural and as easy to use as possible for
`C++` programmers, we want the arguments to be converted implicitly and safely
to the types that the method requires. For example, if a parameter is passed by
reference we want to get a reference to the value passed as argument. On the
other hand, if the parameter is passed by value we want a copy of the value. The
best place to implement these conversion is the `VariantValue` class. We can see
some of the conversions that we would like to support in listing 2.

Listing 2. Requirements for VariantValue

```
1
2   VariantValue v("5"); // initialize
3   std::string s = v.convertTo<std::string>(); // copy
4   std::string& sr = v.convertTo<std::string&>(); // get reference
5   std::string* sp = v.convertTo<std::string*>(); // get pointer
6   int n = v.convertTo<int>(); // convert to to integer
```

The main issue faced when building an infrastructure of meta-data for `C++`
is the sheer number of possibilities. For example, a method can be virtual or
not. It can be const qualified or volatile qualified, or even be static (in that
case, it is really a function). Parameters may be passed by value, by pointer
or by reference. For all these options, the const and volatile qualifiers may be
applied. A reflection `API` must cope with most of these special cases in order to be
useful.

3   Overview of Relevant C++ Features

In this section, we will analyze what features of `C++` are relevant to the implementation of the reflection `API`. We start by analyzing the type information `C++`
gives us at runtime and end with the type information available at compile-time.

3.1   Runtime Type Information

To build a reflection `API` that shields the application code from the definitions of
reflected types we must introduce a layer that hides these types. At some point,
however, we need to recover the abstracted type information in order to use it.
For example, the user of the reflection `API` wraps a value inside a `VariantValue`
and passes it to the method call mechanisms. The implementation of this method
call mechanism must be able to verify if the wrapped value can be converted to
the expected type and recover the value. In this section we will analyze what
tools the language has to offer and how we can employ them to safely inquire
the types of values defined in another translation unit.

`C++` provides some forms of introspection, collectively known as runtime type
information (`rtti`). The most commonly used `rtti` operation is the `dynamic_cast`
that permits the programmer to navigate in a class hierarchy. The `dynamic_cast`
can be seen as a built-in template function which takes a pointer to a polymorphic object and a destination type as template parameter. It thus takes two
types as parameters: the origin type implicitly specified by the pointer argument, and the explicitly specified destination type. If the object referred to by the

argument pointer is an instance of the requested class, a pointer of the correct type, pointing to that same object, is returned. Otherwise, a null pointer is returned. Therefore the dynamic_cast enables us to ask if the object pointed to is an instance of the destination type, with the restriction that both types must be in a the same hierarchy of polymorphic classes. And this is where the problem lies because we can't use this cast to find out if a void pointer points to an integer value. And even if it were possible, both types must be provided at the same source location. What we want is to take the type information of a value whose type is known in one translation unit and use it in another translation unit, which leads us to the next form of rtti: the type_info.

C++ provides a special operator called typeid that returns a reference to type_info, a type defined by the standard library. The standard library also provides a special operator== to compare two references to type_info. If this comparison operator returns true, both type_infos refer to the same type. The type_info works for all types and we can compare instances even if the represented type is not known, so we could use it to compare the type af a generic reference to a unknown type. The problem is that type_info is agnostic to class hierarchies. Because of this, typeid(A) == typeid(B) evaluates to false even if B inherits A.

The last form of rtti is rather surprising because it is not usually seen as such, but it is really the most powerful one. Because in C++ anything is throwable, the exception machinery must include the type information to guarantee that the correct catch statement is called. Listing 3 shows how the dynamic_cast can be implemented with exception handling.

Listing 3. A cast implementation using exception handling

```
1   template<class Orig, class Dest>
2   Dest* dyn_cast(Orig* o) {
3     try {
4        throw o;
5     } catch (Dest* d) {
6        return d;
7     } catch (...) {
8        return nullptr;
9     }
10  }
```

In fact, the above dyn_cast is more powerful than the dynamic_cast because Orig and Dest need not be in an inheritance relation. Of course, this is an abuse of exception handling for a totally different purpose, so we cannot expect it to be as efficient as the other forms of rtti. The advantage of this mechanism is that the code that throws can be defined in one translation unit and the catching code in another. Better yet is the fact that the catching code does not need to know the type that is effectively thrown and, conversely, the throwing code does not need to know the types that appear in the catch statement.[2] In section 4.1 we show how we can make use of exception handling type information.

---

[2] By "knowing a type" we mean that, at a certain code location, the entire textual declaration of the type is available to the compiler.

3.2   Template Metaprogramming

With the intention of allowing reusable data structures and algorithms, the designers of C++ introduced a Turing-complete compile-time language. This has originated a number of interesting techniques called template metaprogramming, which was exploited to generate optimal linear algebra code[5], create concrete products out of product lines[6] and implement object-oriented design patterns efficiently [7]. The introduction of templates that accept a variable number of arguments, known as *variadic templates*, has greatly improved the programming style for an unknown number of arguments.

The basis for template metaprogramming is template specialization which works like a compile-time *if*, as seen in listing 4

Listing 4. Static if

```
1  template<class T>
2  struct is_a_pointer {
3      enum { value = false };
4  }
5
6  template<class T>
7  struct is_a_pointer<T*> {
8      enum { value = true };
9  }
```

Listing 5. Static recursion

```
1  template<int N>
2  struct fact {
3      enum { value = N*fact<N-1>::value };
4  }
5
6  template<>
7  struct fact<0> {
8      enum { value = 1 };
9  }
```

And since integer constants may be used as template arguments, we have recursion as well, as shown in listing 5

C++ may not have runtime reflection, but templates do provide some compile-time reflection. Using these techniques, we can query if a class has a default constructor, if it is polymorphic, if a method is const qualified, and much more. The compile-time type information and the runtime type information can be applied in a complementary manner to implement a big part of a runtime introspection supports. The only things lacking are the iteration over all existing classes and within them, the iteration over their attributes and methods.

4   API Implementation

As we seen, there are two parts to the reflection API: the active one and the descriptive one. The active part is tricky to implement in a language with such a diversity of options as C++ and, therefore, its implementation takes the greatest part of this section. We made use of several of the new features introduced by the new C++ standard, especially variadic templates. Without this feature the syntax required merely to use it would so convoluted that macros would be needed simplify its API. The remainder of this section deals with how we gather all this type information form the source files.

4.1   Variant

Variants are like void pointers enhanced with type information and life-cycle management. They are essential for normalizing the parameter and return values for generic method calls and are, therefore, a central piece in our reflection system. Most variants are implemented either using unions, as described by Alexandrescu[8], or a template class implementing an abstract interface, a technique called *type erasure* [9] described by Henney[10]. boost::any and boost::variant[11] are good examples of both alternatives. The problem of the union approach is that the variant is restricted to a finite set of types, so our variant implementation follows the type erasure approach due to its greater flexibility, but incorporates several improvements from Alexandrescu's approach. Our variant can hold objects of concrete types by value. The object can be constructed in place and it does not need to have default or copy constructors. Because the constructor of the variant is a variadic template, any constructor of the selected type can be used. Variants holding references to objects are also supported. The object held can be accessed by copy, by reference or by pointer. Most importantly objects can be accessed by references and pointers to base classes. Additionally, it is detected at compile time if the type is convertible to std::string or arithmetic types. If this is the case, conversions to any arithmetic type or std::string are automatically implemented. The arithmetic type conversion is very convenient because it allows us to pass a variant containing a

Listing 6. Conversion of variants

```
1   class VariantValue
2     unique_ptr<IValueHolder> m_impl;
3
4     template<class ValueType>
5     typename strip_reference<ValueType>::ptr_type
6     isA_priv() const {
7       try {
8         m_impl->throwCast();
9       } catch(typename strip_reference<ValueType>::ptr_type ptr) {
10        return ptr;
11      } catch (...) {
12        return nullptr;
13      }
14    }
15
16  public:
17    template<class ValueType>
18    ValueType value() const {
19      auto ptr = isA_priv< ValueType >();
20      if (ptr == nullptr) {
21        // throw (error handling omitted)
22      }
23      return *ptr;
24    }
25    // other methods...
26  };
27
28  template<class ValueType>
29  class ValueHolder: public IValueHolder {
30    ValueHolder m_value;
31  public:
32    virtual void throwCast() const {
33      throw &m_value;
34    }
35  private:
36  };
```

char where an int is expected, just like the compiler would accept for temporary values. The philosophy of our variant in this respect is like Qt's QVariant's[12]: what matters most is not the real type hidden inside the variant, but the types it can be converted to. This frees us from painstakingly constructing variants of an exact type.

In listing 12 we can see the essential aspects of our Variant implementation. We have a front-end called **VariantValue** (line 1) with value-semantics that holds a pointer to the abstract base class **IValueHolder** which in turn is implemented by the class template **ValueHolder** (line 28). (The abstract base class has been omitted to avoid redundancy)

It is here that the flexibility of exception handling **rtti** is used. At line 33 in method **throwCast**, where the type of the contained value is known, we throw a pointer to it. At line 8 we call the **throwCast** method and an line 9 we try to catch a pointer to a type provided by the user. If the catch is successful we return the pointer, else we return a null pointer.

4.2 Call Forwarding

We want to generate a uniform interface to call methods with an arbitrary number of parameters, the tools we have are variants and pointers-to-methods. The main idea is to capture the parameters into a vector of variants and unpack the variant into the argument list of the function call expression. The first thing is to take a variable number of arguments, pack each of them in a variant, and place it in a vector. We can use variadic templates to do this:

Listing 7. Packing of parameters

```
1
2   inline void emplace(std::vector<VariantValue>& v ) { }
3
4   template<class T, class... U>
5   inline void emplace(std::vector<VariantValue>& v, T&& t, U&&... u )
6   {
7     v.emplace_back(t);
8     emplace(v, u...);
9   }
10
11  class Method {
12  public:
13    template<class... Args>
14    VariantValue call(VariantValue& object, const Args&... args) const
        {
15      ::std::vector<VariantValue> vargs;
16      emplace(vargs, args...);
17      return callArgArray(object, vargs );
18    }
19    // other methods and attributes...
20  }
```

In listing 7 at line 17 **callArgArray** forwards the two parameters to the **call** method of **MethodImpl**, seen in listing 8 at line 9.

Listing 8. Dispatching the parameters

```
1   typedef VariantValue (*boundmethod)(
2     const volatile VariantValue&, const vector<VariantValue>& args);
3
4   class MethodImpl {
5     boundmethod m_method;
6   public:
7
8     VariantValue call(VariantValue& object, const vector<VariantValue
          >& args)
9     {
10        if (args.size() < m_numArgs) {
11          // throw exception
12        }
13        return m_method(object, args); // call function pointer
14      }
15      // other methods and attributes...
16  };
```

The m_method at line 6 attribute is simply a pointer to a function that is used to normalize a pointer to method. Its type is declared at line 1. Because the type of a method pointer depends on the entire signature, it would be impossible for a non-templated class to have such a pointer as member. However, in addition to types and integer constants, pointers to functions and methods can be used as template arguments. We can use this to capture each pointer to method as a template parameter of a function template with a uniform signature.

The next step is to implement this function template that does the real method invocation. It has to know the number of arguments and their types, as well as the return type (there are other subtleties as well, such as the constness of a method, but for the sake of simplicity we will ignore them for now). Again, we use variadic templates to pass these types to the call function.

It is difficult to manipulate unexpanded parameter packs and pass them as argument to other templates, but we can employ a helper template called Typelist, due to Alexandrescu[7]. Basically, Typelists use a head and tail structure to encode a sequence of types as a type. They are very useful to group together a list of unrelated types, such as the argument types of a function. Alexandrescu showed how to implemented algorithms to find types in typelists, insert new types, query types by position and sort them from the most abstract to the most derived. The only drawback in his implementation was that C++98 did not support variadic templates or at least variadic macros, which made its use somewhat cumbersome. Using the new variadic templates, we designed a more natural Typelist that is used to implement the functions that forward the arguments vector of variants. We use it to compute to which type each argument in the variant vector should be converted.

With the vector of wrapped arguments and the Typelist containing the expected types we have all the information that is necessary to invoke a method. The next problem to be addressed is how to expand the arguments inside the parentheses of the call expression. We cannot use iteration inside the parentheses. We could somehow capture the arguments to the typelist as an unexpandend parameter, and pack and re-expand them. However, types cannot be used to index the elements of a vector. The answer is to use a helper template call Indices, an idea by Preney[13] to handle the problem of passing the content of an std::tuple as parameters to a function call. Indices are just a way to encode a sequence of numbers as a type. Because integers can be used to implement compile-time recursion, we are able to generate a type containing the numbers from 0 to N. If we capture the unexpanded pack of integers, we can use it to generates indices for the typelist and the vector at the same time. We use the expansion of an expression containing the indices to emplace the arguments at the correct place. The simplified templates can be seen in listing 9

Listing 9. Unpacking the parameters and calling the method

```
1   template<class _Method>
2   struct method_type;
3
4   // We use specialization to capture the
5   // parameter pack inside a method pointer declaration
6
7   template<class _Clazz, class _Result, class... Args>
8   struct method_type<_Result(_Clazz::*)(Args...)> {
9
10      typedef _Result (_Clazz::* ptr_to_method)(Args...);
11      typedef TypeList<Args...> Arguments;
12
13      static VariantValue
14      bindcall(VariantValue& object, const vector<VariantValue>& args)
15      {
16          return call_helper<typename make_indices<sizeof...(Args)>::type,
17              Result>::call(ref, ptr, args);
18      }
19
20      template<class Ind, class RType>
21      struct call_helper;
22
23      template< size_t... I, template< size_t...> class Ind, class RType
          >
24      struct call_helper<Ind<I...>, RType> {
25          static VariantValue
26          call(ClazzRef object, ptr_to_method ptr, const vector<
              VariantValue>& args)
27          {
28              // This is where the magic happens
29              return (object.* ptr)(args[I].
30                  moveValue<typename type_at<Arguments, I>::type>()...);
31          }
32      };
33
34  };
```

Forwarding functions and constructor calls is simpler but uses the same mechanism, so for the sake of brevity we will not discuss them. In reality, the method_type template has more specializations to detect if a method is const-qualified, volatile-qualified or static. The result of all this work is that we can call methods of objects of unknown types in a very natural way. An example usage can be seen in listing 10.

Listing 10. Example usage

```
1
2  Class a              = Class :: forname("A");
3  Constructor c        = a.constructors().front();
4  VariantValue instance = c.call("test", 1);
5  Method m             = a.methods().front();
6  VariantValue result  = m.call(instance, 4, 6);
```

Listing 11 presents an equivalent sequence of calls for Java's `java.lang.reflect` API.

Listing 11. Equivalent Java reflection usage

```
1
2  Class a         = Class.forName("A");
3  Constructor c   = a.getDeclaredConstructors()[0];
4  Object instance = c.newInstance("test", 1);
5  Method m        = a.getDeclaredMethods()[0];
6  Object result   = m.invoke(instance, 4, 6);
```

As the reader might have noticed we have chosen to use a template function for each method call instead of having a template `MethodImpl` implementing a `AbstractMethodIml` abstract base class. We will explain the reason why in the evaluation section.

4.3   Meta-data Declarations

At this stage, the only missing piece for our introspection API is how we extract all the meta-data from source and feed it to our library. As previously stated, what C++ lacks is a way to discover declarations from within the language, so this information must be provided in another way. For each kind of declaration, there is a corresponding meta-data class, so, for each declaration, a global instance of the corresponding meta-data class must be instantiated. To make the meta-data definitions more readable, we provide a set of macros which can be easily used by the programmer:

Listing 12. Meta-data input

```
1  BEGIN_CLASS(TextFile)
2  SUPERCLASS(File)
3  METHOD(write, int, const std::string&)
4  CONST_METHOD(size, int)
5  END_CLASS
```

When many classes and method declarations must be defined, writing all these declarations can be a very labour-intensive and error-prone task. Because of this, we have built a program that parses C++ header files and produces the meta-data for all usable declarations. This program is built around `clang`'s parser libraries [14]. Basically, `clang` parses the files and returns an abstract syntax tree (AST). Since we are only interested in the interface of C++ entities, we only read public declarations. The private sections and function bodies are ignored. We also ignore definitions that generate no symbols, such as global static functions and everything inside private namespaces. In C++, classes can be forward-declared if they are used only as parameter types, return types, pointers and references. However, in order to generate the method call code, our reflection system needs the full declaration of all types used in parameter or return types. When a declaration is not available, our parser prints a warning and ignores the entity that depended on it. In `clang`, there is an interaction between the "forward declarable" and the template instantiation rules. Whenever a template instance name is used where a forward declaration is sufficient, `clang` does not generate the AST nodes for it. If we want to generate meta-data for this template class instance, we need this piece of the AST and, therefore, we force its instantiation, effectively modifying the AST. The output of the parser is a `C++` code file containing all meta-data that must be compiled by a `C++11` conforming compiler. We have not tested it but, in principle, the meta-data code could be compiled into a separate dynamic library that could be shipped separately and loaded only if needed.

5   Evaluation

Inevitably the meta-data introduces a memory usage overhead. A quite reasonable way to calculate this overhead is to look at the size of the compiled translation unit containing the meta-data, but keeping in mind that the operating systems may never load the unused parts into working memory. As an example, we have generated the meta-data for qtextedit.h, a file shipped with Qt's `C++` SDK, once with forced template instantiation and once without. We have selectively suppressed the generation of certain kinds of meta-data to see how each one contributes on terms of space usage. The result can be seen in the tables 1 and 2. In both tables, classes, methods, attributes and functions refer to the number of reflected entities of each kind.

Table 1. qtextedit.h with templates

Mesurement	result
object file size	2.9MB
classes	71
public methods	3262
public attributes	2
functions	0
rtti	486KB (16.5%)
method call code	1.2MB (42.8%)
code per method	395 bytes
type spellings	9KB (0.32%)

Table 2. qtextedit.h without templates

Measurement	result
object file size	200KB
classes	3
public methods	154
public attributes	2
functions	0
rtti	25KB (12.6%)
method call code	101KB (42.8%)
code per method	675 bytes
type spellings	1KB (0.54%)

From the numbers, the information that stands out the most is the percentage of space dedicated to method call forwarding. Because of the way `C++` method pointers work, for each combination of class, return type, parameter types and qualifiers, the whole method procedure call must be generated again. The size of a single method call function is below 1K, which is acceptable if we consider how much work is involved in converting every variant to the correct type. But, because it is very difficult to share the same code for different methods, we have no choice but repeating it for every method. That is not to say that there is no difference in the code generated for a method with three parameters and one with four, but, for example, there should be no difference in the machine code generated for two methods of the same class with almost the same signature, differing only in constness. Experience with existing compilers suggests that one could cast a method pointer to another one of a similar type [15] and call it without problems if certain restrictions are observed. The casting of method pointers could be used to reduce the repetition of equal code, but we would no longer be standards-conforming, as the standard states that calling a converted method pointer results in undefined behavior.

Another relevant observation is the percentage of space used for `type_info` data. Our system makes no use of this information internally, it is only there for the `API` and can be disabled with a compiler flag if the user does not need it. For example, if the `API` is used through a binding for another language such as `Lua`, the `type_info rtti` is useless. The type spellings, that is the textual representation of parameter and return types, take a negligible amount of space, but are very useful for language bindings because the code in another language can make textual comparisons to check the parameter types of a method.

We can see that there is a great difference both in the number of code entities as in translation unit size when all templates are instantiated. We remind the reader that, in `C++`, a template method that is not used does not generate code. However, taking the address of a template's method, forces the compiler to fully instantiate that code. Additionally, as at this stage the compiler has no clue whether the template classes are already defined in other translation units or not, it has no choice but generating all their code into the current one. This certainly accounts for some of the size of the resulting file, but it is difficult to measure exactly how much. The template instances included in this example are instances of QList<class T>, QList<class T>::iterator and QList<class T>::const_iterator.

Finally, we note that the amount of the code generated per method call is smaller for the file with more methods. We can only speculate about why this happens, but perhaps the compiler is more likely to reuse the same piece of code for different methods.

Having this discussion in mind, we can explain why we did not use the type erasure technique for the meta-data classes. In fact, this was our first approach, but the result was not very encouraging. With the type erasure approach, the compiler had to generate a new class for each method, which means a new *vtable*, a new set of methods, etc. With all this unnecessary code, the object file for qtextedit.h's meta-data surpassed the size of 30MB, what was clearly unacceptable.

We have not yet done benchmarks to measure the call overhead in CPU time, but inevitably there will be a considerable cost for all the extra flexibility. In any case, the call mechanism is not meant to be used in tight inner loops, but to facilitate the configuration and composition of software components, which typically are done only at start-up.

6 Related Work

SEAL Reflex [3] is a very detailed reflection library including meta-data for *typedefs*, scopes, primitives and arrays. It has a method call construct but it is not type-safe as arguments are passed as an array of void pointers. Internally it uses method call functions generated in plain text by a meta-data generation tool.

Devadithya et. al. [4] present a reflection system similar to SEAL. It uses template classes to hold method pointers and do the calls. The number of of arguments is limited to the number of template specializations implemented in the library. The exact types of arguments and return types must be known, which has as consequence that the end user code needs their complete definitions.

PocoCapsule[16] is not a reflection library but a IoC container for C++ that uses an interesting approach to deal with method calls and attributes. The C++ parser takes as input both the source files and the XML configuration file, so XML binding code is only generated for the methods that are actually used. After the binding's generation, parameters like string or integer constants can be changed but calls to previously unused methods require re-compilation.

Reflection for C++ [17] proposes the gathering of meta-data out of debug information generated by compilers. This has the advantage that the meta-data can be extracted of executable files. The drawback is that the code must be compiled in debug mode. Also each compiler uses a different representation for debug information.

And finally there are invasive approaches that require code modifications for reflected classes [17]. Other approaches require extensions of C++. For example, Microsoft supports an extended C++ for their common language runtime, which provides reflection for all supported languages [18]. Qt's signals and slots mechanisms adds a few keywords to C++ and depends on a separate tool to generate standard C++ code for these features [12].

7 Conclusion

We have presented a type introspection API for C++, similar to Java's, but respecting the characteristics of the language. The reflection API makes heavy use of some features new to C++11, so compiler support may be an issue. We have successfully compiled the code with g++ 4.7 and clang++ 3.1. We also made a binding for Lua that enables us to instantiate and use C++ objects. The usage in C++ is very natural as it requires no manual "boxing" of parameter types into variants in method calls. No modifications of existing code are required and the meta-data can be compiled separately. The most serious problem is the space overhead incurred by the method call code if we consider that, in most situations, probably less than 10% of these methods will be called. We believe that we have gone as far in reducing its size as possible in a standards conforming way. However, it might be interesting to investigate the possibility of generating the required code on demand at runtime for a standard `ABI` such as the `Itanium ABI` used by `gcc` and `clang`, among other compilers. Possibilities include JIT compilation using clang or creating the call frames with libffi.

The entire source code can be found at `https://github.com/maxdebayser/reflection`

References

1. Fowler, M.: Inversion of control containers and the dependency injection pattern, `http://martinfowler.com/articles/injection.html`
2. dos Reis, V.Q., Cerqueira, R.: Controlling processing usage at user level: a way to make resource sharing more flexible. Concurr. Comput.: Pract. Exper. 22(3), 278–294 (2010)
3. Roiser, S., Mato, P.: The seal c++ reflection system. In: Proceedings of CHEP 2004, Interlaken, Switzerland, September 24-October 1, CERN-2005-02, vol. 1, p. 437. International Standard; Programming Languages - C++; ISO/IEC 14882:2003(E); 2nd edn. (October 15, 2003); ISO, CH-1211 Geneva 20 (2004)
4. Devadithya, T., Chiu, K., Lu, W.: C++ reflection for high performance problem solving environments. In: Proceedings of the 2007 Spring Simulation Multiconference - SpringSim 2007, vol. 2, pp. 435–440. Society for Computer Simulation International, San Diego (2007)
5. Veldhuizen, T.: Using template metaprograms. C++ Report 7, 26–31 (1995)
6. Czarnecki, K.: Generative Programming. Phd. thesis, Technical University of Ilmenau (1998)
7. Alexandrescu, A.: Modern C++ Desing. Addison-Wesley (2001)
8. Alexandrescu, A.: Discriminated unions. C/C++ Users Journal (April 2002)
9. Becker, T.: On the tension between object-oriented and generic programming in C++ and what type erasure can do about it, `http://www.artima.com/cppsource/type_erasure2.html`
10. Henney, K.: Valued conversions. C++ Report (July-August 2000)
11. Boost C++ libraries, `http://www.boost.org/`
12. Qt library, `http://doc.qt.nokia.com/4.7/`
13. Preney, P.: Applying std::tuple to functors efficiently, `http://preney.ca/paul/archives/486`
14. Clang C language family frontend for LLVM, `http://clang.llvm.org/`
15. Clugston, D.: Member function pointers and the fastest possible C++ delegates, `http://clang.llvm.org/`
16. Pococapsule/C++ ioc, `http://www.pocomatic.com/prod-docs.html`
17. Knizhnik, K.: Reflection for C++, `http://www.garret.ru/cppreflection/docs/reflect.html`
18. MSDN: Reflection in C++, `http://msdn.microsoft.com/en-us/library/y0114hz2(v=vs.80).aspx`

Model-Based Programming Environments
for Spreadsheets*

Jácome Cunha[1,3], João Saraiva[1], and Joost Visser[2]

[1] HASLab / INESC TEC, Universidade do Minho, Portugal
{jacome,jas}@di.uminho.pt
[2] Software Improvement Group & Radboud University Nijmegen, The Netherlands
j.visser@sig.eu
[3] Escola Superior de Tecnologia e Gestão de Felgueiras, IPP, Portugal

Abstract. Although spreadsheets can be seen as a flexible programming environment, they lack some of the concepts of regular programming languages, such as structured data types. This can lead the user to edit the spreadsheet in a wrong way and perhaps cause corrupt or redundant data.

We devised a method for extraction of a relational model from a spreadsheet and the subsequent embedding of the model back into the spreadsheet to create a model-based spreadsheet programming environment. The extraction algorithm is specific for spreadsheets since it considers particularities such as layout and column arrangement. The extracted model is used to generate formulas and visual elements that are then embedded in the spreadsheet helping the user to edit data in a correct way.

We present preliminary experimental results from applying our approach to a sample of spreadsheets from the EUSES Spreadsheet Corpus.

1 Introduction

Developments in programming languages are changing the way in which we construct programs: naive text editors are now replaced by powerful programming language environments which are specialized for the programming language under consideration and which help the user throughout the editing process. Helpful features like highlighting keywords of the language or maintaining a beautified indentation of the program being edited are now provided by several text editors. Recent advances in programing languages extend such naive editors to powerful language-based environments [1–6]. Language-based environments use *knowledge* of the programming language to provide the users with more powerful mechanisms to develop their programs. This knowledge is based on the *structure* and the *meaning* of the language. To be more precise, it is based on the syntactic and (static) semantic characteristics of the language. Having this

---

* The authors would like to thank Martin Erwig and his team for providing us the code from the UCheck project. This work is funded by ERDF - European Regional Development Fund through the COMPETE Programme (operational programme for competitiveness) and by National Funds through FCT - Fundação para a Ciência e a Tecnologia (Portuguese Foundation for Science and Technology) within project FCOMP-01-0124-FEDER-010048. The first author is supported by the FCT grant SFRH/BPD/73358/2010.

F.H. de Carvalho Junior and L.S. Barbosa (Eds.): SBLP 2012, LNCS 7554, pp. 117–133, 2012.

knowledge about a language, the language-based environment is not only able to high-light keywords and beautify programs, but it can also detect features of the programs being edited that, for example, violate the properties of the underlying language. Fur-thermore, a language-based environment may also give information to the user about properties of the program under consideration. Consequently, language-based environ-ments guide the user in writing correct and more reliable programs.

Spreadsheet systems can be viewed as programming environments for non-profes-sional programmers. These so-called *end-user* programmers vastly outnumber profes-sional programmers [7].

In this paper, we propose a technique to enhance a spreadsheet system with mecha-nisms to guide end users to introduce correct data. A background process adds formulas and visual objects to an existing spreadsheet, based on a relational database schema. To obtain this schema, or model, we follow the approach used in language-based envi-ronments: we use the *knowledge* about the data already existing in the spreadsheet to guide end users in introducing correct data. The knowledge about the spreadsheet under consideration is based on the *meaning* of its data that we infer using data mining and database normalization techniques.

Data mining techniques specific to spreadsheets are used to infer *functional depen-dencies* from the spreadsheet data. These functional dependencies define how certain spreadsheet columns determine the values of other columns. Database normalization techniques, namely the use of normal forms [8], are used to eliminate redundant func-tional dependencies, and to define a relational database model. Knowing the relational database model induced by the spreadsheet data, we construct a new spreadsheet en-vironment that not only contains the data of the original one, but that also includes advanced features which provide information to the end user about correct data that can be introduced. We consider three types of advanced features: *auto-completion of column values, non-editable columns* and *safe deletion of rows*.

Our techniques work not only for database-like spreadsheets, like the example we will use throughout the paper, but they work also for realistic spreadsheets defined in other contexts (for example, inventory, grades or modeling). In this paper we present our first experimental results obtained by considering a large set of spreadsheets included in the EUSES Spreadsheet Corpus [9].

This paper is organized as follows. Section 2 presents an example used throughout the paper. Section 3 presents our algorithm to infer functional dependencies and how to construct a relational model. Section 4 discusses how to embed assisted editing features into spreadsheets. A preliminary evaluation of our techniques is present in Section 5. Section 6 discusses related work and Section 7 concludes the paper.

2   A Spreadsheet Programming Environment

In order to present our approach we shall consider the following well-known example taken from [10] and modeled in a spreadsheet as shown in Figure 1.

This spreadsheet contains information related to a housing rental system. It gathers information about clients, owners, properties, prices and rental periods. The name of each column gives a clear idea of the information it represents. We extend this example

	A	B	C	D	E	F	G	H	I	J	K	L
1	clientNr	propNr	cName	pAddress	country	rentStart	rentFinish	days	rent	total	ownerNr	oName
2	cr76	pg4	john	6 Lawrence	UK	01/07/00	08/31/01	602	50	30100	co40	tina
3	cr76	pg16	john	5 Novar Dr.	UK	09/01/01	09/01/02	365	70	25550	co93	tony
4	cr56	pg4	aline	6 Lawrence	UK	09/02/99	06/10/00	282	50	14100	co40	tina
5	cr56	pg36	aline	2 Manor Rd	UK	10/10/00	12/01/01	417	60	25020	co93	tony
6	cr56	pg16	aline	5 Novar Dr.	UK	11/01/02	08/10/04	648	70	45360	co93	tony

Fig. 1. A spreadsheet representing a property rental system

with three additional columns, named *days* (that computes the total number of rental days by subtracting the column *rentStart* to *rentFinish*), *total* (that multiplies the number of rental days by the rent per day value, *rent*) and *country* (that represents the property's country). As usually in spreadsheets, the columns *days* and *rent* are expressed by formulas.

This spreadsheet defines a valid model to represent the information of the rental system. However, it contains redundant information: the displayed data specifies the house rental of two clients (and owners) only, but their names are included five times, for example. This kind of redundancy makes the maintenance and update of the spreadsheet complex and error-prone. A mistake is easily made, for example, by mistyping a name, thus corrupting the data on the spreadsheet.

Two common problems occur as a consequence of redundant data: *update anomalies* and *deletion anomalies* [11]. The former problem occurs when we change information in one place but leave the same information unchanged in the other places. The problem also occurs if the update is not performed exactly in the same way. In our example, this happens if we change the rent of property number pg4 from 50 to 60 only one row and leave the others unchanged, for example. The latter problem occurs when we delete some data and lose other information as a side effect. For example, if we delete row 5 in the our example all the information concerning property pg36 is lost.

The database community has developed techniques, such as data normalization, to eliminate such redundancy and improve data integrity [11, 12]. Database normalization is based on the detection and exploitation of functional dependencies inherent in the data [13]. Can we leverage these database techniques for spreadsheets systems so that the system eliminates the update and deletion anomalies by guiding the end user to introduce correct data? Based on the data contained in our example spreadsheet, we would like to discover the following functional dependencies which represent the four entities involved in our house rental system: *countries*, *clients*, *owners* and *properties*.

$$country \quad \rightharpoonup$$
$$clientNr \rightharpoonup cName$$
$$ownerNr \rightharpoonup oName$$
$$propNr \quad \rightharpoonup pAddress, rent, ownerNr$$

A functional dependency $A \rightharpoonup B$ means that if we have two equal inhabitants of A, then the corresponding inhabitants of B are also equal. For instance, the client number functionally determines his/her name, since no two clients have the same number. The right hand side of a functional dependency can be an empty set. This occurs, for example, in the *country* functional dependency. Note that there are several columns (labeled *rentStart*, *rentFinish*, *days* and *total*) that are not included in any functional dependency. This happens because their data do not define any functional dependency.

Using these functional dependencies it is possible to construct a relational database schema. Each functional dependency is translated into a table where the attributes are the ones participating in the functional dependency and the primary key is the left hand side of the functional dependency. In some cases, foreign keys can be inferred from the schema. The relational database schema can be normalized in order to eliminate data redundancy. A possible normalized relational database schema created for the house rental spreadsheet is presented bellow.

> *country*
> *clientNr*, *cName*
> *ownerNr*, *oName*
> *propNr*, *pAddress*, *rent*, *ownerNr*

This database schema defines a table for each of the entities described before. Having defined a relational database schema we would like to construct a spreadsheet environment that respects that relational model, as shown in Figure 2.

	A	B	C	D	E	F	G	H	I	J	K	L	M
1	clientNr	propNr	cName	pAddress	country	rentStart	rentFinish	days	rent	total	ownerNr	oName	
2	cr76	pg4	john	6 Lawrence	UK	01/07/00	08/31/01	602	50	30100	co40	tina	Delete
3	cr76	pg16	john	5 Novar Dr.	UK	09/01/01	09/01/02	365	70	25550	co93	tony	Delete
4	cr56	pg4	aline	6 Lawrence	UK	09/02/99	06/10/00	282	50	14100	co40	tina	Delete
5	cr56	pg36	aline	2 Manor Rd	UK	10/10/00	12/01/01	417	60	25020	co93	tony	Delete
6	cr56	pg16	aline	5 Novar Dr.	UK	11/01/02	08/10/03	282	70	19740	co93	tony	Delete
7	cr76 ▾	pg4 ▾	john	6 Lawrence	UK ▾				50		co40 ▾	tina	Delete

Fig. 2. A spreadsheet with auto-completion based on relational tables

For example, this spreadsheet would not allow the user to introduce two different properties with the same property number *propNr*. Instead, we would like that the spreadsheet offers to the user a list of possible properties, such that he can choose the value to fill in the cell. Figure 3 shows a possible spreadsheet environment where possible properties can be chosen from a *combo box*.

Using the relational data base schema we would like that our spreadsheet offers the following features:

	A	B	C	D
1	clientNr	propNr	cName	pAddress
2	cr76	pg4	john	6 Lawrence
3	cr76	pg16	john	5 Novar Dr.
4	cr56	pg4	aline	6 Lawrence
5	cr56	pg36	aline	2 Manor Rd
6	cr56	pg16	aline	5 Novar Dr.
7	cr76 ▾	pg4	▾ john	6 Lawrence
8		pg4 ▲		
9		pg36		
		pg16		

Fig. 3. Selecting possible values of columns using a combo box

Auto-completion of Column Values: The columns corresponding to primary keys in the relational model determine the values of other columns; we want the spreadsheet environment to be able to automatically fill those columns provided the end -user defines the value of the primary key.

For example, the value of the property number (*propNr*, column B) determines the values of the address (*pAddress*, column D), rent per day (*rent*, column I), and owner number (*ownerNr*, column K). Consequently, the spreadsheet environment should be able to automatically fill in the values of the columns D, I and K, given the value of column B. Since *ownerNr* (column K) is a primary key of another table, transitively the value of *oName* (column L) is also defined. This auto-completion mechanism has been implemented and is presented in the spreadsheet environment of Figure 2.

Non-Editable Columns: Columns that are part of a table but not part of its primary key must not be editable. For example, column L is part of the owner table but it is not part of its primary key. Thus, it must be protected from being edited. The primary key of a table must not be editable also since it can destroy the dependency. This feature prevents the end user from introducing potentially incorrect data and, thus, producing update anomalies. Figure 4 illustrates this edit restriction.

Safe Deletion of Rows: Another usual problem with non-normalized data is the deletion problem. Suppose in our running example that row 5 is deleted. In such scenario, all the information about the pg36 property is lost. However, it is likely that the user wanted to delete the rental transaction represented by that row only. In order to prevent this type of deletion problems, we have added a button per spreadsheet row (see Figure 2). When pressed, this button detects whether the end user is deleting important information included in the corresponding row. In case important information is removed by such deletion, a warning window is displayed, as shown in Figure 5.

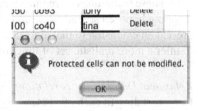

Fig. 4. In order to prevent update anomalies some columns must not be editable

Apart from these new features, the user can still access traditional editing features, and can rely on recalculation of functional dependencies in the background.

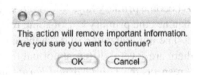

Fig. 5. Window to warn the end user that crucial information may be deleted

Traditional Editing: Advanced programming language environments provide both advanced editing mechanisms and traditional ones (*i.e.*, text editing). In a similar way, a spreadsheet environment should allow the user to perform traditional spreadsheet editing too. In traditional editing the end user is able to introduce data that may violate the relational database model that the spreadsheet data induces.

Recalculation of the Relational Database Model: Because standard editing allows the end user to introduce data violating the underlying relational model, we would like that the spreadsheet environment may enable/disable the advanced features described in this section. When advanced features are disabled, the end user would be able to introduce data that violates the (previously) inferred relational model. However, when the end user returns to advanced editing, then the spreadsheet should infer a new relational model that will be used in future (advanced) interactions.

In this section we have described an instance of our techniques. In fact, the spreadsheet programming environment shown in the Figures 2, 3, 4 and 5 was automatically produced from the original spreadsheet displayed in Figure 1. In the following sections we will present in detail the technique to perform such an automatic spreadsheet refactoring.

3   From Spreadsheets to Relational Databases

This section briefly explains how to extract functional dependencies from the spreadsheet data and how to construct a normalized relational database schema modeling such data. These techniques were introduced in detail in our work on defining a bidirectional mapping between spreadsheets and relational databases [14]. In this section we briefly present an extension to that algorithm that uses spreadsheet specific properties in order to infer a more realistic set of functional dependencies.

Relational Databases: A *relational schema* R is a finite set of attributes $\{A_1, ..., A_k\}$. Corresponding to each attribute A_i is a set D_i called the *domain* of A_i. These domains are arbitrary, non-empty sets, finite or countably infinite. A *relation* (or *table*) r on a relation schema R is a finite set of *tuples* (or *rows*) of the form $\{t_1, ..., t_k\}$. For each $t \in r$, $t(A_i)$ must be in D_i. A *relational database schema* is a collection of relation schemas $\{R_1, ..., R_n\}$. A *Relational Database* (RDB) is a collection of relations $\{r_1, ..., r_n\}$.

Each tuple is uniquely identified by a minimum non-empty set of attributes called a *Primary Key* (PK). On certain occasions there may be more then one set suitable for becoming the primary key. They are designated *candidate keys* and only one is chosen to become primary key. A *Foreign Key* (FK) is a set of attributes within one relation that matches the primary key of some relation.

The normalization of a database is important to prevent data redundancy. Although there are several different normal forms, in general, a RDB is considered normalized if it respects the *Third Normal Form* (3NF) [10].

Discovering Functional Dependencies: In order to define the RDB schema, we first need to compute the functional dependencies presented in a given spreadsheet data. In [14] we reused the well known data mining algorithm, named FUN, to infer such dependencies. This algorithm was developed in the context of databases with the main goal of inferring all existing functional dependencies in the input data. As a result, FUN may infer a large set of functional dependencies depending on the input data. For our example, we list the functional dependencies inferred from the data using FUN:

$$clientNr \;\rightharpoonup\; cName, country$$
$$propNr \;\rightharpoonup\; country, pAddress, rent, ownerNr, oName$$
$$cName \;\rightharpoonup\; clientNr, country$$
$$pAddress \;\rightharpoonup\; propNr, country, rent, ownerNr, oName$$
$$rent \;\rightharpoonup\; propNr, country, pAddress, ownerNr, oName$$
$$ownerNr \;\rightharpoonup\; country, oName$$
$$oName \;\rightharpoonup\; country, ownerNr$$

Note that, data contained in the spreadsheet exhibits all those dependencies. In fact, even the non-natural dependency $rent \rightharpoonup propNr, country, pAddress, ownerNr, oName$ is inferred. Indeed, the functional dependencies derived by the FUN algorithm depend heavily on the quantity and quality of the data. Thus, for small samples of data, or data that exhibits too many or too few dependencies, the FUN algorithm may not produce the desired functional dependencies.

Note also that the *country* column occurs in most of the functional dependencies although only a single country actually appears in a column of the spreadsheet, namely UK. Such single value columns are common in spreadsheets. However, for the FUN algorithm they induce redundant fields and redundant functional dependencies.

In order to derive more realistic functional dependencies for spreadsheets we have extended the FUN algorithm so that it considers the following spreadsheet properties:

- *Single value columns*: these columns produce a single functional dependency with no right hand side (*country* $\rightharpoonup$, for example). This columns are not considered when finding other functional dependencies.
- *Semantic of labels*: we consider label names as strings and we look for the occurrence of words like *code, number, nr, id* given them more priority when considered as primary keys.
- *Column arrangement*: we give more priority to functional dependencies that respect the order of columns. For example, $clientNr \rightharpoonup cName$ has more priority than $cName \rightharpoonup clientNr$.

Moreover, to minimize the number of functional dependencies we consider the smallest subset that includes all attributes/columns in the original set computed by FUN. The result of our spreadsheet functional dependency inference algorithm is:

$$country \;\rightharpoonup$$
$$clientNr \;\rightharpoonup\; cName$$
$$ownerNr \;\rightharpoonup\; oName$$
$$propNr \;\rightharpoonup\; pAddress, rent, ownerNr, oName$$

This set of dependencies is very similar to the one presented in the previous section. The exception is the last functional dependency which has an extra attribute (*oName*).

Spreadsheet Formulas: Spreadsheets use formulas to define the values of some elements in terms of other elements. For example, in the house rental spreadsheet, the column *days* is computed by subtracting the column *rentFinish* from *rentStart*, and it is usually written as follows H3 = G3 - F3. This formula states that the values of G3 and F3 determine the value of H3, thus inducing the following functional dependency: $rentStart, rentFinish \rightharpoonup days$.

Formulas can have references to other formulas. Consider, for example, the second formula of the running example J3 = H3 * I3, which defines the total rent by multiplying the total number of days by the value of the rent. Because H3 is defined by another formula, the values that determine H3 also determine J3. As a result, the two formulas induce the following functional dependencies:

$$rentStart, rentFinish \qquad \rightharpoonup days$$
$$rentStart, rentFinish, rent \rightharpoonup total$$

In general, a spreadsheet formula of the following form $X_0 = f(X_1, \ldots, X_n)$ induces the following functional dependency: $X_1, \ldots, X_n \rightharpoonup X_0$. In spreadsheet systems, formulas are usually introduced by copying them through all the elements in a column, thus making the functional dependency explicit in all the elements. This may not always be the case and some elements can be defined otherwise (e.g. by using a constant value or a different formula). In both cases, all the cells referenced must be used in the antecedent of the functional dependency.

These functional dependencies are useful for the mapping of spreadsheets to databases as presented in [14]. In this work, they are not relevant since the existing formulas are used to fill in those columns.

Normalizing Functional Dependencies: Having computed the functional dependencies, we can now normalize them. Next, we show the results produced by the *synthesize* algorithm introduced by Maier in [15]. The *synthesize* algorithm receives a set of functional dependencies as argument and returns a new set of *compound functional dependencies*. A *compound functional dependency* (CFD) has the form $(X_1, \ldots, X_n) \rightharpoonup Y$, where $X_1, \ldots, X_n$ are all distinct subsets of a scheme R and Y is also a subset of R. A relation r satisfies the CFD $(X_1, \ldots, X_n) \rightharpoonup Y$ if it satisfies the functional dependencies $X_i \rightharpoonup X_j$ and $X_i \rightharpoonup Y$, where $1 \leqslant i$ and $j \leqslant k$. In a CFD, $(X_1, \ldots, X_n)$ is the *left side*, $X_1, \ldots, X_n$ are the *left sets* and Y is the *right side*.

Next, we list the compound functional dependencies computed from the functional dependencies induced by our running example.

$$(\{country\}) \rightharpoonup \{\}$$
$$(\{clientNr\}) \rightharpoonup \{cName\}$$
$$(\{ownerNr\}) \rightharpoonup \{oName\}$$
$$(\{propNr\}) \quad \rightharpoonup \{pAddress, rent, ownerNr\}$$

Computing the Relational Database Schema: Each compound functional dependency defines several candidate keys for each table. However, to fully characterize the relational database schema we need to choose the primary key from those candidates. To find such keys we use a simple algorithm: we produce all the possible tables using each candidate key as the primary key; we then use the same algorithm that is used to choose the initial functional dependencies to choose the best table. Note that before applying the *synthesize* algorithm, all the functional dependencies with antecedents' attributes representing formulas should be eliminated since a primary key must not change over time. The final result is listed bellow.

country
clientNr, cName
ownerNr, oName
propNr, pAddress, rent, ownerNr

This relational database model corresponds exactly to the one shown in Section 2. Note that the synthesize algorithm removed the redundant attribute $oName$ that occurred in the last functional dependency.

4 Building Spreadsheet Programming Environments

This section presents techniques to refactor spreadsheets into powerful spreadsheet programming environments as described in Section 2. This spreadsheet refactoring is implemented as the embedding of the inferred functional dependencies and the computed relational model in the spreadsheet. This embedding is modeled in the spreadsheet itself by standard formulas and visual objects: formulas are added to the spreadsheet to guide end users to introduce correct data.

Before we present how this embedding is defined, let us first define a spreadsheet. A spreadsheet can be seen as a partial function $S : A \rightarrow V$ mapping addresses to spreadsheet values. Elements of S are called *cells* and are represented as (a, v). A cell address is taken from the set $A = \mathbb{N} \times \mathbb{N}$. A value $v \in V$ can be an input plain value $c \in C$ like a string or a number, references to other cells using addresses or formulas $f \in F$ that can be applied to one or more values: $v \in V ::= c \mid a \mid f(v, \ldots, v)$.

Auto-completion of Column Values: This feature is implemented by embedding each of the relational tables in the spreadsheet. It is implemented by a spreadsheet formula and a combo box visual object. The combo box displays the possible values of one column, associated to the primary key of the table, while the formula is used to fill in the values of the columns that the primary key determines.

Let us consider the table $ownerNr, oName$ from our running example. In the spreadsheet, $ownerNr$ is in column K and $oName$ in column L. This table is embed in the spreadsheet introducing a combo box containing the existing values in the column K (as displayed in Figure 2). Knowing the value in the column K we can automatically introduce the value in column L. To achieve this, we embed the following formula in row 7 of column L:

$$S(L, 7) = \textbf{if } (\textbf{isna } (\textbf{vlookup } (K7, K2 : L6, 2, 0)), \text{" "}, \textbf{vlookup } (K7, K2 : L6, 2, 0))$$

This formula uses a (library) function **isna** to test if there is a value introduced in column K. In case that value exists, it searches (with the function **vlookup**) the corresponding value in the column L and references it. If there is no selected value, it produces the empty string. The combination of the combo box and this formula guides the user to introduce correct data as illustrated in Figure 2.

We have just presented a particular case of the formula and visual object induced by a relational table. Next we present the general case. Let $minr$ be the very next row after the existing data in the spreadsheet, $maxr$ the last row in the spreadsheet, and $r1$ the first row with already existing data. Each relational database table $\underline{a_1}, ..., \underline{a_n}, c_1, ..., c_m$, with $a_1, ..., a_n, c_1, ..., c_m$ column indexes of the spreadsheet, induces firstly, a combo box defined as follows:

$$\forall\, c \in \{a_1, ..., a_n\}, \forall\, r \in \{minr, ..., maxr\}:$$
$$S\,(c, r) = combobox := \{\, linked\_cell \;\; := (c, r);$$
$$source\_cells := (c, r1):(c, r-1)\}$$

secondly, a spreadsheet formula defined as:

$$\forall\, c \in \{c_1, ..., c_m\}, \forall\, r \in \{minr, ..., maxr\}:$$
$$S\,(c, r) = \textbf{if } (\textbf{if } (\textbf{isna}\ (\textbf{vlookup}\ ((a_1, r), (a_1, r1):(c, r-1), r - a_1 + 1, 0)),$$
$$\text{" "},$$
$$\textbf{vlookup}\ ((a_1, r), (a_1, r1):(c, r-1), r - a_1 + 1, 0))$$
$$==$$
$$\textbf{if } (\textbf{isna}\ (\textbf{vlookup}\ ((a_2, r), (a_2, r1):(c, r-1), r - a_2 + 1, 0)),$$
$$\text{" "},$$
$$\textbf{vlookup}\ ((a_2, r), (a_2, r1):(c, r-1), r - a_2 + 1, 0))$$
$$==$$
$$...$$
$$==$$
$$\textbf{if } (\textbf{isna}\ (\textbf{vlookup}\ ((a_n, r), (a_n, r1):(c, r-1), r - a_n + 1, 0)),$$
$$\text{" "},$$
$$\textbf{vlookup}\ ((a_n, r), (a_n, r1):(c, r-1), r - a_n + 1, 0)),$$
$$\textbf{vlookup}\ ((a_1, r), (a_1, r1):(c, r-1), r - a_1 + 1, 0),$$
$$\text{" "})$$

This formula must be used for each non primary key column created by our algorithm. Each conditional **if** inside the main **if** is responsible for checking a primary key column. In the case a primary key column value is chosen, **isna** (**vlookup** (...)), the formula calculates the corresponding non primary key column value, **vlookup** (...). If the values chosen by all primary key columns are the same, then that value is used in the non primary key column. This formula considers tables with primary keys consisting of multiple attributes (columns). Note also that the formula is defined in each column associated to non-key attribute values.

The example table analysed before is an instance of this general one. In the table _ownerNr, oName_, _ownerNr_ is a_1, _oName_ is c_1, c is L, $r1$ is 2, $minr$ is 7. The value of $maxr$ is always the last row supported by the spreadsheet system.

Foreign keys pointing to primary keys become very helpful in this setting. For example, if we have the relational tables $\underline{A}, B$ and $\underline{B}, C$ where B is a foreign key from the second table to the first one, then when we perform auto-completion in column A, both B and C are automatically filled in. This was the case presented in Figure 2.

Non-Editable Columns: To prevent wrong introduction of data, and thus, producing update anomalies, we protect some columns from edition. A relational table, such as $\underline{a_1}, ..., \underline{a_n}, c_1, ..., c_m$, induces the non-edition of columns $a_1, ..., a_n, c_1, ..., c_m$. That is to say that all columns that form a table become non-editable. Figure 4 illustrates such a restriction. In the case where the end user really needs to change the value of such protected columns, we provide traditional editing (explained below).

Safe Deletion of Rows: Another usual problem with non-normalized data is the deletion of data. Suppose in our running example that row 5 is deleted. All the information about property pg36 is lost, although the user would probably want to delete that rental transaction only. To correctly delete rows in the spreadsheet, a button is added to each row in the spreadsheet as follows: for each relational table $\underline{a_1}, ..., \underline{a_n}, c_1, ..., c_m$ each button checks, on its corresponding row, the columns that are part of the primary key, $a_1, ..., a_n$. For each primary key column, it verifies if the value to remove is the last one.

Let $c \in \{a_1, ..., a_n\}$, let r be the button row, $r1$ be the first row of column c with data and rn be the last row of column c with data. The test is defined as follows:

if (**isLast** $((c, r), (c, r1) : (c, rn))$, **showMessage**, **deleteRow** (r))

If the value is the last one, the spreadsheet warns the user (**showMessage**) as can be seen in Figure 5. If the user presses the OK button, the spreadsheet will remove the row. In the other case, Cancel, no action will be performed. In the case the value is not the last one, the row will simply be removed, **deleteRow** (r). For example, in column *propNr* of our running example, the row 5 contains the last data about the house with code pg36. If the user tries to delete this row, the warning will be triggered.

Traditional Editing: Advanced programming language environments provide both advanced editing mechanisms and traditional ones (*i.e.*, text editing). In a similar way, a spreadsheet environment should allow the user to perform traditional spreadsheet editing too. Thus, the environment should provide a mechanism to enable/disable the advanced features described in this section. When advanced features are disabled, the end user is be able to introduce data that violates the (previously) inferred relational model. However, when the end user returns to advance editing, the spreadsheet infers a new relational model that will be used in future (advanced) interactions.

4.1   HaExcel Add-in

We have implemented the FUN algorithm, the extensions described in this paper, the *synthesize* algorithm, and the embedding of the relational model in the HASKELL programming language [16]. We have also defined the mapping from spreadsheet to relational databases in the same framework named HaExcel [14]. Finally, we have extended this framework to produce the visual objects and formulas to model the relational tables in the spreadsheet. An Excel add-in as been also constructed so that the end user can use spreadsheets in this popular system and at the same time our advanced features.

5   Preliminary Experimental Results

In order to evaluate the applicability of our approach, we have performed a preliminary experiment on the EUSES Corpus [9]. This corpus was conceived as a shared resource to support research on technologies for improving the dependability of spreadsheet programming. It contains more than 4500 spreadsheets gathered from different sources and developed for different domains. These spreadsheets are assigned to eleven different categories. including financial (containing 19% of the total number of spreadsheets), inventory (17%), homework (14%), grades (15%), database (17%) and modeling (17%) (the remaining 1% represents other spreadsheets). Among the spreadsheets in the corpus, about 4.4% contain macros, about 2.3% contain charts, and about 56% do not have formulas being only used to store data.

In our preliminary experiment we have selected the first ten spreadsheets from each of the eleven categories of the corpus. We then applied our tool to each spreadsheet, with different results (see also Table 1): a few spreadsheets failed to parse, due to glitches in the Excel to Gnumeric conversion (which we use to bring spreadsheets into a processable form). Other spreadsheets were parsed, but no tables could be recognized in them, *i.e.*, their users did not adhere to any of the supported layout conventions. The layout conventions we support are the ones presented in the UCheck project [17]. This was the case for about one third of the spreadsheets in our item. The other spreadsheets were parsed, tables were recognized, and edit assistance was generated for them. We will focus on the last groups in the upcoming sections.

Processed Spreadsheets: The results of processing our sample of spreadsheets from the EUSES corpus are summarized in Table 1. The rows of the table are grouped by category as documented in the corpus. The first three columns contain size metrics on the spreadsheets. They indicate how many tables were recognized, how many columns are present in these tables, and how many cells. For example, the first spreadsheet in the *financial* category contains 15 tables with a total of 65 columns and 242 cells.

Table 1. Preliminary results of processing the selected spreadsheets

File name	Recognized tables	Cols.	Cells	FDs	Cols. w/ safe insertion & deletion	Auto-compl. cols.	Non-editab. cols.
cs101							
Act4_023_capen	5	24	402	0	0	0	0
act3_23_bartholomew	6	21	84	1	8	1	9
act4_023_bartholomew	6	23	365	0	0	0	0
meyer_Q1	2	8	74	0	0	0	0
posey_Q1	5	23	72	0	8	0	8
database							
%5CDepartmental%20Fol#A8...	2	4	3463	0	0	0	0
00061r0P802-15_TG2-Un...69	23	55	491	0	18	4	21
00061r5P802-15_TG2-Un...6C	30	83	600	25	21	5	26
0104TexasNutrientdb	5	7	77	1	1	1	2
01BTS_framework	52	80	305	4	23	2	25
03-1-report-annex-5	20	150	1599	12	15	8	22
filby							
BROWN	5	14	9047	2	3	1	4
CHOFAS	6	48	4288	3	3	1	4

continues on the next page

Table 1. (*continued*)

File name	Recognized tables	Cols.	Cells	FDs	Cols. w/ safe insertion & deletion	Auto-compl. cols.	Non-editab. cols.
financial							
03PFMJOURnalBOOKSFina...	15	65	242	0	7	0	7
10-formc	12	20	53	8	5	4	9
forms3							
ELECLAB3.reichwja.xl97	1	4	44	0	0	0	0
burnett-clockAsPieChart	3	8	14	0	1	0	1
chen-heapSortTimes	1	2	24	0	0	0	0
chen-insertSortTimes	1	2	22	0	0	0	0
chen-lcsTimes	1	2	22	0	0	0	0
chen-quickSortTimes	1	2	24	0	0	0	0
cs515_npeg_chart.reichwja.xl97	7	9	93	0	0	0	0
cs515_polynomials.reichwja.xl97	6	12	105	0	0	0	0
cs515_runtimeData.reichwja.X...	2	6	45	0	0	0	0
grades							
0304deptcal	11	41	383	19	18	17	28
03_04ballots1	4	20	96	6	4	0	4
030902	5	20	110	0	0	0	0
031001	5	20	110	0	0	0	0
031501	5	15	51	31	3	1	4
homework							
01_Intro_Chapter_Home#A9171	6	15	2115	0	1	0	1
01readsdis	4	16	953	5	4	3	6
02%20fbb%20medshor	1	7	51	0	0	0	0
022timeline4dev	28	28	28	0	0	0	0
026timeline4dev	28	28	30	0	2	0	2
03_Stochastic_Systems#A9172	4	6	48	0	2	0	2
04-05_proviso_list	79	232	2992	0	25	0	25
inventory							
02MDE_framework	50	83	207	10	31	1	32
02f202assignment%234soln	37	72	246	7	20	1	21
03-1-report-annex-2	5	31	111	10	5	5	8
03singapore_elec_gene#A8236	9	45	153	3	5	2	7
0038	10	22	370	0	0	0	0
modeling							
%7B94402d63-cdd8-4cc3#A...	1	3	561	0	0	0	0
%EC%86%90%ED%97%8C...	1	10	270	13	7	5	9
%EC%9D%98%EB%8C%80...	1	7	1442	4	4	5	6
%EC%A1%B0%EC%9B%90...	2	17	534	18	13	5	15
%ED%99%98%EA%B2%B...	3	7	289	2	1	2	3
0,10900,0-0-45-109057-0,00	4	14	6558	9	9	2	10
00-323r2	24	55	269	31	9	6	15
00000r6xP802-15_Docum#A...	3	13	3528	10	9	3	11
003_4	25	50	2090	0	0	0	0

The fourth column shows how many functional dependencies were extracted from the recognized tables. These are the non-trivial functional dependencies that remain after we use our extension to the FUN algorithm to discard redundant dependencies. The last three columns are metrics on the generated edit assistance. In some cases, no edit assistance was generated, indicated by zeros in these columns. This situation occurs when no (non-trivial) functional dependencies are extracted from the recognized tables. In the other cases, the three columns respectively indicate:

– For how many columns a combo box has been generated for *controlled insertion*. The same columns are also enhanced with the *safe deletion of rows* feature.
– For how many columns the *auto-completion of column values* has been activated, *i.e.*, for how many columns the user is no longer required to insert values manually.
– How many columns are locked to prevent edit actions where information that does not appear elsewhere is deleted inadvertently.

For example, for the first spreadsheet of the *inventory* category, combo boxes have been generated for 31 columns, auto-completion has been activated for 1 column, and locking has been applied to 32 columns. Note that for the categories *jackson* and *personal*, no results were obtained due to absent or unrecognized layout conventions or to the size of the spreadsheets (more than 150,000 cells).

Observations: On the basis of these preliminary results, a number of interesting observations can be made. For some categories, edit assistance is successfully added to almost all spreadsheets (e.g. *inventory* and *database*), while for others almost none of the spreadsheets lead to results (e.g. the *forms/3* category). The latter may be due to the small sizes of the spreadsheets in this category. For the *financials* category, we can observe that in only 2 out of 10 sample spreadsheets tables were recognized, but edit assistance was successfully generated for both of these.

The *percentage* of columns for which edit assistance was generated varies. The highest percentage was obtained for the second spreadsheet of the *modeling* category, with 9 out of 10 columns (90 %). A good result is also obtained for the first spreadsheet of the *grades* category with 28 out of 41 columns (68.3 %). On the other hand, the 5th of the *homework* category gets edit assistance for only 2 out of 28 columns (7.1 %). The number of columns with combo boxes often outnumbers the columns with auto-completion. This may be due to the fact that many of the functional dependencies are small, with many having only one column in the antecedent and none in consequent.

Evaluation: Our preliminary experiment justifies two preliminary conclusions. Firstly, the tool is able to successfully add edit assistance to a series of non-trivial spreadsheets. A more thorough study of these and other cases can now be started to identify technical improvements that can be made to the algorithms for table recognition and functional dependency extraction. Secondly, in the enhanced spreadsheets a large number of columns are generally affected by the generated edit assistance, which indicates that the user experience can be impacted in a significant manner. Thus, a validation experiment can be started to evaluate how users experience the additional assistance and to which extent their productivity and effectiveness can be improved.

6 Related Work

Our work is strongly related to a series of techniques by Abraham *et al.*. Firstly, they designed and implemented an algorithm that uses the labels within a spreadsheet for *unit checking* [18, 19]. By typing the cells in a spreadsheet with unit information and tracking them through references and formulas, various types of users errors can be caught. We have adopted the view of Abraham *et. al.* of a spreadsheet as a collection of tables and we have reused their algorithm for identifying the spatial boundaries of these tables. Rather than exploiting the labels in the spreadsheet to reconstruct implicit user intentions, we exploit redundancies in data elements. Consequently, the errors caught by our approach are of a different kind. Secondly, Abraham *et. al.* developed a type system and corresponding inference algorithm that assigns types to values, operations, cells, formulas, and entire spreadsheets [20]. The type system can be used to catch errors in spreadsheets or to infer spreadsheet models that can help to prevent future errors. We have used such spreadsheet models, namely the ClassSheet models [21], to realize model-driven software evolution in the context of spreadsheets [22–28].

In previous work we presented techniques and tools to transform spreadsheets into relational databases and back [14]. We used the FUN algorithm to construct a relational model, but rather than generating edit assistance, the recovered information was used to perform spreadsheet *refactoring*. The algorithm for extracting and filtering spreadsheets presented in the current paper is an improvement over the algorithm that we used previously.

We provided a short user-centered overview of the idea of generating edit assistance for spreadsheets via extraction of functional dependencies in a previous short paper [29]. In the current paper, we have provided the technical details of the solution, including the improved algorithm for extraction and filtering functional dependencies. Also, we have provided the first preliminary evaluation of the approach by application to a sample of spreadsheets from the EUSES corpus.

7 Conclusions

Contributions: We have demonstrated how implicit structural properties of spreadsheet data can be exploited to offer edit assistance to spreadsheet users. To discover these properties, we have made use of our improved approach for mining functional dependencies from spreadsheets and subsequent synthesis of a relational database. On this basis, we have made the following contributions:

- Derivation of formulas and visual elements that capture the knowledge encoded in the reconstructed relational database schema.
- Embedding of these formulas and visual elements into the original spreadsheet in the form of features for auto-completion, guarded deletion, and controlled insertion.
- Integration of the algorithms for reconstruction of a schema, for derivation of corresponding formulas and visual elements, and for their embedding into a *add-in* for spreadsheet environments.

A spreadsheet environment enhanced with our *add-in* compensates to a significant extent for the lack of the structured programming concepts in spreadsheets. In particular, it assists users to prevent common update and deletion anomalies during edit actions.

Future Work: There are several extensions of our work that we would like to explore. The algorithms running in the background need to recalculate the relational schema and the ensuing formulas and visual elements every time new data is inserted. For larger spreadsheets, this recalculation may incur waiting time for the user. Several optimizations of our algorithms can be attempted to eliminate such waiting times, for example, by use of incremental evaluation. Our approach could be integrated with similar, complementary approaches to cover a wider range of possible user errors. In particular, the work of Abraham *et al.* [20, 30] for preventing range, reference, and type errors could be combined with our work for preventing data loss and inconsistency. We have presented some preliminary experimental results to pave the way for a more comprehensive validation experiments. In particular, we intend to set up a structured experiment for testing the impact on end-user productivity, and effectiveness.

References

1. Saraiva, J.: Design, Implementation and Animation of Spreadsheets in the Lrc System. In: Erwig, M. (ed.) Int. Workshop on Foundations of Spreadsheet. ENTCS (2004)
2. Kuiper, M., Saraiva, J.: Lrc - A Generator for Incremental Language-Oriented Tools. In: Koskimies, K. (ed.) CC 1998. LNCS, vol. 1383, pp. 298–301. Springer, Heidelberg (1998)
3. Reps, T., Teitelbaum, T.: The synthesizer generator. SIGSOFT Softw. Eng. Notes 9(3), 42–48 (1984)
4. van den Brand, M., Klint, P., Olivier, P.: Compilation and Memory Management for ASF+SDF. In: Jähnichen, S. (ed.) CC 1999. LNCS, vol. 1575, pp. 198–215. Springer, Heidelberg (1999)
5. Saraiva, J., Swierstra, S.D.: Generating Spreadsheet-Like Tools from Strong Attribute Grammars. In: Pfenning, F., Smaragdakis, Y. (eds.) GPCE 2003. LNCS, vol. 2830, pp. 307–323. Springer, Heidelberg (2003)
6. Holzner, S.: Eclipse. O'Reilly (May 2004)
7. Scaffidi, C., Shaw, M., Myers, B.: Estimating the numbers of end users and end user programmers. In: VLHCC 2005: Proceedings of the 2005 IEEE Symposium on Visual Languages and Human-Centric Computing, pp. 207–214 (2005)
8. Codd, E.F.: A relational model of data for large shared data banks. Commun. ACM 13(6), 377–387 (1970)
9. Fisher II, M., Rothermel, G.: The EUSES Spreadsheet Corpus: A shared resource for supporting experimentation with spreadsheet dependability mechanisms. In: Proceedings of the 1st Workshop on End-User Software Engineering, pp. 47–51 (2005)
10. Connolly, T., Begg, C.: Database Systems, A Practical Approach to Design, Implementation, and Management, 3rd edn. Addison-Wesley (2002)
11. Ullman, J.D., Widom, J.: A First Course in Database Systems. Prentice Hall (1997)
12. Date, C.J.: An Introduction to Database Systems. Addison-Wesley (1995)
13. Beeri, C., Fagin, R., Howard, J.: A complete axiomatization for functional and multivalued dependencies in database relations. In: Proc. of the ACM SIGMOD Int. Conf. on Management of Data, pp. 47–61 (1977)
14. Cunha, J., Saraiva, J., Visser, J.: From spreadsheets to relational databases and back. In: PEPM 2009: Proc. of the 2009 ACM SIGPLAN Workshop on Partial Evaluation and Program Manipulation, pp. 179–188. ACM (2009)
15. Maier, D.: The Theory of Relational Databases. Computer Science Press (1983)
16. Peyton Jones, S.: Haskell 98: Language and libraries. J. Funct. Program. 13(1), 1–255 (2003)

17. Abraham, R., Erwig, M.: UCheck: A spreadsheet type checker for end users. J. Vis. Lang. Comput. 18(1), 71–95 (2007)
18. Erwig, M., Burnett, M.: Adding Apples and Oranges. In: Adsul, B., Ramakrishnan, C.R. (eds.) PADL 2002. LNCS, vol. 2257, pp. 173–191. Springer, Heidelberg (2002)
19. Abraham, R., Erwig, M.: Header and unit inference for spreadsheets through spatial analyses. In: 2004 IEEE Symposium on Visual Languages and Human Centric Computing, pp. 165–172 (September 2004)
20. Abraham, R., Erwig, M.: Type inference for spreadsheets. In: Bossi, A., Maher, M.J. (eds.) Proceedings of the 8th Int. ACM SIGPLAN Conference on Principles and Practice of Declarative Programming, Venice, Italy, July 10-12, pp. 73–84. ACM (2006)
21. Engels, G., Erwig, M.: ClassSheets: automatic generation of spreadsheet applications from object-oriented specifications. In: ASE 2005: Proc. of the 20th IEEE/ACM International Conference on Automated Software Engineering, pp. 124–133. ACM (2005)
22. Cunha, J., Erwig, M., Saraiva, J.: Automatically inferring classsheet models from spreadsheets. In: VL/HCC 2010: IEEE Symp. on Visual Languages and Human-Centric Computing, pp. 93–100. IEEE Computer Society (2010)
23. Beckwith, L., Cunha, J., Paulo Fernandes, J., Saraiva, J.: End-users productivity in model-based spreadsheets: An empirical study. In: Proceedings of the Third International Symposium on End-User Development, IS-EUD 2011, pp. 282–288 (2011)
24. Cunha, J., Fernandes, J.P., Mendes, J., Saraiva, J.: Towards an Evaluation of Bidirectional Model-driven Spreadsheets. In: USER 2012: User evaluation for Software Engineering Researchers (to appear, 2012)
25. Cunha, J., Fernandes, J.P., Mendes, J., Pacheco, H., Saraiva, J.: Bidirectional Transformation of Model-Driven Spreadsheets. In: Hu, Z., de Lara, J. (eds.) ICMT 2012. LNCS, vol. 7307, pp. 105–120. Springer, Heidelberg (2012)
26. Cunha, J., Fernandes, J.P., Mendes, J., Saraiva, J.: MDSheet: A framework for model-driven spreadsheet engineering. In: ICSE 2012: Proc. of the 34th International Conference on Software Engineering, pp. 1412–1415. ACM (2012)
27. Cunha, J., Visser, J., Alves, T., Saraiva, J.: Type-Safe Evolution of Spreadsheets. In: Giannakopoulou, D., Orejas, F. (eds.) FASE 2011. LNCS, vol. 6603, pp. 186–201. Springer, Heidelberg (2011)
28. Cunha, J., Mendes, J., Fernandes, J.P., Saraiva, J.: Extension and implementation of classsheet models. In: VL/HCC 2012: IEEE Symposium on Visual Languages and Human-Centric Computing. IEEE Computer Society (2011) (to appear)
29. Cunha, J., Saraiva, J., Visser, J.: Discovery-based edit assistance for spreadsheets. In: Proceedings of the 2009 IEEE Symposium on Visual Languages and Human-Centric Computing (VL/HCC), VLHCC 2009, pp. 233–237. IEEE Computer Society, Washington, DC (2009)
30. Abraham, R., Erwig, M.: Inferring templates from spreadsheets. In: Proc. of the 28th Int. Conf. on Software Engineering, pp. 182–191. ACM, New York (2006)

A Quantitative Assessment of Aspectual Feature Modules for Evolving Software Product Lines

Felipe Nunes Gaia[1], Gabriel Coutinho Sousa Ferreira[1], Eduardo Figueiredo[2], and Marcelo de Almeida Maia[1]

[1] Federal University of Uberlândia, Brazil
[2] Federal University of Minas Gerais, Brazil
{felipegaia,gabriel}@mestrado.ufu.br,
figueiredo@dcc.ufmg.br, marcmaia@facom.ufu.br

Abstract. Feature-Oriented Programming (FOP) and Aspect-Oriented Programming (AOP) are programming techniques based on composition mechanisms, called refinements and aspects, respectively. These techniques are assumed to be good variability mechanisms for implementing Software Product Lines (SPLs). Aspectual Feature Modules (AFM) is an approach that combines advantages of feature modules and aspects to increase concern modularity. Some guidelines of how to integrate these techniques have been established in some studies, but these studies do not focus the analysis on how effectively AFM can preserve the modularity and stability facilitating SPL evolution. The main purpose of this paper is to investigate whether the simultaneous use aspects and features through the AFM approach facilitates the evolution of SPLs. The quantitative data were collected from a SPL developed using four different variability mechanisms: (1) feature modules, aspects and aspects refinements of AFM, (2) aspects of aspect-oriented programming (AOP), (3) feature modules of feature-oriented programming (FOP), and (4) conditional compilation (CC) with object-oriented programming. Metrics for change propagation and modularity stability were calculated and the results support the benefits of the AFM option in a context where the product line has been evolved with addition or modification of crosscutting concerns.

Keywords: Software product lines, feature-oriented programming, aspect-oriented programming, aspectual feature modules, variability mechanisms.

1 Introduction

Software Product Line (SPL) refers to an emerging engineering technique that aims to establish the systematic reuse of a common core and shared modules by several software products [11]. Optional features define points of variability and their role is to permit the instantiation of different products by enabling or disabling them. SPL products share the same application domain and have points of variability among them. The potential benefits of SPLs are achieved through the reuse of the core in different products, enabling higher quality and productivity.

F.H. de Carvalho Junior and L.S. Barbosa (Eds.): SBLP 2012, LNCS 7554, pp. 134–149, 2012.
© Springer-Verlag Berlin Heidelberg 2012

During the software life cycle, change requests are not only inevitable, but also highly frequent [19] in SPL since they target several different products. These change requests must be accommodated since they include demands from multiple stakeholders [15].

Variability mechanisms play a crucial role when considering evolving SPLs. They must guarantee the architecture stability and, at the same time, facilitate future changes in the SPL. Therefore, variability mechanisms should not degenerate modularity and should minimize the need of future changes. This can be reached through non-intrusive and self-contained changes that favor insertions and do not require deep modifications into existing components. The inefficacy of variability mechanisms to accommodate changes might lead to several undesirable consequences related to the product line stability, including invasive wide changes, significant ripple effects, artificial dependences between core and optional features, and the lack of independence of the optional code [16, 27].

Our work aims at better understanding how contemporary variability mechanisms contribute to the mentioned SPL evolution practices. To this aim, this paper presents a case study that evaluates comparatively four mechanisms for implementing variability on evolving product lines: conditional compilation (CC), aspect-oriented programming (AOP), feature-oriented programming (FOP), and aspectual feature modules (AFM). Our investigation focuses on the evolution of six versions of a software product line (Section 3), called WebStore.

In Section 2, the implementation mechanisms used in the case study are presented. Section 3 describes the study settings, including the target SPL and change scenarios. Section 4 analyzes changes made in the WebStore SPL and how they propagate through its releases. Section 5 discusses the modularity of WebStore while Section 6 presents some limitations of this work. Section 7 presents some related work and points out directions for future work. Finally, Section 8 concludes this paper.

2   Variability Mechanisms

This section presents some concepts about the four techniques evaluated in the study: conditional compilation (CC), aspect-oriented programming (AOP), feature-oriented programming (FOP), and aspectual feature modules (AFM). Our main goal is to compare the different composition mechanisms available to understand their strengths and weaknesses. Although conditional compilation is not a new variability mechanism, we decide to include it in this study because it is a state-of-the-practice option adopted in SPL industry, and can serve as a baseline for comparison [1, 33].

2.1   Conditional Compilation

The CC approach used in this work is a well-known technique for handling software variability [1, 4, 21]. It has been used in programming languages like C for decades and it is also available in object-oriented languages such as C++. Basically, the preprocessor directives indicate pieces of code that should be compiled or not, based on the value of preprocessor variables. The pieces of code can be marked at granularity of a single line of code or to a whole file.

The code snippet below shows the use of conditional compilation mechanisms by inserting the pre-processing directives.

```
1   public class ControllerServlet extends HttpServlet {
2     public void init() {
3         actions.put("goToHome", new GoToAction("home.jsp"));
4         //#if defined(BankSlip)
5         actions.put("goToBankSlip",
                          new GoToAction("bankslip.jsp"));
6         //#endif
7         //#if defined(Logging)
8         Logger.getRootLogger().addAppender(new ConsoleAppender(
              new PatternLayout("[%C{1}] Method %M
                                      executed with success.")));
9         //#endif
10    }
11  }
```

Listing 1. Example of variability management with conditional compilation

In the example above, there are some directives that characterize the CC way of handling variability. On line 4 there is a directive `//#if defined (BankSlip)` that indicates the beginning of the code belonging to BankSlip feature. In line 7,6 there is a `#endif` directive that determines the end of the code associated to this feature. The identifiers used in the construction of these directives, in this case "Bank-Slip", are defined in a configuration file and are always associated with a boolean value. This value indicates the presence of the feature in the product, and consequently the inclusion of the bounded piece of code in the compiled product. The same reasoning applies to the bounded piece of code that belongs to Logging feature.

2.2   Feature-Oriented Programming

Feature-oriented programming (FOP) [31] is a paradigm for software modularization by considering features as a major abstraction. This work relies on AHEAD [9, 10] which is an approach to support FOP based on step-wise refinements. The main idea behind AHEAD is that programs are constants and features are added to programs using refinement functions. The code snippets in Listings 2-4 show examples of a class and a class refinement used to implement variation points.

```
1   public class ControllerServlet extends HttpServlet {
2     public void init() {
3         actions.put("goToHome", new GoToAction("home.jsp"));
5     }
6   }
```

Listing 2. Example of variability mechanism with FOP (base class)

```
1  layer bankslip;
2  refines class ControllerServlet {
3    public void init() {
4      Super().init();
5      actions.put("goToBankSlip",
                new GoToAction("bankslip.jsp"));
6    }
7  }
```

Listing 3. Example of variability mechanism with FOP (bankslip class refinement)

The example in Listing 2 shows an ordinary base class that implements a default action for *going to home* and Listing 3 presents the respective FOP class refinement that considers going to *bank slip payment* in checkout. Line 1 of Listing 3 is a clause that indicates a layer of the class refinements. The `bankslip` identifier in line 1 is used to compose the layers according to some pre-established order in the SPL configuration script that creates a specific product.

```
1  layer logging;
2  refines class ControllerServlet {
3    public void init() {
4      Super().init();
5      Logger.getRootLogger().addAppender(new ConsoleAppender(
          new PatternLayout("[%C{1}] Method %M
                              executed with success.")));
6    }
7  }
```

Listing 4. Example of variability mechanism with FOP (logging class refinement)

Listing 4 provides another class refinement to include the behavior of feature *logging* in the class. This feature is designed to register successful execution of public methods.

2.3   Aspect-Oriented Programming

Aspect-oriented programming has been proposed to modularize crosscutting concerns. The main mechanism of modularization is the aspect, which encapsulate a concern code that would be tangled with and scattered across the code of other concerns. An extension of Java for AOP is AspectJ [23]. Listing 5 shows how an aspect can modularize the BankSlip payment feature. An aspect usually needs to provide the interception points in the base code in order to get the code adequately weaved. Line 3 shows an example of intercepting the execution of the method `init` of `ControllerServlet`. Line 5 shows how and what will be executed in that interception point (pointcut).

```
1  public privileged aspect BankSlipAspect {
2    pointcut init(ControllerServlet controller):
3    execution(public void ControllerServlet.init())&&
               this(controller) && args();
4    after(ControllerServlet controller): init(controller) {
5      controller.actions.put("goToBankSlip",
        new GoToAction("bankslip.jsp"));
6  }
```

Listing 5. Example of variability mechanism with AOP (aspect)

2.4   Aspectual Feature Modules

Aspectual feature modules (AFM) are an approach to implement the symbiosis of FOP and AOP [5, 6, 7]. An AFM encapsulates the roles of collaborating classes and aspects that contribute to a feature. In other words, a feature is implemented by a collection of artifacts, e.g., classes, refinements and aspects. Typically, an aspect inside an AFM does not implement a role. Usually, a refinement is more adequate for this task. Aspects in AFM usually are used to do what they are good for, and in the same way of AOP: modularize code that otherwise would be tangled with or scattered across other concerns. It is important to note that an aspect is a legitimate part of a feature module and so, is applied and removed together with the feature it belongs to. First enabled features are composed using AHEAD, after aspects belonging to these features are weaved using AspectJ.

3   Case Study

This section describes the study based on the analysis of the evolution of a software product line. This SPL was developed from the scratch. The study was conducted to answer the following research questions.

> **RQ1.** Does the use of AFM have smoother change propagation impact than using CC, FOP, or AOP?

> **RQ2.** Does the use of AFM provide more stable design of the SPL features than using CC, FOP, or AOP during the evolution?

3.1   Infrastructure Setting

The independent variable of this study is the variability mechanism used to implement SPLs, namely, Conditional Compilation (CC), Feature-oriented programming (FOP), Aspect-oriented programming (AOP), and Aspectual Feature Modules (AFM). A subject system is used to analyze the behavior of the dependent variables: change propagation and modularity metrics. The study was organized in four phases: (1) construction of the subject SPL with complete releases that correspond to their respective change scenarios using the four techniques aforementioned for each release (2) feature source code shadowing of all produced source code, (3) measurement and metrics calculation, and (4) quantitative and qualitative analysis of the results. In the first phase, the first two authors implemented the WebStore SPL from the scratch using all different variability mechanisms resulting in 24 different versions of the SPL. In the second phase, all code was marked according to each designed feature. The concrete result of this phase was text files, one for each code file, marked with the corresponding feature. In the third phase, changes propagation [32] was measured and modularity metrics [15] were calculated. Finally, the results were analyzed in the fourth phase. The next sections present the analyzed target SPL WebStore, and discuss their change scenarios.

3.2   The Evolved WebStore SPL

The target SPL was developed to represent major features of an interactive web store system. It was designed for academic purpose, but focusing on real features available in typical web store systems. We have also designed representative changes scenarios (the same for all studied techniques – CC, FOP, AOP and AFM), considered important, that could exercise the SPL evolution.

WebStore is an SPL for applications that manage products and their categories, show products catalog, control access, and payments. Table 1 provides some measures about the size of the SPL implementation in terms of number of components, methods, and lines of source code (LOC). Classes, class refinements, and aspects were accounted as components. The number of components varies from 23 (CC) to 85 (FOP).

Table 1. WebStore SPL implementation

	CC						FOP					
	R.1	R.2	R.3	R.4	R.5	R.6	R.1	R.2	R.3	R.4	R.5	R.6
#Components	23	23	26	26	26	32	28	32	38	40	44	85
#Methods	138	139	165	164	167	197	142	147	175	177	182	394
LOC (aprox.)	885	900	1045	1052	1066	1496	915	950	1107	1121	1149	2181
	AOP						AFM					
	R.1	R.2	R.3	R.4	R.5	R.6	R.1	R.2	R.3	R.4	R.5	R.6
#Components	23	46	48	53	52	53	30	34	40	42	46	50
#Methods	138	143	171	171	176	212	130	135	163	165	170	206
LOC (aprox.)	885	924	1080	1081	1105	1371	784	819	976	990	1018	1284

Figure 1 presents a simplified view of the WebStore SPL feature model [8]. Examples of core features are CategoryManagement and ProductManagement. In addition, some optional features are DisplayByCategory and BankSlip. We use numbers in the top right-hand corner of a feature in Figure 1 to indicate in which release the feature was included (see Table 2).

The WebStore versions are very similar from the architecture design point-of-view, even though they are implemented using four distinct variability mechanisms. In all versions the Release 1 contains the core of the target SPL. All subsequent releases were designed to incorporate the required changes in order to include the corresponding feature. For instance, the FOP version was developed trying to maximize the decomposition of the product features. This explains why Release 1 in FOP contains more artifacts than Release 1 that uses CC. All new scenarios were incorporated by including, changing, or removing classes, class refinements, or aspects.

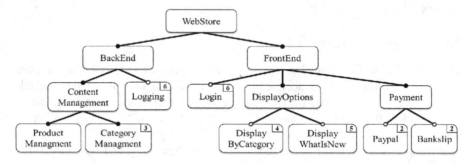

Fig. 1. WebStore Basic Feature Model

3.3   Change Scenarios

As aforementioned, we designed and implemented a set of change scenarios in the first phase of our investigation. A total of five change scenarios were incorporated into WebStore, resulting in six releases. Table 2 summarizes changes made in each release. The scenarios comprised different types of changes involving mandatory and optional features. Table 2 also presents which types of change each release encompassed. The purpose of these changes is to exercise the implementation of the feature boundaries and, so, to assess the design stability of the SPL.

Table 2. Summary of change scenarios in WebStore

Release	Description	Type of Change
R1	WebStore core	
R2	Two types of payment included (Paypal and BankSlip)	Inclusion of optional feature
R3	New feature included to manage category	Inclusion of optional feature
R4	The management of category was changed to mandatory feature and new feature included to display products by category	Changing optional feature to mandatory and inclusion of optional feature
R5	New feature included to display products by nearest day of inclusion	Inclusion of optional feature
R6	Two crosscutting features included (Login and Logging)	Inclusion of optional feature

4   Propagation Analysis

This section presents a quantitative analysis to answer RQ1. In particular, we are interested to know how different variability mechanisms affect changes in software product line evolution. The quantitative analysis uses traditional measures of change impact [32], considering different levels of granularity: components, methods, and lines of source code (Table 1). A general interpretation is that lower number of modified and removed artifacts suggests more stable solution, possibly supported by the variability mechanisms. In the case of additions, we expect that a higher addition of artifacts indicates the conformance with the Open-Closed principle. In this case, the lowest number of additions may suggest that the evolution is not being supported by non intrusive extensions.

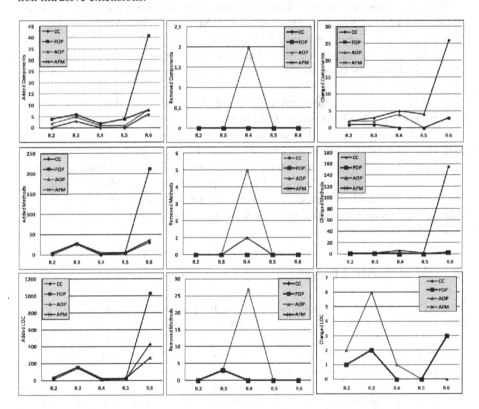

Fig. 2. Additions, Removals and Changes in WebStore versions

Figure 2 in the first column shows the number of added components, methods, and lines of code, respectively, in Releases 2 to 6 of the WebStore SPL. The CC mechanism has the lowest number of added components compared to the other approaches. Concerning the number of methods and lines of code, there is no sharp difference between the measures of the four mechanisms. An important exception is for the implementation of Release 6. In that case, there is a substantial higher number of methods and LOCs with FOP. This can be explained because the implementation of the Logging concern required a class refinement for each component what almost doubled the number of components in FOP implementation of Release 6. It is also important to note that AOP and AFM solution of Release 6 required the lowest number of line additions.

The middle column of Figure 2 shows the number of removed components, methods, and lines of code in Releases 2 to 6 of the WebStore SPL. Release 4 using AOP had a significant difference because the numbers of components, methods and lines removed were significantly higher than in other approaches. This is because the feature change from optional to mandatory, resulting in removing the aspect components that allow enabling this feature and code distribution of it by the system.

The right column of Figure 2 shows the number of changed components, methods and lines of code in Releases 2 to 6 of the WebStore SPL. The AFM and FOP mechanism has a lower number of modified components than AOP (except in Releases 5 and 6) and CC. The number of lines changes is quantitatively irrelevant for all versions. The changes in components and methods were due to insertions that occurred inside them.

Considering some specific releases, we could observe that the addition of crosscutting concerns with FOP is a painful task. In this case, we could clearly see the importance of AFM to overcome this situation. On the other hand, aspects did not work well when transforming an optional feature into mandatory.

Considering all releases, one finding in the change propagation is that CC releases have consistently lower number of added components than the others. Considering that there is no notably difference in changes and removals when all releases are considered, we conclude that CC does not adhere as closely to the Open-Close principle as the other mechanisms do.

5   Modularity Analysis

This section presents and discusses the results for the analysis of the stability of the SPLs design throughout the implemented changes. To support our analysis, we used a suite of metrics for quantifying feature modularity [37]. This suite measures the degree to which a single feature of the system maps to: (i) components (i.e. classes, class refinements and aspects) – based on the metric Concern Diffusion over Components (CDC), (ii) operations (i.e. methods and advices) – based on the metric Concern Diffusion over Operations (CDO) and (iii) lines of code – based on the metrics Concern Diffusion over Lines of Code (CDLOC) and Number of Lines of Concern Code (LOCC) [16]. We choose these metrics because they have been used and validated in several previous empirical studies [12, 13, 14, 17, 18, 20].

Optional features are the locus of variation in the SPLs and, therefore, they have to be well modularized. On the other hand, mandatory features also need to be investigated in order to assess the impact of changes on the core SPL architecture. From the analysis of the measures, three interesting situations, discussed below, naturally emerged with respect to which type of modularization paradigm presents superior modularity and stability. The data was collected and organized in one spreadsheet for each metric. For WebStore, each sheet of one studied metric has 8435 lines, i.e., one line for each combination of feature, version, technique and artifact.

Figure 3 presents CDC, CDO, CDLOC and LOCC mean values for each release of the subject SPL. The CDC mean values for FOP and AFM were consistently the lowest in all releases. The values for AOP stayed in between, while CC had the worst values. The CDLOC mean values for FOP were also consistently the lowest in all releases. The CDLOC mean values for AFM were slightly better than AOP in Releases 4, 5, and 6. CDLOC values for CC were the worst ones, especially in Release 6. For CDO and LOCC there was no significant difference between releases or techniques, except in Release 6 where the CC values were significantly the worst ones.

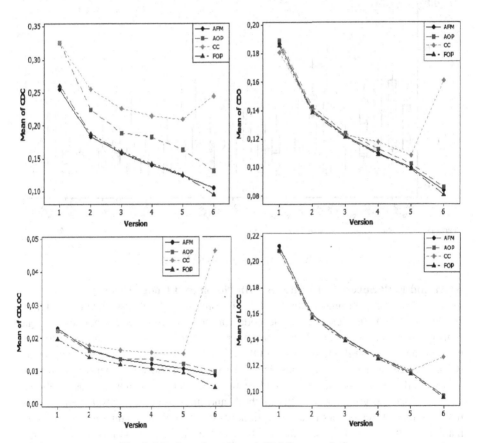

Fig. 3. Metrics values through WebStore evolution

Since Figure 3 shows only mean values, it is not possible to understand the variation occurred in that data. Figure 4 show the boxplot of the corresponding data, allowing us to visualize the variation on the CDC concerning the several features and components. FOP and AFM have consistently lower variation than AOP and CC, which supports our analysis that the CDC mean is confidently lower for FOP and AFM. Moreover, this boxplot shows interesting outliers in Release 6 for CC and FOP. The cause of those outliers is the crosscutting feature introduced in Release 6 that produced undesirable consequence in the CDC values of CC and FOP, as expected. The boxplots for the other metrics are omitted because they produce the same pattern of variation, which enables us to interpret the mean values adequately.

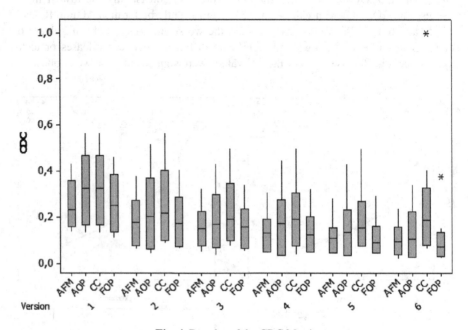

Fig. 4. Boxplot of the CDC Metric

AFM and FOP Succeed in Features with No Shared Code. This situation was observed with three optional features of WebStore SPL (Bankslip, Paypal, and DisplayWhatIsNew). In these cases, the code for these features were independent (no sharing) and then, AFM and FOP solutions presented lower values and superior stability in terms of tangling, specially FOP (CDLOC) and scattering over components (CDC) which explain the previous data. The results of the other metrics (CDO and LOCC) did not follow the same trend of the CDC metric, which can be explained because since the granularity of the methods and lines of code is lower, then the distribution of features occurs in a proportional fashion in all mechanisms. On the other hand, since the granularity of components is higher, the impact ón modularity metrics is higher too.

When Crosscutting Concerns Are Present in the Solution AFM Are Recommended over FOP. Another interesting finding that emerged from our analysis is that FOP does not cope well with crosscutting concerns. In this case, AFM provided an adequate solution, because it did not forced the use of aspects to modularize features with no shared code, but still did not force painful scattered refinements to implement a crosscutting feature.

CC Compilation Should Be Avoided Whenever Possible. Although conditional compilation is still widely used in large scale projects, our data have shown that its use does not produced a stable architecture and should be avoided specially in situations where changes are frequent.

6   Threats to Validity

Even with the careful planning of the study, some factors should be considered in the evaluation of the results validity. Concerning the conclusion validity, since 33740 data points were collected the reliability of the measurement process is an issue, which was alleviated because most of the measurements were independently checked by one of the authors that did not collect the respective data. Concerning the internal validity, the versions of the SPLs used in this study were constructed by some of the authors. There is a reasonably large space for different designs, so different designs would produce different results. However, all designs of WebStore were carefully constructed to take the best of each implementation technique and at the same time to maintain a similar division of components. Concerning the external validity, some other factors limit the generalization of the results, such as, the special purpose subject system and evolution scenarios. Also, the languages and tools used limit the generalization. Finally, concerning the construct validity, one issue is on how much support modularity metrics offer to produce robust answers to the design stability problem. As a matter of fact, these metrics offers a limited view on the overall quality of design. They are mostly related to the quality of modularization of features, which are notably important for SPLs. The scope of this study has been narrowed to SPLs systems in order to cope with this issue.

7   Related Work

Recent research work has also analyzed stability and reuse of SPLs [12, 15]. Figueiredo et al. [15] performed an empirical study to assess modularity, change propagation, and feature dependency of two evolving SPLs. Their study focused on aspect-oriented programming while we analyzed variability mechanisms available in feature-oriented programming in this study. Dantas and his colleagues [12] conducted an exploratory study to analyze the support of new modularization techniques to implement SPLs. However, their study aimed at comparing the advantage and drawbacks of different techniques in terms of stability and reuse. Although Dantas also used a FOP language, named CaesarJ [28], we focused on different goals and on a different language: AHEAD [9]. Other studies also analyzed the variability management of SPLs and benefits of using FOP in software reuse [5, 29].

Apel and others [5], who have proposed the Aspectual Feature Modules [6, 7] approach , have also used size metrics to quantify the number of components and lines of code in an SPL implementation. Their study, however, did not consider a significant suite of software metrics and did not address SPL evolution and stability. In other work Greenwood et al. [20] used similar suites of metrics to ours to assess the design stability of an evolving application. However, they did not target at assessing the impact of changes in the core and variable features of SPLs.

Other studies focused on challenges in software evolution field [19, 27]. These works have in common the concern about measuring different artifacts through software evolution, which relies directly on the use of reliable software metrics [22]. Furthermore, there is a shared sense about software metrics on engineering perspective: they are far from being mature and are constantly the focus of disagreements [22, 26, 34].

Several studies have investigated variability management on SPLs [2, 3, 24, 30]. Batory et al. have reported an increased flexibility in changes and significant reduction in program complexity measured by number of methods, lines of code, and number of tokens per class [10]. Simplification in evolving SPL architecture has also been reported in [29, 32], as consequence of variability management.

In our previous study [14], we analyzed and compared variability mechanisms to evolve SPLs, using FOP, Design Patterns and Conditional Compilation. The evaluation was also based on the change propagation and modularity stability metrics. In that work, the result was mostly favorable for FOP. It is important to consider that crosscutting concerns were not considered in the subject system analyzed in that study.

8   Concluding Remarks and Future Work

This study evolved a SPL in order to assess the capabilities of contemporary variability mechanisms to provide SPL modularity and stability in the presence of change requests. Such evaluation included two complementary analyses: change propagation and feature modularity. The use of variability mechanisms to develop SPLs largely depends on our ability to empirically understand their positive and negative effects through design changes.

Some interesting results emerged from our analysis. First, the AFM and FOP designs of the studied SPL tend to be more stable than the other approaches. This advantage of AFM and FOP is particularly observable when a change targets optional features. Second, we observed that AFM and FOP class refinements adhere more closely the Open-Closed principle. Furthermore, such mechanisms usually scale well for dependencies that do not involve shared code and facilitate multiple different product instantiations. However, FOP does not cope well when crosscutting concerns must be addressed. In this case, AFM provides a better scenario concerning the propagation of changes.

Our results also indicate that conditional compilation (CC) may not be adequate when feature modularity is a major concern in the evolving SPL. For instance, the addition of new features using CC mechanisms usually causes the increase of feature tangling and scattering. These crosscutting features destabilize the SPL architecture and make it difficult to accommodate future changes.

For the future work, the study of other metrics and its relationship to other quality attributes in SPLs, such as robustness and reuse could be an interesting way. We also aim to replicate this study with additional SPLs.

Acknowledgments. This work was partially supported by FAPEMIG, grants APQ-02932-10 and APQ-02376-11, and CNPq grant 485235/2011-0.

References

1. Adams, B., De Meuter, W., Tromp, H., Hassan, A.E.: Can we Refactor Conditional Compilation into Aspects? In: 8th ACM International Conference on Aspect-oriented Software Development, AOSD 2009, pp. 243–254. ACM, New York (2009)
2. Adler, C.: Optional Composition - A Solution to the Optional Feature Problem? Master thesis, University of Magdeburg, Germany (February 2011)
3. Ali Babar, M., Chen, L., Shull, F.: Managing variability in software product lines. IEEE Software 27, 89–91 (2010)
4. Alves, V., Neto, A.C., Soares, S., Santos, G., Calheiros, F., Nepomuceno, V., Pires, D., Leal, J., Borba, P.: From Conditional Compilation to Aspects: A Case Study in Software Product Lines Migration. In: First Workshop on Aspect-Oriented Product Line Engineering (AOPLE), Portland, USA (2006)
5. Apel, S., Batory, D.: When to Use Features and Aspects? A Case Study. In: GPCE, Portland, Oregon (2006)
6. Apel, S., et al.: Aspectual Mixin Layers: Aspects and Features in Concert. In: Proceedings of ICSE 2006, Shanghai, China (2006)
7. Apel, S., Leich, T., Saake, G.: Aspectual feature modules. IEEE Trans. Softw. Eng. 34, 162–180 (2008)
8. Batory, D.: Feature Models, Grammars, and Propositional Formulas. In: Obbink, H., Pohl, K. (eds.) SPLC 2005. LNCS, vol. 3714, pp. 7–20. Springer, Heidelberg (2005)
9. Batory, D.: Feature-Oriented Programming and the AHEAD tool suite. In: 26th International Conference on Software Engineering, ICSE 2004, pp. 702–703. IEEE Computer Society, Washington (2004)
10. Batory, D., Sarvela, J., Rauschmayer: Scaling step-wise refinement. IEEE Transactions on Software Engineering 30(6), 355–371 (2004)
11. Clements, P., Northrop, L.: Software Product Lines: Practices and Patterns. Addison-Wesley (2002)
12. Dantas, F., Garcia, A.: Software Reuse versus Stability: Evaluating Advanced Programming Techniques. In: 23rd Brazilian Symposium on Software Engineering, SBES 2010 (2010)
13. Eaddy, M., et al.: Do Crosscutting Concerns Cause Defects? IEEE Trans. on Software Engineering (TSE) 34, 497–515 (2008)
14. Ferreira, G., Gaia, F., Figueiredo, E., Maia, M.: On the Use of Feature-Oriented Programming for Evolving Software Product Lines – a Comparative Study. In: Proc. of the XV Brazilian Symposium on Programming Languages, São Paulo, pp. 121–135

15. Figueiredo, E., Cacho, N., Sant'Anna, C., Monteiro, M., Kulesza, U., Garcia, A., Soares, S., Ferrari, F., Khan, S., Castor Filho, F., Dantas, F.: Evolving Software Product Lines with Aspects: An Empirical Study on Design Stability. In: 30th International Conference on Software Engineering, ICSE 2008, pp. 261–270. ACM, New York (2008)
16. Figueiredo, E., et al.: On the Maintainability of Aspect-Oriented Software: A Concern-Oriented Measurement Framework. In: Proc. of European Conf. on Soft. Maint. and Reeng. (CSMR), Athens (2008)
17. Figueiredo, E., Sant'Anna, C., Garcia, A., Lucena, C.: Applying and Evaluating Concern-Sensitive Design Heuristics. In: 23rd Brazilian Symposium on Software Engineering (SBES), Fortaleza, Brazil (2009)
18. Garcia, A., Sant'Anna, C., Figueiredo, E., Kulesza, U., Lucena, C., von Staa, A.: Modularizing design patterns with aspects: a quantitative study. In: Proceedings of the 4th International Conference on Aspect-Oriented Software Development, AOSD 2005, pp. 3–14. ACM, New York (2005)
19. Godfrey, M., German, D.: The past, present, and future of software evolution. In: Frontiers of Software Maintenance, pp. 129–138 (2008)
20. Greenwood, P., Bartolomei, T., Figueiredo, E., Dosea, M., Garcia, A., Cacho, N., Sant'Anna, C., Soares, S., Borba, P., Kulesza, U., Rashid, A.: On the Impact of Aspectual Decompositions on Design Stability: An Empirical Study. In: Bateni, M. (ed.) ECOOP 2007. LNCS, vol. 4609, pp. 176–200. Springer, Heidelberg (2007)
21. Hu, Y., Merlo, E., Dagenais, M., Lague, B.: C/C++ Conditional Compilation Analysis Using Symbolic Execution. In: Proceedings of the IEEE International Conference on Software Maintenance, ICSM (2000)
22. Jones, C.: Software metrics: good, bad and missing. Computer 27, 98–100 (1994)
23. Kästner, C., Apel, S., Batory, D.: A Case Study Implementing Features using AspectJ. In: International SPL Conference (2007)
24. Lee, K., Kang, K.C., Koh, E., Chae, W., Bokyoung, K., Choi, B.W.: Domain-oriented engineering of elevator control software: a product line practice. In: Proceedings of the First Conference on Software Product Lines: Experience and Research Directions, pp. 3–22. Kluwer Academic Publishers (2000)
25. Maletic, J., Kagdi, H.: Expressiveness and effectiveness of program comprehension: thoughts on future research directions. In: Frontiers of Software Maintenance, pp. 31–40 (2008)
26. Mayer, T., Hall, T.: A critical analysis of current OO design metrics. Softw. Qual. J. 8, 97–110 (1999)
27. Mens, T., Wermelinger, M., Ducasse, S., Demeyer, S., Hirschfield, R., Jazayeri, M.: Challenges in software evolution. In: IWPSE 2005: Proceedings of the Eighth International Workshop on Principles of Software Evolution, pp. 13–22. IEEE Computer Society (2005)
28. Mezini, M., Ostermann, K.: Conquering Aspects with Caesar. In: 2nd International Conference on Aspect-Oriented Software Development (AOSD), Boston, USA (2003)
29. Mezini, M., Ostermann, K.: Variability Management with Feature-Oriented Programming and Aspects. In: 12th ACM SIG-SOFT Twelfth International Symposium on Foundations of Software Engineering, SIGSOFT 2004/FSE-12, pp. 127–136. ACM, New York (2004)
30. Pettersson, U., Jarzabek, S.: Industrial experience with building a web portal product line using a lightweight, reactive approach. In: Proceedings of the 10th European Software Engineering Conference Held Jointly with 13th ACM SIGSOFT International Symposium on Foundations of Software Engineering, pp. 326–335. ACM (2005)

31. Prehofer, C.: Feature-Oriented Programming: A Fresh Look at Objects. In: Aksit, M., Auletta, V. (eds.) ECOOP 1997. LNCS, vol. 1241, pp. 419–443. Springer, Heidelberg (1997)

32. Sant'Anna, C., et al.: On the Reuse and Maintenance of Aspect-Oriented Software: An Assessment Framework. In.: Brazilian Symposium on Software Engineering (SBES), pp. 19–34 (2003)

33. Svahnberg, M., van Gurp, J., Bosch, J.: A taxonomy of variability realization techniques. Software—Practice and Experience 35, 705–754 (2005)

34. Yau, S.S., Collofello, J.S.: Design Stability Measures for Software Maintenance. IEEE Transactions on Software Engineering 11(9), 849–856 (1985)

Attribute Grammar Macros

Marcos Viera[1] and Doaitse Swierstra[2]

[1] Instituto de Computación, Universidad de la República
Montevideo, Uruguay
mviera@fing.edu.uy
[2] Department of Computer Science, Utrecht University
Utrecht, The Netherlands
doaitse@cs.uu.nl

Abstract. Having extensible languages is appealing, but raises the question of how to construct extensible compilers and how to compose compilers out of a collection of pre-compiled components.

Being able to deal with attribute grammar fragments as first-class values makes it possible to describe semantics in a compositional way; this leads naturally to a plug-in architecture, in which a core compiler can be constructed as a (collection of) pre-compiled component(s), and to which extra components can safely be added as need arises.

We extend *AspectAG*, a Haskell library for building strongly typed first-class attribute grammars, with a set of combinators that make it easy to describe semantics in terms of already existing semantics in a macro-like style, just as syntax macros extend the syntax of a language. We also show how existing semantics can be redefined, thus adapting some aspects from the behavior defined by the macros.

1   Introduction

Since the introduction of the very first programming languages, and the invention of grammatical formalisms for describing them, people have investigated how an initial language definition can be extended by someone else than the original language designer by providing separate language-definition fragments.

The simplest approach starts from the *text* which describes a compiler for the base language. Just before the compiler is compiled, several extra ingredients may be added textually. In this way we get great flexibility and there is virtually no limit to the things we may add. The Utrecht Haskell Compiler [5] has shown the effectiveness of this approach by composing a large number of attribute grammar fragments textually into a complete compiler description. This approach however is not very practical when defining relatively small language extensions; we do not want an individual user to have to generate a completely new compiler for each small extension. Another problematic aspect of this approach is that, by making the complete text of the compiler available for modification or extension, we also loose important safety guarantees provided by e.g. the type system; we definitely do not want everyone to mess around with the delicate internals of a compiler for a complex language.

F.H. de Carvalho Junior and L.S. Barbosa (Eds.): SBLP 2012, LNCS 7554, pp. 150–164, 2012.

So the question arises how we can reach the effect of textual composition, but without opening up the whole compiler source. The most commonly found approach is to introduce so-called *syntax macros* [8], which enable the programmer to add *syntactic sugar* to a language by defining new notation *in terms of already existing syntax*.

In this paper we will focus on how to provide such mechanisms *at the semantic level* [9] too. As a running example we take a minimal expression language described by the grammar:

$$expr \;\; \rightarrow \;\; \texttt{"let"} \; var \; \texttt{"="} \; expr \; \texttt{"in"} \; expr \mid term \; \texttt{"+"} \; expr \mid term$$
$$term \;\; \rightarrow \; factor \; \texttt{"*"} \; term \mid factor$$
$$factor \rightarrow int \mid var$$

with the following abstract syntax (as a Haskell data type):

data $Root = Root \,\{\, expr :: Expr \,\}$
data $Expr = Cst \;\;\{\, cv \;\;\; :: Int \,\} \mid Var \,\{\, vnm :: String \,\}$
$\qquad\qquad \mid \; Mul \;\{\, me1 :: Expr, \;\; me2 :: Expr \,\}$
$\qquad\qquad \mid \; Add \;\{\, ae1 \;\; :: Expr, \;\; ae2 \;\; :: Expr \,\}$
$\qquad\qquad \mid \; Let \;\;\{\, lnm :: String, val \;\; :: Expr, body :: Expr \,\}$

Suppose we want to extend the language with one extra production for defining the square of a value. A syntax macro aware compiler might accept definitions of the form $square \,(se :: Expr) \Rightarrow Mul \; se \; se$, translating the new syntax into the existing abstract syntax.

Althought this approach may be very effective and seems attractive, such transformational programming [3] has its shortcomings too; as a consequence of mapping the new constructs onto existing constructs and performing any further processing such as type checking on this simpler, but often more detailed program representation, feedback from later stages of the compiler is given in terms of the intermediate program representations in which the original program structure if often hard to recognise. For example, if we do not change the pretty printing phase of the compiler, the expression *square* 2 will be printed as 2 * 2. Hence the implementation details shine through, and the produced error messages can be confusing or even incomprehensible. Similar problems show up when defining embedded domain specific languages: the error messages from the type system are typically given in terms of the underlying representation [6].

In a previous paper [16] we introduced AspectAG[1], a Haskell library of first-class attribute grammars, which can be used to implement a language semantics and its extensions in a safe way, i.e. by constructing a core compiler as a (collection of) pre-compiled component(s), to which extra components can safely be added at will. In this paper we show how we can define the semantics of the right hand side in terms of existing semantics, in the form of *attribute grammar macros*.

---

[1] `http://hackage.haskell.org/package/AspectAG`

We also show how, by using first class attribute grammars, the already defined semantics can easily be *redefined* at the places where it makes a difference, e.g. in pretty printing and generating error messages.

The functionality provided by the combination of attribute grammar macros and redefinition is similar to the *forwarding attributes* [14] technique for higher-order attribute grammars, implemented in the Silver AG system [15]. We however implement our proposal as a set of combinators embedded in Haskell, such that the correctness of the composite system is checked by the Haskell type checker.

In Section 2 we give a top-level overview of our approach. In Section 3 we describe our approach to first-class attribute grammars, and in Section 4 we show how to define semantic macros and how to redefine attributes. We close by presenting our conclusions and future work.

2   Attribute Grammar Combinators

Before delving into the technical details, we show in this section how the semantics of our running example language and some simple extensions can be implemented using our approach. We have chosen our example to be very simple, in order to help the understanding of the technique. For a more involved example, including an implementation of the Oberon-0 language [17] using macros to represent the **FOR** and **CASE** statements in terms of a core sub-language, we refer to the web page of the AspectAG project[2].

The semantics are defined by two aspects: pretty printing, realized by a synthesized attribute *spp*, which holds a pretty printed document, and expression evaluation, realized by two attributes: a synthesized *sval* of type *Int*, which holds the result of an expression, and an inherited *ienv* which holds the environment ($[[(String, Int)]]$) in which an expression is to be evaluated. We show how the attributes are directly definable in Haskell using the functions *syndefM* and *inhdefM* from the AspectAG library, which define a single synthesized or inherited attribute respectively. Figure 1 lists some of the rule definitions of the semantics of our example. In our naming convention a rule with name *attProd* defines the attribute *att* for the production *Prod*. The rule *sppAdd* for the attribute *spp* of the production *Add* looks for its children attributions and binds them ($e_i \leftarrow at\ ch\_ae_i$) and then combines the pretty printed children e_i # *spp* with the string "+" using the pretty printing combinator (>#<) for horizontal (beside) composition, from the *uulib*[3] library. The rule *ienvLet* specifies that the *ienv* value coming from the parent (*lhs* stands for "left-hand side") is copied to the *ienv* position of the child *val*; the *ienv* attribute of the *body* is this environment extended with a pair composed of the name (*lnm*) associated with the first child and the value (the *sval* attribute) of the second child.

In Figure 2 we show for each production of the example how we combine the various aspects introduced by the attributes using the function *ext*.

---

[2] http://www.cs.uu.nl/wiki/bin/view/Center/AspectAG
[3] http://hackage.haskell.org/package/uulib

```
    -- Pretty-Printing
sppRoot  = syndefM spp $ liftM (#spp) (at ch_expr)
...

sppAdd   = syndefM spp $ do e₁ ← at ch_ae₁
                            e₂ ← at ch_ae₂
                            return $ e₁ # spp >#< "+" >#< e₂ # spp
...

    -- Environment
ienvRoot = inhdefM ienv { nt_Expr } $
           do return {{ ch_expr .=. ([] :: [(String, Int)]) }}
...

ienvLet  = inhdefM ienv { nt_Expr } $
           do lnm ← at ch_lnm
              val ← at ch_val
              lhs ← at lhs
              return {{ ch_val  .=. lhs # ienv
                      , ch_body .=. (lnm, val # sval) : lhs # ienv }}
    -- Value
svalRoot = syndefM sval $ liftM (#sval) (at ch_expr)
...

svalVar  = syndefM sval $ do vnm ← at ch_vnm
                             lhs ← at lhs
                             return $ fromJust (lookup vnm (lhs # ienv))
...
```

Fig. 1. Fragments of the specification of the example's semantics using the AspectAG library

The semantics we associate with an abstract syntax tree is a function which maps the inherited attributes of the root node to its synthesized attributes. So for each production that may be applied at the root node of the tree we have to construct a function that takes the semantics of its children and uses these to construct the semantics of the complete tree. We will refer to such functions as *semantic functions*. The hard work is done by the function *knit*, that "ties the knot", combining the attribute computations (i.e. the data flow at the node) with the semantics of the children trees (describing the flow of data from their inherited to their synthesized attributes) into the semantic function for the parent. The following code defines the semantic functions of the production *Add*:

$$semExpr\_Add\ sae1\ sae2 = knit\ aspAdd\ \{\{\ ch\_ae_1\ .=.\ sae1, ch\_ae_2\ .=.\ sae2\ \}\}$$

where the function *knit* is applied to the combined attributes for the production.

The resulting semantic functions can be associated with the concrete syntax by using parser combinators [13] in an applicative style:

$$
\begin{aligned}
aspRoot &= sppRoot \text{ `ext`} svalRoot \text{ `ext`} ienvRoot \\
aspCst &= sppCst \text{ `ext`} svalCst \\
aspVar &= sppVar \text{ `ext`} svalVar \\
aspMul &= sppMul \text{ `ext`} svalMul \text{ `ext`} ienvMul \\
aspAdd &= sppAdd \text{ `ext`} svalAdd \text{ `ext`} ienvAdd \\
aspLet &= sppLet \text{ `ext`} svalLet \text{ `ext`} ienvLet
\end{aligned}
$$

Fig. 2. Composition of the semantics

$$
\begin{aligned}
pExpr \quad &= \; semExpr\_Let \;\; \texttt{<\$}\; pKeyw \;\texttt{"let"}\; \texttt{<*>}\; pString \\
&\qquad \texttt{<*}\; pKeyw \;\texttt{"="}\; \quad \texttt{<*>}\; pExpr \\
&\qquad \texttt{<*}\; pKeyw \;\texttt{"in"}\; \quad \texttt{<*>}\; pExpr \\
&\texttt{<|>}\; semExpr\_Add \;\texttt{<\$>}\; pTerm \;\; \texttt{<*}\; pKeyw \;\texttt{"+"}\; \texttt{<*>}\; pExpr \;\texttt{<|>}\; pTerm \\
pTerm \quad &= \; semExpr\_Mul \;\texttt{<\$>}\; pFactor \;\texttt{<*}\; pKeyw \;\texttt{"*"}\; \texttt{<*>}\; pTerm \;\texttt{<|>}\; pFactor \\
pFactor &= \; semExpr\_Cst \;\texttt{<\$>}\; pInt \;\texttt{<|>}\; semExpr\_Var \;\texttt{<\$>}\; pString
\end{aligned}
$$

Thus far we have described a methodology to define the static semantics of a language. The goal of this paper is to show how we can define new productions by combining existing productions, while probably updating some of the aspects. We want to express the semantics of new productions *in terms of already existing semantics* and *by adapting parts of the semantics* resulting from such a composition.

To show our approach we will extend the language of our example with some extra productions; one for defining the square of a value, one for defining the sum of the squares of two values, and one for doubling a value:

$$
expr \rightarrow \dots \mid \texttt{"square"}\; expr \mid \texttt{"pyth"}\; expr\; expr \mid \texttt{"double"}\; expr
$$

In the rest of this section we define the semantic functions $semExpr\_Sq$, $semExpr\_Pyth$ and $semExpr\_Double$, of the new productions, in a macro style, although providing specific definitions for the pretty-printing attributes. Thus, if the expressions' parser is extended with these new productions:

$$
\begin{aligned}
pExpr = \; &\dots \; \texttt{<|>}\; semExpr\_Sq \qquad \texttt{<\$}\; pKeyw \;\texttt{"square"}\; \texttt{<*>}\; pExpr \\
&\texttt{<|>}\; semExpr\_Pyth \quad \texttt{<\$}\; pKeyw \;\texttt{"pyth"}\; \quad \texttt{<*>}\; pExpr \;\texttt{<*>}\; pExpr \\
&\texttt{<|>}\; semExpr\_Double \;\texttt{<\$}\; pKeyw \;\texttt{"double"}\; \texttt{<*>}\; pExpr
\end{aligned}
$$

the semantic action associated to parse, for example, `"square 2"` returns the value 2 for the attribute *sval* and `"square 2"` for *spp*.

Thus far, when extending the example language with a *square* production, we would have to define its semantics from scratch, i.e we had to define all its attributes in the same way we did for the original language. Thus, if the semantics of a language are defined by about twenty attributes[4] (to perform pretty-printing, name binding, type checking, optimizations, code generation,

---

[4] As is the case in the UHC Haskell compiler.

etc.), a definition of all these twenty attributes has to be provided. To avoid this, we introduce *attribute grammar macros* in Figure 3 to define the extensions of the example.

The square of a value is the multiplication of this value by itself. Thus, the semantics of multiplication can be used as a basis, by passing to it the semantics of the only child (ch_se) of the square production both as ch_me_1 and ch_me_2. We do so in the definition of $aspSq$ in Figure 3; we declare an attribute grammar macro based on the attribute computations for the production Mul, defined in $aspMul$, with its children (ch_me_1 and ch_me_2) mapped to the new child ch_se.

$$
\begin{aligned}
aspSq &= agMacro\,(aspMul\ ,\ \ ch\_me_1 \hookrightarrow ch\_se \\
&\qquad\qquad\qquad\ \texttt{<>}\ ch\_me_2 \hookrightarrow ch\_se) \\
aspPyth &= agMacro\,(aspAdd\ ,\ \ ch\_ae_1 \Longrightarrow (aspSq,\ ch\_se \hookrightarrow ch\_pe_1) \\
&\qquad\qquad\qquad\ \texttt{<>}\ ch\_ae_2 \Longrightarrow (aspSq,\ ch\_se \hookrightarrow ch\_pe_2)) \\
aspDouble &= agMacro\,(aspMul\ ,\ \ ch\_me_1 \Longrightarrow (aspCst, ch\_cv \rightsquigarrow 2) \\
&\qquad\qquad\qquad\ \texttt{<>}\ ch\_me_2 \hookrightarrow ch\_de)
\end{aligned}
$$

Fig. 3. Language Extension

Attribute macros can map children to other macros, and so on. For example, in the definition of $aspPyth$ (sum of the squares of ch_pe_1 and ch_pe_2) the children are mapped to macros based on the semantics of square ($aspSq$).

When defining a macro based on the semantics of a production which has literal children, these children can be mapped to literals. In the definition of $aspDouble$ the child ch_me_1 of the multiplication is mapped to a constant, which is mapped to the literal 2.

In some cases we may want to introduce a specialized behavior for some specific attributes of an aspect defined by a macro. For example, the pretty printing attribute spp of the macros of Figure 3 currently is expressed in terms of the base rule. Thus when pretty printing *square x*, instead $x * x$ will be shown. Fortunately it turns out to be very easy to overwrite the definition of some specific attribute instead of adding a new one. This is implemented by the functions $synmodM$ and $inhmodM$.

In Figure 4 we show how the pretty printing attributes of the language extensions we defined in Figure 3 can be redefined to reflect their original appearance in the input program:

3   AspectAG

In this section we describe AspectAG, a library for defining first-class attribute grammars. The key technique underlying our embedded approach lies in using the HList library [7] for typed heterogeneous collections (extensible polymorphic

$$
\begin{aligned}
sppSq &= synmodM \; spp \; \$ \; \textbf{do} \; de \leftarrow at \; ch\_de \\
&\qquad\qquad\qquad\qquad return \; \$ \; \texttt{"square"} \; \texttt{>\#<} \; de \; \# \; spp \\
aspSq' &= sppSq \; `ext` \; aspSq \\
sppPyth &= synmodM \; spp \; \$ \; \textbf{do} \; e_1 \leftarrow at \; ch\_pe_1 \\
&\qquad\qquad\qquad\qquad e_2 \leftarrow at \; ch\_pe_2 \\
&\qquad\qquad\qquad\qquad return \; \$ \; \texttt{"pyth"} \; \texttt{>\#<} \; e_1 \; \# \; spp \; \texttt{>\#<} \; e_2 \; \# \; spp \\
aspPyth' &= sppPyth \; `ext` \; aspPyth \\
sppDouble &= synmodM \; spp \; \$ \; \textbf{do} \; de \leftarrow at \; ch\_de \\
&\qquad\qquad\qquad\qquad return \; \$ \; \texttt{"double"} \; \texttt{>\#<} \; de \; \# \; spp \\
aspDouble' &= sppDouble \; `ext` \; aspDouble
\end{aligned}
$$

Fig. 4. Redefiniton of the *spp* attribute

records) for representing collections of attributes, and expressing the AG well-formedness conditions by type-level predicates (i.e., type-class constraints), thus mimicking dependently typed programming techniques in Haskell [10].

Heterogeneous lists are constructed using the functions (.∗.) and *hNil*, modeling the structure of a normal list both at the value and the type level. An *extensible record* is an heterogeneous list of uniquely labeled fields marked with the type *Record*. A field (l .=. v) relates a (first-class) label l with the value v. Extensible records can be constructed with the functions (.∗.) and *emptyRecord*; where (.∗.) is overloaded to not only extend the list both at type and value level, but also to impose by (type class) constraints that elements in a record are uniquely labeled. In order to keep our programs readable we will use the some syntactic sugar to denote lists and records in the rest of the paper:

- { $v_1, ..., v_n$ } for (v_1 .∗. ... .∗. v_n .∗. *hNil*)
- {{ $f_1, ..., f_n$ }} for (f_1 .∗. ... .∗. f_n .∗. *emptyRecord*)

Thus, if $label_1$ and $label_2$ are labels, the following is the definition of a record (myR) with the elements *True* and `"bla"`:

$$myR = \{\!\{ \; label_1 \; \text{.=.} \; True, \; label_2 \; \text{.=.} \; \texttt{"bla"} \; \}\!\}$$

The operator ($\#$) is used to retrieve the value part corresponding to a specific label from a record, statically enforcing that the record indeed has a field with this label. The expression ($myR \# label_2$) returns the string `"bla"`, while, given a label $label_3$, the expression ($myR \# label_3$) does not compile.

3.1 Rules

In this subsection we show how attributes and their defining rules are represented. An *attribution* is a finite mapping from attribute names to attribute values, represented by a *Record*, in which each field represents the name and value of an attribute.

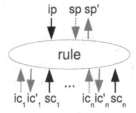

Fig. 5. Rule: black arrows represent input and gray arrows represent output; dotted gray arrows represent the already constructed output which can be used to compute further output elements (hence the direction of the arrow)

When inspecting what happens at a production (a node of the abstract syntax tree) we see that information flows from the inherited attribute of the parent (ip) and the synthesized attributes of the children (sc) to the synthesized attributes (sp) of the parent and the inherited attributes of the children (ic). Henceforth the attributes ip and sc together are called *input family* while the attributes sp and ic are called *output family*, both represented by:

data *Fam children parent* = *Fam children parent*

A *Fam* contains a single attribution for the parent and a collection of attributions for the children. Hence the type *parent* will always be a *Record* with fields labeled by attribute names; the type of *children* is a *Record* with fields labeled by children names and attributions (*Records*) as values. The labels of the children can be defined out of the abstract syntax using the Template Haskell function *deriveAG*. For our example, the call $(deriveAG$ "*Root*) generates the labels *ch_expr*, *ch_cv*, *ch_vnm*, ch_me_1, ch_me_2, ch_ae_1, ch_ae_2, *ch_lnm*, *ch_val* and *ch_body*.

Attributes are defined by *rules* [4], where a rule is a mapping from an input family (the inherited attributes of the parent and the synthesized attributes of the children) to a function which extends the output family (the inherited attributes of the children and the synthesized attributes of the parent) with the new elements defined by this rule:

type *Rule sc ip ic sp ic' sp'* = *Fam sc ip* → (*Fam ic sp* → *Fam ic' sp'*)

Figure 5 shows a graphic representation of a rule; each rule describes a node of a data flow graph which has an underlying tree-shaped structure induced by the abstract syntax tree at hand.

Rule Definition. The functions *syndefM* and *inhdefM* are versions of *syndef* and *inhdef*, that use a *Reader* monad to make definitions look somewhat "prettier".

The function *syndef* adds the definition of a synthesized attribute. It takes a label *att* representing the name of the new attribute, a value *val* to be assigned to this attribute, and it builds a function which updates the output for the parent as constructed thus far (sp):

$$syndef\ att\ val\ (Fam\ ic\ sp) = Fam\ ic\ (att\ .=.\ val\ .*.\ sp)$$

$$syndefM\ att\ mval\ inpFam = syndef\ att\ (runReader\ mval\ inpFam)$$

Let us take a look at how the rule definition *sppAdd* of the attribute *spp* for the production *Add* is defined using *syndef* instead of *syndefM*:

$$sppAdd\ (Fam\ sc\ ip)$$
$$= syndef\ spp\ \$\ ((sc\ \#\ ch\_ae_1)\ \#\ spp)\ >\#<\ "+"\ >\#<\ ((sc\ \#\ ch\_ae_2)\ \#\ spp)$$

The children ch_ae_1 and ch_ae_2 are retrieved from the input family so we can subsequently retrieve the attribute *spp* from these attributions, and construct the computation of the synthesized attribute *spp*. The function *inhdef* introduces new inherited attributes for a collection of non-terminals at the same time, all with the same name.

$$inhdef\ ::\ Defs\ att\ nts\ vals\ ic\ ic'$$
$$\Rightarrow att \to nts \to vals \to (Fam\ ic\ sp \to Fam\ ic'\ sp)$$

It results in a function which updates the output constructed thus far and takes the following parameters: the attribute *att* which is being defined, the list *nts* of non-terminals with which this attribute is being associated, and a record *vals* labeled with child names and containing values, describing how to compute the attribute being defined at each of the applicable child positions. The class *Defs* introduces a type-level function used to iterate over the record *vals* and to compute the new record of inherited attributes *ic'*, extending the record *ic* with the inherited attributes defined thus far.

Thus, in the rule *ienvLet*, described before, we give a definition for the attribute *ienv* for each child of which the semantic category is in the list {{ *nt_Expr* }}, and these are stored in an extensible record labeled by the names of the children. It is the possibility of defining such functions in Haskell which shows the advantages of expressing one's attribute grammars using an embedded domain specific language.

Rules Composition. The composition of two rules is the composition of the two functions resulting from applying each of them to the input family:

$$ext\ ::\ Rule\ sc\ ip\ ic'\ sp'\ ic''\ sp'' \to Rule\ sc\ ip\ ic\ sp\ ic'\ sp'$$
$$\to Rule\ sc\ ip\ ic\ sp\ ic''\ sp''$$
$$(rule1\ `ext`\ rule2)\ input = rule1\ input \circ rule2\ input$$

Figure 6 represents a composition *rule1* `ext` *rule2*, of rules with two children. By inspecting the labyrinths of this figure, it can be seen how the inputs (black arrows) are shared and the outputs are combined by using the outputs of *rule2* (solid gray) as output constructed thus far of *rule1* (dotted gray). Thus, the outputs constructed thus far (dotted gray) of the composed rule are passed to *rule2* and the resulting outputs (solid gray) of the composed rule are equivalent to the resulting outputs of *rule1*.

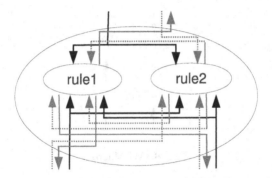

Fig. 6. Rules Composition: produces a new rule, represented by the external oval

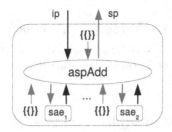

Fig. 7. Rule Knitting: produces a semantic function (external rounded rectangle)

Semantic Functions. Figure 7 represents the resulting semantic function for the production *Add*. Notice that the function *knit* initializes the already constructed outputs with empty records ($\{\{\ \}\}$).

4   Attribute Grammar Macros

An attribute grammar macro is determined by a pair with the *base rule* ($rule_b$) of the macro and the mapping (*chMap*) between the children of this rule and their newly defined semantics, and returns a *macro rule*. As shown in Figure 8, *chMap* (rectangle) is an interface between the children of the base rule (inner oval) and the children of the macro rule (outer oval). The number of children of the macro rule (below *chMap* in the figure) does not need to be the same as the number of children of the base rule.

The function *agMacro* constructs the macro rule; it performs the "knitting" of $rule_b$, by applying this rule to its input and the output produced thus far. These elements have to be obtained from the corresponding elements of the macro rule and the mapping *chMap*. To keep the code clear, we will use the subindex b for the elements of the base rule and m for the elements of the macro rule. Thus, the macro rule takes as input the family ($Fam\ sc_m\ ip_m$) and updates the output family constructed thus far ($Fam\ ic_m\ sp_m$) to a new output family ($Fam\ ic_m''\ sp_m'$):

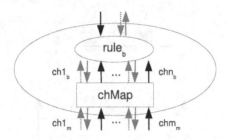

Fig. 8. AG Macro

$$agMacro\ (rule_b, chMap)\ (Fam\ sc_m\ ip_m)\ (Fam\ ic_m\ sp_m) =$$
$$\textbf{let}\ ip_b = ip_m$$
$$sp_b = sp_m$$
$$(Fam\ ic'_b\ sp'_b) = rule_b\ \ (Fam\ sc_b\ ip_b)\ (Fam\ ic_b\ sp_b)$$
$$(ic'_m, ic_b, sc_b) = chMap\ (sc_m, ic_m)\ (ic'_b, emptyRecord, emptyRecord)$$
$$ic''_m = hRearrange\ (recordLabels\ ic_m)\ ic'_m$$
$$sp'_m = sp'_b$$
$$\textbf{in}\ (Fam\ ic''_m\ sp'_m)$$

The inherited and synthesized attributes of the parent of the base rule (ip_b and sp_b) respectively correspond to ip_m and sp_m, the inherited and synthesized attributes of the parent of the macro rule. The inherited and synthesized attributes of the children of the base rule (ic_b and sc_b), as well as the updated inherited attributes of the children of the macro rule (ic'_m), are generated by the children mapping function $chMap$. The function $chMap$ takes as input a pair (sc_m, ic_m) with the synthesized attributes and the inherited attributes constructed thus far of the children of the macro rule, and returns a function that updates a triple with the updated inherited attributes (ic'_m) of the children of the macro rule and the inherited (ic_b) and synthesized (sc_b) attributes of the children of the base rule. We start with an "initial" triple composed of the updated inherited attributes of the children of the base rule (ic'_b), which has been converted into ic'_m, and two empty records (to be extended to ic_b and sc_b). Notice that the attributes we pass to $chMap$ are effectively the ones indicated by the incoming arrows in Figure 8.

The rearranging of ic'_m is just a technical detail stemming from the use of HList; by doing this we make sure that the children in ic_m and ic'_m are in the same order, thus informing the type system that both represent the same production. The synthesized attributes of the parent of the macro rule (sp'_m) are just sp'_b, the synthesized attributes of the parent of the base rule.

Mapping functions resemble rules in the sense that they take an input and return a function that updates its "output", that in this case is the triple (ic'_m, ic_b, sc_b) instead of an output family. Thus, they can be combined in the same way as rules are combined; the combinator (<.>), used in Figure 3, is exactly the same as the *ext* function but with a different type:[5]

---

[5] To avoid confusion with rule combination, instead of using apostrophes to denote updates we use numeric suffixes.

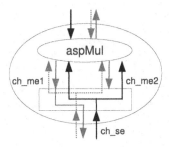

Fig. 9. aspSq

$$(<.>) :: ((sc_m, ic_m) \to ((ic'1_m, ic1_b, sc1_b) \to (ic'2_m, ic2_b, sc2_b)))$$
$$\to ((sc_m, ic_m) \to ((ic'0_m, ic0_b, sc0_b) \to (ic'1_m, ic1_b, sc1_b)))$$
$$\to ((sc_m, ic_m) \to ((ic'0_m, ic0_b, sc0_b) \to (ic'2_m, ic2_b, sc2_b)))$$
$$(chMap1 <.> chMap2) \; inp = chMap1 \; inp \circ chMap2 \; inp$$

We use the combinator ($\hookrightarrow$) to map a child lch_b of the base rule to a child lch_m of the macro rule.

$$lch_b \hookrightarrow lch_m = \lambda(sc_m, ic_m) \; (ic'0_m, ic0_b, sc0_b) \to$$
$$\textbf{let } ic'1_m = hRenameLabel \; lch_b \; lch_m \; (hDeleteAtLabel \; lch_m \; ic'0_m)$$
$$icl_b \quad = lch_b \; .=. \; (ic_m \; \# \; lch_m) \; .*. \; ic0_b$$
$$scl_b \quad = lch_b \; .=. \; (sc_m \; \# \; lch_m) \; .*. \; sc0_b$$
$$\textbf{in } (ic'1_m, ic1_b, sc1_b)$$

The updated inherited attributes for the child lch_m correspond to the updated inherited attributes of the child lch_b. Thus, the new ic'_m ($ic'1_m$) is the original one with the field lch_b renamed to lch_m. Since more than a single child of the base rule can be mapped to a child of the macro rule, like in $aspSq$ of Figure 3, we have to avoid duplicates in the record by deleting a possible previous occurrence of lch_m. This decision fixes the semantics of multiple occurrences of a child in a macro: the child will receive the inherited attributes of its left-most mapping. We represent this behavior in Figure 9 with the gray arrow, which corresponds to the inherited attributes of ch_me_2, pointing nowhere outside the mapping. In the cases of the initial inherited attributes and the synthesized attributes, they have to be extended with a field corresponding to the child lch_b with the attributions for the child lch_m from the inherited and synthesized attributes, respectively, of the macro rule.

Inside a macro a child can be mapped to some other macro ($rule_c, chMap$), where the subindex c stands for child. This is the case of the definitions of $aspPyth$ and $aspDouble$, graphically represented in Figure 10 and Figure 11, where the rectangles representing the children mappings have rules (ovals) inside.

$$lch_b \Longrightarrow (rule_c, chMap) = \lambda(sc_m, ic_m) \; (ic'0_m, ic0_b, sc0_b) \to$$
$$\textbf{let } (Fam \; ic'_c \; sp'_c) = agMacro \; (rule_c, chMap) \; (Fam \; sc_m \; (ic'0_m \; \# \; lch_b))$$
$$(Fam \; ic_m \; emptyRecord)$$

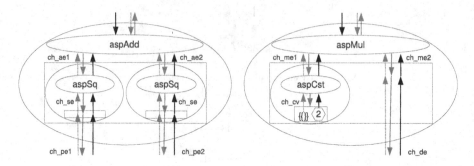

Fig. 10. aspPyth   **Fig. 11.** aspDouble

$$ic'1_m = hLeftUnion\ ic'_c\ (hDeleteAtLabel\ lch_b\ ic'0_m)$$
$$icl_b\ \ = lch_b\ .=.\ emptyRecord\ .*.\ ic0_b$$
$$scl_b\ \ = lch_b\ .=.\ sp'_c\ \qquad\qquad .*.\ sc0_b$$
$$\mathbf{in}\ \ (ic'0_m, icl_b, scl_b)$$

In this case, the inner macro has to be evaluated using *agMacro*. The children of the inner macro will be included in the children of the outer macro; thus the synthesized attributes of the inner macro are included in sc_m, and the new inherited attributes of the children have to extend ic_m. The inherited attributes of the parent of the inner macro are the inherited attributes of the child lch_b of the base rule of the outer macro. The synthesized attributes of the parent of the inner macro are initialized with an empty attribution. The child lch_b is removed from $ic'0_m$, because the macro rule will not include it. On the other hand, the inherited attributes of the children of the inner macro (ic'_c) have to be added to the inherited attributes of the children of the macro. With the function *hLeftUnion* from HList we perform an union of records, choosing the elements of the left record in case of duplication. We initialize the inherited attributes for lch_b with an empty attribution, since it cannot be seen "from the outside". The synthesized attributes are initialized with the resulting synthesized attributes of the inner rule.

With the combinator ($-\rightsquigarrow$) we define a mapping from a child with label *lch* to a literal value *cst*. For the base rule, the initial synthesized attributes of the child lch_b are fixed to the literal *cst*.

$$lch_b\ -\rightsquigarrow cst = \lambda(\_,\_)\ (ic'0_m, ic0_b, sc0_b) \rightarrow$$
$$\quad \mathbf{let}\ ic'1_m = hDeleteAtLabel\ lch\ ic'0_m$$
$$\qquad icl_b\ \ = lch_b\ .=.\ emptyRecord\ .*.\ ic0_b$$
$$\qquad scl_b\ \ = lch_b\ .=.\ cst \qquad\qquad .*.\ sc0_b$$
$$\quad \mathbf{in}\ \ (ic'1_m, icl_b, scl_b)$$

The (internal) macro associated to the mapping of the child ch_me_1 in Figure 11 shows the semantics of the combinator ($-\rightsquigarrow$). The synthesized attributes of ch_cv are fixed to the constant (hexagon) 2. Since the child is mapped to a constant, the inherited attributes are ignored (the arrow points nowhere). Although, we have to provide a (empty) set of inherited attributes constructed thus far to the rule *aspCst*.

4.1 Attribute Redefinitions

We have shown how to introduce new syntax and how to express its meaning in terms of existing constructs. In this section we show how we can *redefine* parts of the just defined semantics by showing how to redefine attribute computations.

The function *synmod* (and its monadic version *synmodM*) modifies the definition of an existing synthesized attribute:

$$synmod\ att\ val\ (Fam\ ic\ sp) = Fam\ ic\ (hUpdateAtLabel\ att\ val\ sp)$$

Note that the only difference between *syndef*, from subsection 3.1, and *synmod*, is that the latter updates an existing field of the attribution *sp*, instead of adding a new field. With the use of the HList's function *hUpdateAtLabel* we enforce (by type class constraints) the record *sp*, which contains the synthesized attributes of the parent constructed thus far, indeed contains a field labeled *att*. Thus, a rule created using *synmod* has to extend, using *ext*, some other rule that has already defined the synthesized attribute this rule is *redefining*.

The AspectAG library also provides functions *inhmodM* and *inhmod*, analogous to *inhdefM* and *inhdef*, that modify the definition of an inherited attribute for all children coming from a specified collection of semantic categories.

5 Conclusions and Future Work

Building on top of a set of combinators that allow us to formulate extensions to semantics as first class attribute grammars (i.e. as plain typed Haskell values), we introduced in this paper a mechanism which allows us to express semantics in terms of already existing semantics, without the need to use higher order attributes.

The programmer of the extensions does not need to know the details of the implementation of every attribute. In order to implement a macro or a redefinition for a production he only needs the names of the attributes used and the names of the children of the production, the latter being provided by the definition of the abstract syntax tree.

This work is part of a bigger plan, involving the development of a series of techniques [1,2,12,13] to deal with the problems involved in both syntactic and semantic extensions of a compiler by composing compiled and type-checked Haskell values. In this way we leverage the type checking capabilities of the Haskel world into such specifications, and we profit from all the abstraction mechanisms Haskell provides.

We already think that the current approach is to be preferred over stacking more and more monads when defining a compositional semantics as is conventionally done in the Haskell world [11].

References

1. Baars, A.I., Doaitse Swierstra, S., Viera, M.: Typed transformations of typed abstract syntax. In: TLDI 2009, pp. 15–26. ACM (2009)
2. Baars, A.I., Doaitse Swierstra, S., Viera, M.: Typed transformations of typed grammars: The left corner transform. In: LDTA 2009. ENTCS (2009)
3. Bravenboer, M., Kalleberg, K.T., Vermaas, R., Visser, E.: Stratego/XT 0.17. A language and toolset for program transformation. Science of Computer Programming 72(1-2), 52–70 (2008)
4. de Moor, O., Backhouse, K., Doaitse Swierstra, S.: First-class attribute grammars. Informatica (Slovenia) 24(3) (2000)
5. Dijkstra, A., Fokker, J., Doaitse Swierstra, S.: The architecture of the Utrecht Haskell compiler. In: Haskell 2009, pp. 93–104. ACM (2009)
6. Heeren, B., Hage, J., Doaitse Swierstra, S.: Scripting the type inference process. In: ICFP 2003, pp. 3–13. ACM Press (2003)
7. Kiselyov, O., Lämmel, R., Schupke, K.: Strongly typed heterogeneous collections. In: Haskell 2004, pp. 96–107. ACM Press (2004)
8. Leavenworth, B.M.: Syntax macros and extended translation. Commun. ACM 9(11), 790–793 (1966)
9. Maddox, W.: Semantically-sensitive macroprocessing. Technical report, Berkeley, CA, USA (1989)
10. McBride, C.: Faking it simulating dependent types in Haskell. J. Funct. Program. 12(5), 375–392 (2002)
11. Schrijvers, T., Oliveira, B.C.d.S.: Monads, zippers and views: virtualizing the monad stack. In: ICFP 2011, pp. 32–44. ACM (2011)
12. Doaitse Swierstra, S.: Parser combinators: from toys to tools. In: Haskell Workshop (2000)
13. Doaitse Swierstra, S.: Combinator Parsing: A Short Tutorial. In: Bove, A., Barbosa, L.S., Pardo, A., Pinto, J.S. (eds.) LerNet 2008. LNCS, vol. 5520, pp. 252–300. Springer, Heidelberg (2009)
14. Van Wyk, E., de Moor, O., Backhouse, K., Kwiatkowski, P.: Forwarding in Attribute Grammars for Modular Language Design. In: Horspool, R.N. (ed.) CC 2002. LNCS, vol. 2304, pp. 128–142. Springer, Heidelberg (2002)
15. Van Wyk, E., Bodin, D., Gao, J., Krishnan, L.: Silver: an extensible attribute grammar system. Science of Computer Programming 75(1-2), 39–54 (2010)
16. Viera, M., Doaitse Swierstra, S., Swierstra, W.: Attribute grammars fly first-class: how to do aspect oriented programming in Haskell. In: ICFP 2009, pp. 245–256. ACM (2009)
17. Wirth, N.: Compiler construction. International computer science series. Addison-Wesley (1996)

Author Index

Printed in the United States
by Baker & Taylor Publisher Services